BACK WORDS AND FORE WORDS

BACK WORDS
AND FORE WORDS

An Author's Year-Book
1893-1945

★

*A Selection
in Chronological Order from the
Plays, Poems, & Prose Writings
of*
LAURENCE HOUSMAN

JONATHAN CAPE
THIRTY BEDFORD SQUARE
LONDON

FIRST PUBLISHED 1945

JONATHAN CAPE LTD.   30 BEDFORD SQUARE, LONDON
AND 91 WELLINGTON STREET WEST, TORONTO

THIS BOOK IS PRODUCED IN COM-
PLETE   CONFORMITY   WITH   THE
AUTHORIZED ECONOMY STANDARDS

PRINTED IN GREAT BRITAIN IN THE CITY OF OXFORD
AT THE ALDEN PRESS
BOUND BY A. W. BAIN & CO. LONDON

CONTENTS

CONTENTS

APPENDIX

PREFACE

In my fifty years of authorship, I have written more books than I should have done had I given more time to second thoughts; or, at any rate, they would have contained less matter, better expressed. Some of them (which are now out of print) I have no wish to recall to second life; but occasionally inquiries reach me as to what has become of them, or of others which have changed hands, or gone into collected editions under fresh titles; so that would-be readers often find a difficulty in tracing them. And one of my reasons for compiling this record of my seven ages as an author has been to remove that difficulty.

But apart from my wish to provide would-be readers with a guide to my past writings, I have another and a more personal one. I am aware that, in my interests and my outlook on life, I have greatly changed during the past fifty years. When I began writing, I had (for literary purposes) very little interest in the world of to-day; in politics I was a home-grown Conservative, in religion a medievalist, and my whole bent, as a writer, lay in the direction of fancy, fairy-tale, and legend. There was, indeed, one short break-away, which, coming when it did, still surprises me: The first book I ever wrote, *Gods, and their Makers*, I might have written to-day — better, I hope, and differently, but in its main purport the same. It was iconoclastic. And having come to regard my later libertarianism in matters religious, social and political, as more genuinely my own than what went before, I have given it more space in the pages that follow, and have added an appendix of Prefaces and Footnotes in which some of these later views find more direct expression.

When a man looks at himself in the glass, he sees only the man he has become: all its earlier reflections have slipped away — only in memory does any trace of them remain. But when an author looks back into that more permanent reflection of himself — the books that he has written — he finds himself confronted not only with the man that he has become, but with all the stages by which he has found his way into that state of life to which it has pleased his gods to call him: however much he has altered, there is his past, still alive before his eyes — a mental reflection from which he cannot get away. If he was a sincere writer, every one of those books was part of himself; and yet he may be very much aware that

PREFACE

it would be impossible for him to write them now, so much has his mind changed.

That is my case; the books which I wrote up to the age of forty, or thereabouts, I could write no longer. When a sharpened interest in political events afflicted me with a social conscience, I shed a good deal of my romanticism; also (in matters of religious belief) my medievalism. And though my *Little Plays of St. Francis*, which I did not begin to write till ten years later, may seem to contradict that statement, is it not true that of all the medieval saints, St. Francis of Assisi remains the most wonderfully alive to-day, and the most universally attractive in this rather untheological age, not primarily because he was a great Saint but because he was a great humanist? It was that unmedieval, and untheological side of him which drew me to the dramatizing of St. Francis in the forty-five *Little Plays* which bear his name. And though I have written an even longer series (fifty-four in all) of scenes from the life of Queen Victoria, she is more of a back-number to-day than that 'glorious poor little one', who died more than seven hundred years ago.

Those plays, and others written before and after, mark a further separation between my present and my past. For in that earlier period I had not written a single play; whereas now it is mostly plays that I write. Drama, dialogue, and satire have become my main interest, as providing the best possible medium for portrayal of human nature in its infinite variety — the good and the bad, the wise and the foolish, the noble and the ridiculous.

In this selection, from my books, ranging over so many years, I have expressed my own preferences not so much in the short extracts (which had to be included in order to make the selection representative) as in those of greater length, most of which are of comparatively recent dates; and though an author is not reckoned to be a good judge of his own work, I will venture the opinion that *The man who did not pray* is the best story I have ever written; *The Rain Child*, my best fairy-tale; *The Instrument* (written twenty-four years ago), my best piece of prophecy; and *Nunc Dimittis*, the most hopeful expression of my rather doubtful belief in a future life.

I have been able to make this collection as complete as, within certain limitations, was possible, through the generous kindness of all those of my Publishers who still hold the copyrights. I am especially indebted to the

8

two firms of Jonathan Cape and Sidgwick & Jackson for the large call
they have allowed me to make on the books (see Book List, page 11)
published under their imprints. My thanks are also due to the Publishers
of the following books, for the extracts which they have allowed me to
make from them:

An Englishwoman's Love-Letters   (Mr. John Murray)
Bethlehem, A Nativity Play   "   "
Gods, and Their Makers   (Messrs. George Allen & Unwin Ltd.)
Ploughshare and Pruning-hook   "   "   "   "
False Premises — A book of plays   (Messrs. Basil Blackwell)
Turn-again Tales   "   "
What-o'Clock Tales   "   "
Amabel and Amoris   (Messrs. Chatto & Wind us)
Ways and Means — Five Plays of Domestic Character
         (Messrs. H. F. W. Deane & Sons)
War-Letters of Fallen Englishmen   (Messrs. Victor Gollancz Ltd.)
*The Sheepfold: The story of A Shepherdess and Her Sheep, and how she
   lost them*   (Messrs. Gerald Duckworth & Co. Ltd.)

Finally I have to thank Messrs. Williams & Norgate Ltd. for permission
to quote from my Preface to *A New Way with Crime* by A. Fenner Brockway, and the London University College Dramatic Society, for permission
to make an entire reprint of my play *Nunc Dimittis* of which they hold all
the rights, literary and dramatic.

To make the following book-list a complete guide to all my earlier
books and to their present whereabouts, I must add a further explanation.
My first four books of fairy-tales are out of print in their original form;
and under the changed titles of *A Doorway in Fairyland* and *Moonshine and
Clover* are now published by Messrs. Jonathan Cape. The same firm has
taken over the publication (in a single volume) of *All Fellows* and the
Cloak of Friendship, and also of my political novel *John of Jingalo* and its
sequel *The Royal Runaway*. Of my seven books of poems, *Green Arras*,
Spikenard, The Little Land, Rue, Mendicant Rhymes, The Heart of Peace,
and *The Love Concealed*, all but the last are now out of print; some, but not
all of them, have been republished by Messrs. Sidgwick & Jackson in
Selected Poems (1908) and *Collected Poems* (1937).

Ploughshare and Pruning-hook has gone from the Swarthmore Press to

Messrs. Allen & Unwin; my *Little Plays of St. Francis* (first and second series) which include most of those published separately under the titles of *Followers of St. Francis*, *The Comments of Juniper* and *Four Plays of St. Clare*, are now published in a three-volume collected edition. My plays of Queen Victoria, which still await final collection, have appeared in instalments under the titles of *Angels and Ministers*, *Palace Plays*, *The Queen's Progress*, *Victoria and Albert*, *Victoria Regina*, *Palace Scenes*, *The Golden Sovereign* and *Gracious Majesty*; a large but not complete selection has also been published under the title of *Happy and Glorious*.

These shifts and changes have misled a friendly critic into accusing me of having written more books than I have lived years. My real output has been more moderate. Eliminating the reprints under changed titles I reckon that I am actually responsible for only sixty-five — plus my half-share in the writing of *Prunella, or Love in a Dutch Garden*, in collaboration with H. Granville-Barker, to whom I owe a word of special thanks for his patient coaching, which enabled me later to become an independent and self-supporting playwright. L. H.

Title	Publisher	Date
The Writings of William Blake with introductory essay	Kegan Paul, Trench, Trubner & Co.	1893
A Farm in Fairyland	,,	1894
The House of Joy	,,	1895
Arthur Boyd Houghton. A selection from his illustrations, with an introductory essay	,,	1896
Green Arras	John Lane	1896
All-Fellows. Seven Legends of Lower Redemption	Kegan Paul, Trench, Trubner & Co.	1896
Gods, and Their Makers	John Lane	1897
The Field of Clover	Kegan Paul, Trench, Trubner & Co.	1898
Spikenard. A Book of Devotional Love Poems	Grant Richards	1898
The Story of the Seven Young Goslings	Blackie & Son	1898
Rue	The Unicorn Press	1899
The Little Land. With Songs from its Four Rivers	Grant Richards	1899
An Englishwoman's Love-Letters	John Murray	1900
★A Modern Antaeus	,,	1901
Bethlehem. A Nativity Play	,,	1902
The Blue Moon	,,	1904
★Sabrina Warham	,,	1904
The Cloak of Friendship	,,	1905
Mendicant Rhymes	The Essex House Press	1906
Prunella, or Love in a Dutch Garden (with H. Granville-Barker)	Sidgwick & Jackson	1906
The Chinese Lantern	,, ,,	1908
Selected Poems	,, ,,	1908
★Articles of Faith in the Freedom of Women	The Woman's Press	1910

*Lysistrata (A Modern Paraphrase)	The Women's Press	1910
The New Child's Guide to Knowledge	Sidgwick & Jackson	1911
Pains and Penalties. The Defence of Queen Caroline	,, ,,	1911
John of Jingalo. The Story of a Monarch in Difficulties	Chapman & Hall	1912
The Royal Runaway. (A sequel to John of Jingalo)	,, ,,	1914
Ploughshare and Pruning-hook ·	The Swarthmore Press	1918
St. Francis Poverello	Sidgwick & Jackson	1918
The Sheepfold	Duckworth	1918
The Heart of Peace	Heinemann	1919
The Wheel. A Trilogy	Sidgwick & Jackson	1919
Little Plays of St. Francis. (First Series)	,, ,,	1921
Angels and Ministers	Jonathan Cape	1921
Possession. (A Peep-show in Paradise)	,,	1921
Dethronements	,,	1922
False Premises	Basil Blackwell	1922
A Doorway in Fairyland	Jonathan Cape	1922
Moonshine and Clover	,,	1922
Followers of St. Francis	Sidgwick & Jackson	1923
Echo de Paris	Jonathan Cape	1923
Trimblerigg. A Book of Revelation	,,	1924
*Odd Pairs	,,	1925
Of Aucassin and Nicolette (A translation in prose and verse) and Amabel and Amoris	Chatto & Windus	1925
The Death of Socrates	Sidgwick & Jackson	1925
The Comments of Juniper	,, ,,	1926
*Ironical Tales	Jonathan Cape	1926
*Uncle Tom Pudd	,,	1927
The Life of H.R.H. The Duke of Flamborough	,,	1927

The Little Plays Handbook	Sidgwick & Jackson	1927
The Love Concealed	,, ,,	1928
Ways and Means	H. F. W. Deane & Sons	1928
Cornered Poets	Jonathan Cape	1929
Palace Plays	,,	1929
War-Letters of Fallen Englishmen	Victor Gollancz	1930
Turn-Again Tales	Basil Blackwell	1930
Little Plays of St. Francis. (Second Series)	Sidgwick & Jackson	1931
The Death of Orpheus	,, ,,	1931
Ye Fearful Saints!	,, ,,	1932
What o'Clock Tales	Basil Blackwell	1932
The Queen's Progress	Jonathan Cape	1932
Victoria and Albert	,,	1933
Victoria Regina	,,	1934
Four Plays of St. Clare	Sidgwick & Jackson	1934
Little Plays of St. Francis, in 3 vols. Complete edition	,, ,,	1935
The Unexpected Years	Jonathan Cape	1936
Palace Scenes	,,	1937
A. E. H. A Memoir	,,	1937
The Golden Sovereign	,,	1937
Collected Poems	Sidgwick & Jackson	1937
What Next?	Jonathan Cape	1938
What can we Believe?	,,	1939
The Preparation of Peace	,,	1940
Gracious Majesty	,,	1941
Palestine Plays	,,	1942
Samuel: the Kingmaker	,,	1944
Nunc Dimittis	(Privately printed 1933)	1944

*N.B. These books are now out of print, and have not yet been republished.

THE KING'S EVIL

On the night which went before His death, we know how Christ gave to His disciples an example of humility, that even to this day is followed by the Kings of certain countries. This is the washing of men's feet, however lowly and poor they may be, done on Maundy Thursday, by which earthly Kings exalt themselves in striving to the pattern of their Lord's great humility.

Now, in a country where they did this, many generations ago, it chanced that the King being an ill ruler and false to his crown oaths, had been driven out and supplanted by his brother, who, if no better at heart than his predecessor, used his means of power more prudently. Thus it came about that, of the two brothers, one was a beggar with no friend to succour him, and the other lord of a great city, and of all the country lying for many leagues around it; and which one hated the other most, he who was supplanted or he who had done the supplanting, it were hard to say.

On the year following this turn-over of their fortunes, it being the morning of Maundy Thursday, the new King entered the palace-court-yard like a servant, girdled with a towel, and carrying a golden ewer in his hands. There, all about the walls, sat the beggars waiting for the King's service; and the King knelt down before each, as the custom was, and poured out water into a gold dish, and washed the feet of all.

And when he came to the last beggar of all, he found that it was his own brother, whom he hated more than aught else in the world, who had brought his feet there to be washed.

Wit ye well, the Devil was at that christening, though not a word did the brothers speak. And the King washed right foot and left foot, and dried them with all care, as if to say, 'See, you are to me even as these, mere beggars, for whom custom makes me do this thing'.

Now this that happened once, happened again each year, on Maundy Thursday, at the washing of the feet: there, last of all, sat the King de-throned, and the brother who had supplanted him came and knelt, and washed his feet as he had done for all the other beggars. And to the one it was the sweetest moment of all the year, and to the other the bitterest. . To the Devil also it became a red-letter feast-day, to cheer him through the dolorous time of Easter, so great was the joy wrought for him by the hatred of the two brothers.

After some years of keeping this bitter anniversary, supplanter and supplanted disappeared from the eyes of men on one and the same day, and went the way their hearts took them. The Devil made them to be his footstool, one under his right foot and one under his left, for he would not have their hatred die for lack of remembrance.

Presently, as time went on, the Devil looked up and laughed. 'Out yonder,' he said, 'your feast-day on earth is beginning. Come, and we will see how the little King keeps the custom that his father and uncle kept so well!'

The Devil clapped a soul into the cleft of each hoof, and went up to earth, like a diver who swims up to the surface of the deep sea.

The young King came down into the palace-courtyard, girdled with a napkin and carrying a golden ewer in his hands. His face was made holy by awe and love, because it was his first time of performing the solemn rite which had its pattern in the humility and love of Christ.

All round the walls sat the beggars with bare feet, and the Devil sat last of them: where hatred had sat all those years before, there he crouched with feet and face folded in the brown robe of a medicant, and waited for the washing to come to his turn.

The King was little more than a child; and to him this worn-out custom was the newest and strangest he had ever had to do with, more strange than the touching for 'the King's evil', which was done on all feast-days. He thought of the disciples in the supper-room, on the night before the Passion; and as he went from beggar to beggar he had in mind Christ with His friends the Saints: so, in each one of the beggars, he washed as it were the feet of some Saint.

'This,' he said of the first, 'must be Peter!' for he was a true child of the Church, and he knew that Peter must ever come foremost. So he washed Peter's feet diligently and humbly, making mental submission to all the dogmas which from then to this had infallibly come from him. Then he passed on. 'And this shall be John!' he thought, at the next, for that saint was ever the one he loved the best. Then he came to James, and then Andrew: and so he went on till he had washed all the feet down to Thomas: then there was one left. 'This must be Judas,' he sighed, as he knelt down to offer water to the last.

The Devil untucked his robe, and let down his two hoofs into the golden dish. The young King drew back his breath, first in disgust, and then in pure pity, at the sight of those deformed feet: and he thought of Judas, and the fiery way his feet had trodden at the last. And he thought, 'To all the others I have prayed; but for this one may I pray?'

Then he laved the right foot tenderly, and the left foot tenderly, and dried them both: and at the end 'O God,' he said, 'make these lame feet whole!' And saying this he stooped forward and kissed them.

The Devil uttered a cry: for the two souls, which he had brought back with him out of Hell, had slipped from his hold, and had passed up into the lowest room of Purgatory.

The Devil drew up his feet painfully, and wrapped them in his robe, while with the best will in the world he let his curse go out on the mortal who had so robbed him. And the young King's lips were all blistered, as he rose up from that washing a white leper.

When the people saw what had befallen, they made sure that it was from God, a sign of His judgment on an evil house in its last generation. Therefore they made haste, and stripped the King of his royal robes, and drove him out beyond the city-walls to a leper's life among the solitary and waste places; and in his room they appointed a magistracy to rule over them, for of the royal line no male of the direct line was left.

The leper King bore all meekly, knowing that his leprosy was but a symbol of the sins of himself and of his father's house: so putting on sackcloth he went out to live in a lonely hut far from the high-road, and not near any of the farms or tilled fields. In a path that ran hard by up to the hill-pastures, he put an earthen bowl, wherein sometimes food for him was set by the charitable, and sometimes not, as might chance. And never did any man see his face.

Only on one day in the seven must he come back to the place where before he had been King; that was when all the bells rang, and at the great church in the city Mass was sung. Then he would cover his face over with a cloth, and hang the leper's bell about his neck, and go along byways, and by a side-gate, and through narrow streets till he was come to the Close and to the chancel's north side where the leper's window was. There he would kneel and look in, and behold the miracle of the Mass, and hear a little of the words; and quickly, after the third bell had been rung, turn and go while the streets were still void. And if at any time he saw a man coming his way he would sound the bell about his neck, and cry 'Un-clean!' So they two would pass upon opposite sides, or else the other would turn, not to meet him, and draw away into a side-street till he had passed by. After a time he became used to that grief and shame; and to go and hear Mass was the one joy he had with God and his fellow-man.

Now it happened, one day of High Mass, that, as he was going along a poor narrow street, there was a child playing upon one of the steep flights of steps that led up to the doors; and as the leper passed the child slipt, and cried, feeling itself falling. Then, forgetting that no help might come from him, the King put out his hand and caught the little one, and set it upon its feet. Its mother within the house, hearing the cry, ran to the door, and saw a leper handling her own flesh and blood. At that sight, between fear and rage, she threw at him the thing that first came, then seizing up a mop-stick made out after him, dealing him many hard knocks with it, and at last casting it after him as a thing that had become unclean for further handling. The leper bowed down his head and went on, stricken to the heart that not for the love of God might he do kind deed to any of his fellow-creatures.

The mother picking up her child carried it in, to wash it clean from any taint of leprosy: but when she was stripping it with shrill scoldings, all at once her voice stopped at mid-word, as her eyes fell on its bared flesh; for there, where before the child had borne the marks of the 'King's evil', the skin was now whole and sound.

The next time the leper went by, a week after, a woman came carrying a child and following him: and she was a sister of the other woman whose child he had caught in its fall. When there was no one else in the street but themselves, she came close: 'Touch my child!' she whispered; and at that the leper moved more quickly, ringing his bell to warn her off. 'I am unclean!' he said. The other did not cease following, but whenever others came in sight she drew back, as if fearful lest she should be seen; then, as soon as they two were alone again, she came, saying, 'For the love of God, touch my child!'

For the love of God! The leper turned his eyes and looked. Through the cloth over his face he saw the mother uncovering the child's throat; and there upon it was the mark of the King's evil. 'For the love of God. Oh, for the love of God!' she wept.

The leper stood still; he reached out his hand trembling, and made the

ALL FELLOWS

sign of the Cross over the scars. Then he turned and ran: nor did he hear the mother's cry of thankfulness, as she blessed God to behold the healing that his touch had brought.

That day he went back out of the city by another way; and always afterwards he crept in by a different gate, and by other streets, till he reached the leper's window within the chancel's north side. But one day as he knelt looking in at the priest saying Mass, he heard footsteps behind, and saw three women coming to where he was; and one was carrying a child in her arms, and one was leading another woman by the hand. When they were near to him the two women stood still, and said, 'For the love of God make these whole!'

'This is my only child,' said one. 'This is my sister,' said the other; 'she is a deaf-mute, the King's evil has been upon her ever since she was born.'

'I am unclean!' said the leper.

'God knows,' said the mother, 'if you can heal my little one, you are not unclean in His sight.'

The King looked in through the leper's window, and saw the priest about to lift up the Host; and with the three women he bowed himself to the ground at the consecration. Then the leper looked towards the Body of Christ and prayed, 'O, Love of God, come by way of the leper's window and give healing to these!' Then he made the sign of the Cross upon each, and turned and went swiftly away.

Presently through all the city the whisper went by stealth how the leper's touch had healing in it, as if he were still King by divine right, and had power such as in old time was given to good Kings to do good to God's poor on earth. So, in a while, the sound of his bell, which was to warn men as he entered any street, served as a summons to those who had need of him to touch them for the King's evil. Yet still, as he went through the poor crowds that blessed him, the leper-king wore the cloth over his face, and cried 'Unclean!'

At first the tale of it had been slow, for there had been doubt and fear that a leper, cut off from all men by the finger of God, should do this thing: but presently, when the secret had passed through more than three hands, the city grew loud with it. And the cry of the poorer people was, 'Give us back our King! for God, though He curses him in his own body, blesses him in all on whom he lays hands.' But for a time the priests and magistrates could not hear of such a thing as for a leper to be upon the throne.

Nevertheless the healing was apparent, for many known cases had been cured; and at last the popular cry could no longer be withstood. For each Sunday, before and after Mass, the whole city was in a tumult, as the leper-king came and went, with his face covered, and his bell ringing about his neck.

At last, seeing that his coming made strife and uproar on God's day, the leper remained in his own hut, in the fields beyond the walls, and listened for the great bell to be rung at the elevation of the Host.

But when it was found that he meant not to come, but would stay in meekness apart from God's altar, then as one man the city rose up, and went and brought him back in triumph, and put on him again the royal robe, and set him upon the throne. And, the thing being done, no voice small or great was lifted up against it.

But the King was a leper still; and still, for all men might say, beneath his crown he wore the cloth over his face, and round his neck the bell to warn men of his coming.

And as he went through the palace where all bowed at his approach, he still cried, 'Unclean, unclean!' nor would he allow any to touch him, save it were for the cure of the King's evil, a thing that he thought to be a special mercy which, in his sins, God had given him. And when he went forth to Mass with a great train, and in all his royal robes, through the streets, at the church-door he and the rest parted; and they went within, but the King passed round to the leper's window on the chancel's north side, and therethrough he heard Mass said. And from touch of him no harm came to any man; though a leper he remained, more loved by all than any king of sound body had been in the world before.

So time went on, and it was Maundy Thursday once more. Into the courtyard came the leper-king, girdled with a towel, and bearing the golden ewer; and there all round the walls sat the beggar-men waiting for their feet to be washed.

The leper over his face was wearing the cloth, and as he moved the bell that was round his neck rang; and he went from one to another thanking God for having put it into his hands to do that solemn service, which he had never hoped could be his to do more. So going the round in meek thanksgiving he came to the last.

That One, at the King's coming, drew up His beggars rags, and set down Feet marred and maimed into the golden dish. The leper, when he saw that, drew in his breath sharp, and trembled with exceedingness of joy; but nothing was said there. Only after the washing he stooped low, and kissed the two Wounds: and still could say no word for the bliss and comfort that had there taken hold of both body and soul. And therefrom never again could he draw his lips away, for in Them mercy and truth were met together, and righteousness and peace kissed each other.

His people, seeing how the King lay low before a beggar's feet, thought he had fallen from some sickness; and going to lift him, first saw they his hands all pure of the leprosy. Then in wonder they drew the face-cloth from his face, and behold, there too all the leprosy was gone. And the bell, as they lifted him, that was about his neck, made no sound as it swung, to tell men that anything unclean was in their midst: but in all ways he was the most beautiful King that ever men swathed for burial.

Within the church, and within the chancel's north side they buried him: where the Wound was in Christ's Side, there in the church they buried him: within the leper's window, in between that and the high altar.

There until now the King's body, which was corrupt in life, stays incorruptible for the final day, when Christ shall at last appear, and lay His Finger upon all the world, and heal it of the King's evil.

Gods, and their Makers   (1897)
     (written in 1889)

CHAPTER I

INTO Peeti's soul had come the vision of his god. In the midst of the night-watches, with eyes straining at the shuffling darkness, he had beheld it; and as his mental appetite took its bite of the unknown, the divine form grew in clearness and definition. With feet planted within the borders of the invisible world, it seemed to be stamping the shape of its godhead on the threshold of the material, apparent already in the stirring of the child's brain, as a manifest reality. The shadows shut and opened like the swaying to and fro of a curtain, deeps darkly disparting, closing again in a greyness more opaque, on the surface of which the form of the god seemed to move. Shiplike the thing drifted over the face of his dreams.

Light of the over-dawn and full awaking came to eye and brain, and Peeti rose carrying with him a consecrated memory of how one, Katchy-wallah of articulated name, had stood over against his bed in the long hours and the darkness, and chattered to him concerning the construction of its own godhead, saying: 'Let me be made of a gourd, and let my countenance be fierce, and for food give me the shedding of men's teeth!' And Peeti, answering by that form of asseveration which among savage races is the most solemn sign of abject and devoted service, had said: 'Thou shalt be made of a gourd; and thy countenance shall be fierce; and for food I will give thee the shedding of men's teeth.'

Conscience and tradition were at strife in Peeti's bosom, as he shook himself up from the continuing slumbers of his tribe at the call of his new-found deity. Conscience said, 'My god is my own god, and he shall be made by me.' Orthodoxy said, 'Up and take your dream to the priests, that they may interpret, fulfil, peradventure dock and curtail this rough vision of a divinity.' Peeti, with the eyes of an advancing mind, had beheld orthodoxy from its hinder parts; presently, in the shove and jostle of contending thoughts, it knocked knees hopelessly, and lay elbowed to the wall.

For here was Peeti's god come to him, minutely defined, the name and the nature of it, and the method of its manufacture. Peeti went over it all bit by bit, till he had it firmly in his vision, and chewed his fists for joy. He planned how a fat gourd could be scooped for a belly, a mouth carved out of wood and coloured a ravenous red; and then he joined to these such a shedding of men's teeth as never was till now.

Was ever possession like to this? Surely his very own should his own god be! As a modern seer has said since, 'My mountains are my own, and I will keep them to myself,' so was Peeti minded to say, as, to his god, the yet unfashioned and invisible, he made consecrate his first vow against the priestly tradition and observance of his tribe. He bowed himself to the coming incarnation and said, 'No hand shall make thee, Katchywallah, but mine alone. Surely, this day thine eyes shall look upon thine own belly which thy servant's hands shall have prepared for thee!'

.   .   .   .   .

CHAPTER XX

WHEN the raft was afloat, they cast thereon food and drink for the journey; and wading waist-deep, took hold of the timbers, cautiously letting themselves drift along the shore till they reached the rocky arch, which spanned the out-going current.

Then, commending themselves to the kindest influence they knew, even the wild spirit of the sea — they cast themselves on board, let the raft swing out into the full push of the current, and clung on for dear life.

The waters roared and swirled about them, dashed them on, in under, and through; then abated their force, and lo — ocean and free sky!

Peeti and Aystah beheld liberty at last. All the sea lay broad and bright before them; and ahead they saw how the current bore away, away, they knew not whither, through what rocks or shoals. The future for them might be dark and imminent as night: or, like the sea, fathomless, but bright and broad.

Whatever Fate had in store for them, life or death, they prepared willingly to take it; having so little to hazard, they hazarded all.

Yet one piteous remnant of the land they left still clung to them, not wishing to be cast away. In their wake there shrilled a plaintive and a feeble cry: 'Take me too! Take me too!'

A poor little fishy god came and put up his gaping mouth and goggle eyes against the side of the raft, and paddled industriously with flapper and fin.

'Oh, let me take him!' said Aystah, touched with compassion. 'Just this one!'

'Oh! take me too! Oh! take me too!' cried the little god.

But Peeti shook his head resolutely. 'Keep in the sea, my friend,' he said, 'when you go back! The Devil is loose in yonder isle; and he eats fish.'

'Take me too! Take me too!' said the little god, disconsolately.

He swam for another mile, falling little by little to the rear; — another mile, and they could only tell by a faint far-off ripple that he still followed them. Over the waters came an attenuated cry, 'Oh! take me too, me too, me too!'

Far away stood the island, blue between the two blues of sky and sea. Fair, very fair, it seemed, with its trees waving away into mist; but in the heart of it went the Devourer—already, if not yet, its sole inhabitant, rapidly approaching the consummation of his aim to become so.

Oh! fish-tailed and finny, go thou, and wait with obsequious cry upon each raft that brings a new god to those shores; point to the land and say, 'Yonder is One waiting and watching like a lion prowling for his prey; and whosoever cometh unto him, shall find in him both food and lodging, nor shall he in anywise be cast out!'

But Peeti and Aystah sail on the great sea-current.

The End

The Story of the Seven Young Goslings   (1898)

[*which here begins*]:

AT the top of a town, on the edge of a wood,
A long time ago a little house stood,
    With a tarred barred gate, and a short court-yard,
And a pump, and a big black water-butt,
And a small front-door that was always shut,
    As though its inside was a Turk's or a Moslem's;
For to privacy owed, 'twas the only abode
    Of a mother goose and her seven young goslimbs.

The goose was a widow: for this and a variety
Of other reasons she never went into society.
    Entombed in a wolf
    Was her husband the gander,
    And the painful event
    Had completely unmanned her.

            .   .   .   .   .

Well! ...
    Hark to the blood-curdling tale that I tell!

Early one morning the mother-goose spread
Her feet into boots, and put bonnet on head;

24

And counting her coin, being gifted with gumption,
Made a list of things wanted for family consumption:
    The chops and the mops,
    And the broccoli-tops;
The jallops and scallops and chocolate-drops;
The ink and the drink, and the pink lollypops,
    And the syrupy sops —
These were the things she must get at the shops.

Then she sat herself down like a tea-cosee,
And gathered her goslings under her knee,
And began for to speak through her beak to this end —
    'Now, children, attend!
You know, for I often have told you so,
Whatever you do, and wherever you go,
'Tis better far to be filial than famous;
So sing me your song of the wise Ignoramus.'

    Then each little gosling looked down its nose,
    And folded its wings, and flattened its toes,
    Looking so pure, and demure, and select,
    And replied to its mother to this effect:

'Oh, you must remember wherever you are,
You are the jam, but your mother's the jar;
You are the twig, but your mother's the trunk;
You are the crumb, but your mother's the chunk.
So you must endeavour, whatever you do,
Not to be clever, nor think it's you;
    But intellect smother,
    And stick to your mother,
And somehow or other she'll pull you through.'

    .   .   .   .   .

[*and which here ends*]:

When the mother-bird heard
How these things had occurred,
She flapped her poor wings, but she uttered no word;

No time did she waste
On the track sorrow traced,
For she knew, through and through, what a mother should do:
So in haste, with hands nimble
    Her work-bag she spread,
Took scissors and thimble,
    Chose needle and thread;
And gnashing the scissors twixt finger and thumb,
With eyes fixed in expression heroic and rum,
    Cried, 'Come!'

The mother-goose called, and the little one came,
Telepathically true, and triumphantly tame;
The mother-goose whistled, the little goose went
Aboundingly bold, and obediently bent;
The mother-goose rushed, and the little goose ran,
As only a goose when she's wolf-hunting can;
    Down the hill,
    Through the town,
To the river they hopped,
And there, with a shiver, the mother-goose stopped.

For there lay the wolf with his nostrils all wide,
And through them went rolling the breath of his pride;
And fat as a football, and tight as a drum,
Post-prandial and full lay his wicked tum-tum.
There he lay sleeping the sleep of the just;
His lying tongue in his cheek was thrust;
    And he worked his paws,
    And jerked his jaws,
And yammered and clamoured, and yelped because
He dreamed of the fat little goslings that he
Had taken and eaten, to sweeten his tea.

    Now hear, and decide,
    Now gaze and see,
How faith, in a competent mother, may be

In competent offspring justified:
For there went a stir in the wolf's inside,
And a sound of tongues that cried and replied;
Out of that place of shadow and shame,
With bubble and squeak the anthem came:

'Oh, you must remember, wherever you are,
You are the jam, but your mother's the jar;
You are the twig, but your mother's the trunk;
You are the crumb, but your mother's the chunk!
So you must endeavour, whatever you do,
Not to be clever, nor think it's you;
    But intellect smother,
    And stick to your mother,
And somehow or other she'll pull you through!'

The old goose heard with motherly pride
Her praises sung in the wolf's inside;
It made her expand, it made her glow,
It nerved her hand for the dreadful blow;
She waited until the words should end,
Then said 'Just so; now, my dears, attend!'
She flourished her scissors, she flashed them wide,
And jabbed them into his wicked inside;
His stomach from end to end she slit,
    And scurry, flurry, flitter, and flutter,
    Before another word she could utter,
Six little goslings leapt out of it!

With uproarious pleasure that overpowered her,
They fell on their mother, and almost devoured her!
They kissed her beak, or her cheek for choice,
They kissed her hands, and the sound of her voice,
They kissed her pillowy, billowy body,
They kissed the shoes she was shod in of shoddy,
They kissed the very ground where she stood,
They kissed her all over because she was good!

Jostling and crowding, pushing and shoving her,
Climbing and clinging, they couldn't stop loving her!

Then cried the mother, to each little chick,
'Run down to the river, and quick, be quick!
Bring six of the largest stones you can fetch,
And let's fill up the paunch of the ravenous wretch:
For fear, when he wakes, he should find himself thinner,
We'll stuff in the stones in the place of his dinner!'
They ran, and they fetched, as their mother had bid,
And what she had promised the mother-goose did;
She stuffed in the stones, and with fingers full nimble,
Stitched him neatly together with needle and thimble.
And back to their home, brimful of content,
The goose and the seven young goslings went.

The wolf, when he woke, felt fit to burst,
He was heavy of head, and consumed by thirst;
    So down to the river, where minnow and perch
Were swimming at will, went he to drink;
And there, so soon as he came to the brink,
    Stretching his throat to the babbling wave,
    All of a sudden the stones gave a lurch,
    And all of a sudden a lurch he gave,
And into the river, neck over crop
Fell he, too heavy to swim to the top, —
    And there found a grave.

And down from the hill, came a song on the breeze,
And the words that sang over his corpse were these:
    'Oh, you must remember, wherever you are,
    You are the jam, but your mother's the jar;
    You are the twig, but your mother's the trunk;
    You are the crumb, but your mother's the chunk!
        So you must endeavour
            Whatever you do,
        Not to be clever,
            Nor think it's you;

> But intellect smother,
> And stick to your mother,
> And somehow or other
> She'll pull you through!'

An Englishwoman's Love-Letters (1900)

I WAS hardly five then, and going up to the nursery from downstairs had my supper-cake in my hand — only a few mouthfuls left. Arthur had been having his bath, and sitting on his nurse's knee was getting into his bed-clothes, when spying me with my cake, he asked to have a share of it. I daresay it would not have been good for him, but of that I thought nothing at all; the cruel impulse took me to make one mouthful of all that was left. He watched it go without crying; but his eyes opened at me in a strange way, wondering at this sudden lesson of the hardness of a human heart. 'All gone!' he said, turning toward nurse, perhaps to see if she too had a like surprise for his small intelligence. I think I have never forgiven myself that: the judging remembrance of it would, I believe, win forgiveness to him for any wrong he might do me now, so unreasonably is my brain scarred where the thought of it still lies. . . .

The other thing came of a less personal greed, and was years later. We were egg-collectors; and in the loft over one of the outhouses there was a swallow's nest too high to be reached by any ladder we could get up there. I was intent on getting the *eggs*, and thought of no other thing that might chance; so I spread a soft fall below, and with a long pole I broke the floor of the nest. Then with a sudden stir of horror I saw soft things falling along with the clay, tiny and feathery. Two were killed by the breakage that fell with them, but one was quite alive and unhurt. I gathered up the remnants of the nest, and set it with the young one in it by the loft-window where the parent birds might see, making clumsy strivings of pity to quiet my conscience. The parent-birds did see, soon enough: they returned — first up to the rafters, then darting round and round, and crying; then to where their little one lay helpless and exposed, hung over it with a nibbling movement of their beaks for a moment, making my miserable heart bound up with hope: then away, away, shrieking into the July sunshine. Once they came back and shrieked at the horror of it all, and fled away not to return. I remained for hours, and did what silly pity could dictate; but of course the young one died: and I — *cleared away all remains, so that nobody might see.* Since then, the poignancy of my regret, when I think of it, has never softened. The question which pride of life and love of make-believe till then had not raised in me: 'Am I a god to kill and make alive?' was answered all at once by an emphatic 'No!' which I never afterwards forgot. But the grief remained all the same, that life — to teach me that blunt truth — should have had to make sacrifice in the mote-hung loft of three frail lives on a clay-altar, and bring to nothing but pain, and a last miserable dart away into the bright sunshine, the spring work of two swift-winged intelligences. Is man we are told to think, not worth many sparrows? Sometimes I doubt it, and would in thought give my life that those swallows in their generation might live again.

A Modern Antaeus   (1901)

LADY PETWYN'S PAST

ONE day he came upon her sitting among heaps of musty documents. A post-mortem mood had seized on her; she had a presentiment, she told him, that she was going to die — prayed it might be with the hounds during the coming winter: and was mindful to spare her executors unnecessary labour. 'If to save trouble were all,' she remarked, 'I might as well put a match to every security I possess, and die intestate; then cousins and the law could wrangle it out at leisure. Executors are usually one's friends: heirs, not necessarily: I've no friend among mine! There are Cooper-Petwyns, and Coopers, who seem to think because I was cooped up with one of them for all the best years of my life and bought up embarrassed property, that I owe it back to them. "It should stay in the family," is the phrase they have in their greedy mouths. I tell them they may buy it back if they want to. Their grievance is that Sir Cooper reaped the benefit of a broken entail, if to pay one's creditors by the sale of one's patrimony be indeed a benefit!

'Burn that, and that, and that!' she gave Tristram dusty bundles to throw to the flames.

Presently a curious perturbation came over her face, as she crackled her fingers on a bunch of notes tied up with pack-thread; self-disgust seemed to predominate.

'Am I into my dotage?' she exclaimed. 'It would seem so. Here have I been hoarding a budget of my Skeleton's letters for over seventeen years without knowing it!'

She glanced her eye through one of them.

'Poor ghost!' she murmured, 'how he gibbers! Ghosts I can't stand; they whine too much about a future life, invoking one to be Christian and charitable. My charity burned a large enough hole in my pocket when it had him to deal with. Thieves got at it then; it's moth and rust now. Help us! What a liar the fellow was: writes he knows I have a kind heart! He knew exactly the contrary, but that was Bones all over: — made love to me when he was dying because he wanted a particular brand to which I had the key, and cursed me in his last will and testament! made a will to do it, I imagine: for he had no money to leave. That's the man my memory has got to deal with! I'm widow to that, my dear; my "Ladyship" I got from him!

'When he did his duty finally, and died, I asked the doctor how long it would take him to become bone. Medical science gave me a date. After he was turned into a bone-man, forgiveness of him became possible! And yet his Christian relatives reproached me for putting him in an earth-to-earth coffin; cremation wasn't to be had in those days. Lord! what moles we all are with our prejudices! You know now why I call him "Bones"; it strips him of his vices. Can you imagine a skeleton taking too much to drink, for instance? No; it's a mercy!

Tristram's sensitiveness showed a shrinking from such a squalid inspection of the past. The old dame's tongue turned a sharp corner.

'I'm going to tell you a love-story,' said she. 'That man kicked to death a friend of mine, and I broke my leg jumping too fast out of window to get at him. Providence seems to have stamped on the wrong foot that time; eh? There's one of the things I have to think him out of the flesh for, for comfort's sake. This is not the love-story, but it comes round to it. Bones used to beat his own dogs every day and all day long, but not my boy — till once. That day I heard curses, and all at once Billy gave a cry. I knew it for his, out of all others, and ran — could run, I tell you, in those days! Out of window I saw my poor beast chained, and my other beast in top-boots kicking him. Murder's a quick brew: two of us got the infection. Ever you've been in a real rage you've felt you could fly. Anyway, a woman before she's forty has her hallucinations at times. That was mine. In reality I came smash. There was I along the cobble-stones; and, over the way, butchery by all the fiends! Bones was doing it: Billy, staunch beast, tugging at his chain to be at him. Soon as he saw me, 'twas a double struggle: — he to get my way, I to get his, — I dragging pain along with me that was like a ton of mustard. Down goes Billy just as I got to him. The last I remembered was having hold of Bones's hand with my teeth where Billy had bitten him just before. And for the result of that day's work Sir Cooper had to do without an heir.

'Five years I shared house with him after that. Think of it, and me lame, hobbling with that thing for a memory! He never struck me; I waited for it; he seemed to know why. That's how it is, my dear, I never murdered him. People who knew what he was, thought me a model of duty; and when I die, as I've made no provision against it, I suppose they will lay me alongside of Bones with all the decorum in the world. Poor Bones, how will he like it, I wonder!'

From this narrative Tristram gathered for the first time the full meaning of a certain tombstone in Little Alwyn churchyard. After many years of neglect Lady Petwyn had one day set herself right with the neighbours by erecting a handsome memorial over the late Baronet's remains. That had been done within Tristram's own brief memory. He remembered the wording of the inscription, and saw now its underlying significance.

'Here rest,' was how it ran, 'the bones of SIR COOPER COOPER PETWYN, Bart., Lord of the Manor of Alwyn, sometime Master of the Tavishire Foxhounds, Justice of the Peace.'

Date of death and date of erection followed; not a word of sentiment or untruth; only the ponderous eloquence of costly stone to say whether this poor dust had not once its value in men's eyes.

'And now,' went on her ladyship, 'how did I come to marry him? It's a life of me you will have to hear.' So, then and there, Tristram heard from hard withered lips, a brave lady's love-story.

The only love her gaoler of a heart had ever let go to man had won freedom behind sound of galloping hoofs on a road leading she knew not whither. The gallant, fine gentleman, pauper, rogue, all rolled into one, who was her companion and tempter in that exploit had beheld her first in a church pew, ranked with the demure misses in their teens of an aristocratic boarding-school; and, more dazzled by her high darting glance than by her fortune — for 'twas whispered there sat an heiress — had come, a stranger, and borne her off under the full stare of day. Adding by a few dexterous strokes ten years to the ten which already made him her senior, he had presented himself in a post-chaise white with the dust of its speed, bearing a missive purporting to tell of a father dying in apoplectic state, as befitted an alderman.

The heiress of two hundred thousand pounds was trustingly confided to a man without a penny that was not borrowed, by a head mistress who had the merit of knowing a gentleman when she saw him.

A mile from the start, being a man of feeling, the gallant dried the young girl's eyes with a broad hint of her father's safety. He bade her look at the bright world that flew past, and draw full breath at being out in it. Did she wish to return?

'Where am I going?' she asked him.

Exactly wherever she liked, he told her, — to Scotland, whose marriages were more made by Heaven than were England's, for preference. He promised her his heart, and white heather instead of orange blossom, yet declared that the decision of the matter rested with her. She tested him at once, bidding him put the chaise about. The thing was done promptly. The sight of the school roofs, and the sound of a bell at that moment giving harsh summons to drudgery from which she was free, made her reverse the order. They arrived very late at the inn which was to be their first resting-place. The lover had insisted, in spite of postilions; had even allowed himself to appear in fear of pursuit. They aroused a sleeping house; and the cause of his solicitude presently appeared in a respectable waiting-woman whom he had engaged beforehand to keep guard over a young girl's reputation. She received her mistress into safe-keeping, and was able to give evidence after, which was the undoing of the whole scheme. 'Heigh ho!' was the poor lady's regretful comment on that incongruity in the midst of an otherwise romantic and promising episode.

The northward miles flew all too briefly; separation followed hard. After an unchurched clinching before witnesses, the lover handed back his wedded wife to the pursuing and enraged relatives, and went gaily off to endure the legal penalty for abduction which he had incurred. Any church ceremony, if they wished for it, could wait his return to liberty. The girl-wife swore faith to his face and behind his back. It was notice-able that she met the parental eye without blushing. Inquiry was started; the waiting-woman was questioned; the gallant himself made a courteous avowal that he had postponed till a more ceremonious occasion the assertion of his indubitable rights. He kissed his hand metaphorically to the mistress of his heart, retiring behind iron bars for the space of two years. The period was long enough for the lady's family to act on hopes destined cruelly to be realized. Supported by certain certificates, proof up to the hilt, a private bill was brought into Parliament and passed, annulling the fly-away marriage. Being a minor the poor girl was left without voice in the matter, and deprived willy-nilly of the man of her heart. Pathetically ignorant to the last as to how her lover's generous scruples had betrayed her, she returned to school and spinsterhood, and became, five years afterwards, the wife of Sir Cooper Petwyn, a man, willing for the sake of compensations, to take over the victim of a dead romance. Thus Lady Petwyn went to her living tomb.

She told Tristram the tale with a dry relish, ironic to the last: yet, with her own fate, had not quite reached the end of her story. After her father's death, being then tied up in decent matrimony, she became the mistress of her own property, and was minded to override such things as private acts of Parliament. Thus she finished her story:

'I saw myself free to be my own mistress — and his. A year or two of Bones had sufficed to make me feel under no bond. Off I went to dis-cover my true mate; hunted, and found him. I had no illusion or romance then. Yet there was a mutual something between us. I knew to my cost that there was loyalty in him. Poor rogue! to pass the time, perhaps to rid himself of a momentary embarrassment, he had married a mere any-body, and between them the precarious couple had come by a baby. The event proved that no life lay in it. I never saw so disappointed a face as his when he found what he had missed for lack of a little patience. Words stopped: we recognized each other's meaning: seeing that new bonds were uppermost, silence was the best medicine for our chagrin.

'I saw the wife: a good little thing, cut out to be the drudge of a brilliant ne'er-do-weel. His truth to her was foolish and touching; there was so little need for it; and he pitied himself so hugely!

'I never saw them again; but it pleased me to dribble out a dole to that

poor domestic squaw about which he was to know nothing. It gave him
an easier conscience to see that, whatever he did or didn't do for her, she
had food enough for her mouth and a roof over her head. He ambled
about, wit, buffoon, and odd-corner man to gay circles; I don't know
what he did to avoid making a living; I should doubt whether he kept
honest. It took him twenty years to catch his death, the one thing he
proved slow over. When he was dying in his own way, I suppose his
wife got soft-hearted and blabbed my name. A child had turned up to
them absurdly just at the last, and the poor woman's betrayal of my
finger in their pie set him naming the thing after me. She sent me word
of it in black edges — I was a widow and a godmother in one — also a
puppy he had had the training of. It came by his last orders, with his
grateful respects, I was to be told. That was poor Billy: the dog only
survived his master two years. Bones! bones! bones! there's three of
them to think about!'

Bethlehem A Nativity Play   (1902)

ACT I

(CHORUS *enters and speaks before the curtain*)

Ye Gentles, that come here to watch our play,
Put, we beseech you, thought of us away!
No standing here have we: in heart we kneel,
With, at our hearts, this prayer, — that ye may feel
How in Love's hands time is a little thing!
And so shall Love to-night your senses bring
Back to the hills of Bethlehem, the fold
Where shepherds watched their sheep, where angels told
Of peace, goodwill to men, in Christ new-born,
By Whom, from Virgin Birth, our flesh goes worn
Also, if we may guide you, ye shall see
The manger where in great humility
Lieth that Babe, the Maker of us all,
By Mary's side, amid the beasts in stall.
And ye shall see the coming of the Kings,
Led by a star; and Gabriel, that brings

Unto Saint Joseph, in a dream by night,
Word of King Herod's fear, and counsels flight.
So, lastly, ye shall see them rise and go,
And the place vacant left. Yet ye shall know
That Love remains, and that Faith sees it so.
So, have ye hope! let Time your trust increase!
Hark, I hear music! Christmas comes; 'tis peace.

A SHEPHERD (*sings*) The world is old, to-night,
    The world is old;
   The stars around the fold
    Do show their light, do show their light.
   And so they did, and so,
   A thousand years ago,
  And so will do, dear love, when you lie cold.

   The world is still, to-night,
    The world is still;
   The snow on vale and hill
    Like wool lies white, like wool lies white.
   And so it was, and so,
   A thousand years ago,
  And so will be, good lads, when we lack will.

ACT II

(*Enter procession of Kings*)

FIRST KING Hear me, O King of Kings,
     And give me my desire!
SECOND KING Hive me beneath Thy wings,
     And guide my feet with fire!
THIRD KING Unto that Holy Mount,
     Where forth from Thee goes Light.
ALL   Whence springs a Living Fount
     To wash the whole world white.
GABRIEL Peace be with you, and hail!
     Where go ye this fair night,
     Travellers, and what seek ye?

FIRST KING We seek from the hill the vale,
        And from the vale the hill.
SECOND KING From the ends of the morning, rest;
        And from the East the West.
THIRD KING In the darkness we seek fire,
        And out of dreams the heart's desire!
        And, if to-day we fail,
        To-morrow we seek it still.
GABRIEL Are ye not weary, seeking so?
        Are ye not laden with care?
FIRST KING We are not weary. If our feet be slow,
        'Tis with the burden of the Love we bear;
        It is our longing for the Light we seek
        Which makes us weak.
GABRIEL What is the longing of each one?
THIRD KING Melchior, wilt thou first speak?
SECOND KING Too slow my footsteps move
        For the goal I seek to prove.
        My body is a waste,
        Through which my soul doth haste,
        Famished until it taste .
        Its nameless new desire!
        A flame my spirit owns,
        Ashes are all my bones,
        Love lights in me such fire!
        I thirst! my throat is dried;
        I ask; — am still denied;
        Cry to be satisfied:
        Yet only as Love will.
        Now, if He comes not first,
        Not death, but ease were worst; —
        Let me die, thirsting still!
GABRIEL And you?
THIRD KING   I have such Love!
        Beauty, I know not of,
        Hath laid on me the vision of its Light.
        When that Light shines, earth's ends

Therein shall all be friends:
They shall not hurt nor kill; but on the height
Named Holy shall be peace.
Then shall all warfare cease,
And every king his crown
Shall at the cradle of a new-born Babe lay down.

GABRIEL   And thou, that standest last,
Say what desire thou hast?

FIRST KING   For Earth's waiting to be done;
For God to send forth His Son,
Godhead and man made one!
That Creation, wrought afresh,
May be finished and made whole;
That the Word may become Flesh,
And Earth receive her soul!
     Pray we for this,
     Seeing well how good it is.

GABRIEL   Behold, this night shall bring you to your bliss.

THIRD KING   Whence comes thy knowledge to make hope so near?

GABRIEL   Oh, let your ears be opened till they hear!
Open your eyes, and mark with fearless sight
The throng of thanksgiving which fills this night:
Nor walks on heaven alone, but earth as well!
Sound in sweet tone, celestial Choirs, and tell!

ANGELS (*appearing*)   Glory to God   In the Highest!
     Who unto man   Now comes nighest.
     Peace be to earth!   Goodwill to all!
     Christ the new Birth   Redeems man's fall.
         (*They disappear*)

FIRST KING   Oh, ye blest sounds, be as the air we breathe!

SECOND KING   Oh, fair things seen, your light to us bequeath!

THIRD KING   And if there be an ending to our quest,
Show, now, where lies our rest!

GABRIEL   O Kings, your quest is ended now, earth joins
To greet her Lord, in Heaven's exultant strains.
Righteousness is the girdle of His loins,
And faithfulness the girdle of His reins.

The Spirit of God shall rest on Him, of might,
Of wisdom, and of counsel, and of fear:
He shall not judge according unto sight,
Neither reprove by the hearing of His ear:
But by His righteousness shall He do right,
And with His equity the meek repay;
Out of His mouth a rod the earth shall smite,
And by His breath the wicked He shall slay.
The wolf shall make his dwelling in the fold,
The leopard and the kid together play,
The young lion with the fatling: and behold
A Little Child shall lead them in the way!
Then like the ox the lion shall eat straw,
The calf and the young bear be in one pen;
The suckling from his hole the asp shall draw,
And the weaned child play by the adder's den.
They shall not hurt in all my Holy Hill,
Nor shall there any more destruction be:
The knowledge of the Lord the earth shall fill,
Even as the water covereth the sea.
And He shall raise His people from their sin.
This is the way of Life: walk ye therein!

The Blue Moon (1904)

[My first three books of fairy-tales were written when I was more of an illustrator than a writer. They are now out of print. Most, but not all of them, have been reissued in two volumes under the titles of *A Doorway in Fairyland* and *Moonshine and Clover*.]

A CAPFUL OF MOONSHINE

On the top of Drundle Head, away to the right side, where the track crossed, it was known that the fairies still came and danced by night. But though Toonie went that way every evening on his road home from work, never once had he been able to spy them.

So one day he said to the old faggot-maker, 'How is it that one gets to see a fairy?' The old man answered, 'There are some to whom it comes by nature; but for others three things are needed — a handful of courage, a mouthful of silence, and a capful of moonshine. But if you would be trying it, take care that you don't go wrong more than twice; for with the third time you will fall into the hands of the fairies and become their bondsman. But if you manage to see the fairies, you may ask whatever you like of them.'

Toonie believed in himself so much that the very next night he took his courage in both hands, filled his cap with moonshine, shut his mouth, and set out.

Just after he had started he passed, as he thought, a priest riding by on a mule. 'God evening to you, Toonie,' called the priest.

'Good evening, your reverence,' cried Toonie, and flourished off his cap, so that out fell his capful of moonshine. And though he went on all the way up over the top of Drundle Head, never a fairy did he spy; for he forgot that, in passing what he supposed to be the priest, he had let go both his mouthful of silence, and his capful of moonshine.

The next night, when he was coming to the ascent of the hill, he saw a little elderly man wandering uncertainly over the ground ahead of him; and he too seemed to have his hands full of courage and his cap full of moonshine. As Toonie drew near, the other turned about and said to him, 'Can you tell me, neighbour, if this be the way to the fairies?'

'Why, you fool,' cried Toonie, 'a moment ago it was! But now you have gone and let go your mouthful of silence!'

'To be sure, to be sure — so I have!' answered the old man sadly; and turning about, he disappeared among the bushes.

As for Toonie, he went on right over the top of Drundle Head, keeping his eyes well to the right; but never a fairy did he see. For he too had on his way let go his mouthful of silence.

Toonie, when his second failure came home to him, was quite vexed with himself for his folly and mismanagement. So that it should not happen again, he got his wife to tie on his cap of moonshine so firmly that it could not come off, and to gag up his mouth so that no word could come out of it. And once more taking his courage in both hands, he set out.

For a long way he went and nothing happened, so he was in good hopes of getting the desire of his eyes before the night was over; and, clenching his fists tight upon his courage, he pressed on.

He had nearly reached the top of Drundle Head, when up from the ground sprang the same little elderly man of the evening before, and began beating him across the face with a hazel wand. And at that Toonie threw up both hands and let go his courage, and turned and tried to run down the hill.

When her husband did not return, Toonie's wife became a kind of widow. People were very kind to her, and told her that Toonie was not dead — that he had only fallen into the hands of the good-folk; but all day long she sat and cried, 'I fastened on his cap of moonshine, and I tied up his tongue; and for all that he has gone away and left me!' And so she cried until her child was born and named Little Toonie in memory of his lost father.

After a while people, looking at him, began to shake their heads; for as he grew older it became apparent that his tongue was tied, seeing that he remained quite dumb in spite of all that was done to teach him; and his head was full of moonshine, so that he could understand nothing clearly by day — only as night came on his wits gathered, and he seemed to find a meaning for things. And some said it was his mother's fault, and some that it was his father's, and some that he was a changeling sent by the fairies, and that the real child had been taken to share his father's bondage. But which of these things was true Little Toonie himself had no idea.

After a time Little Toonie began to grow big, as is the way with children, and at last he became bigger than ever old Toonie had been. But folk still called him Little Toonie, because his head was so full of moonshine; and his mother, finding he was no good to her, sold him to the farmer, by whom, since he had no wits for anything better, he was set to pull at wagon and plough just as if he were a cart-horse; and, indeed, he was almost as strong as one. To make him work, carter and plough-man used to crack their whips over his back; and Little Toonie took it as the most natural thing in the world, because his brain was full of moonshine, so that he understood nothing clearly by day.

But at night he would lie in his stable among the horses, and wonder about the moonlight that stretched wide all over the world and lay free on the bare tops of the hills; and he thought — would it not be good to be there all alone, with the moonbeams laying their white hands down on his head? And so it came that one night finding the door of his stable unlocked, he ran out into the open world a free man.

A soft wind breathed at large, and swung slowly in the black-silver treetops. Over them Little Toonie could see the quiet slopes of Drundle Head, asleep in the moonlight.

Before long, following the lead of his eyes, he had come to the bottom of the ascent. There before him went walking a little shrivelled elderly man, looking to right and left as if uncertain of the road.

As Little Toonie drew near, the other one turned and spoke. 'Can you tell me,' he said, 'if this be the way to the fairies?'

Little Toonie had no tongue to give an answer; so, looking at his questioner, he wagged his head and went on.

Quickening his pace, the old man came alongside and began peering; then he smiled to himself, and after a bit spoke out. 'So you have lost your cap, neighbour? Then you will never be able to find the fairies.' For he did not know that Little Toonie, who wore no cap on his head, carried his capful of moonshine safe underneath his skull, where it had been since the hour of his birth.

The little elderly man slipped from his side, disappearing suddenly among the bushes, and Toonie went on alone. So presently he was more than halfway up the ascent, and could see along the foot-track of the thicket the silver moonlight lying out over the open ahead.

He had nearly risen to the top of the hill, when up from the ground sprang up the little elderly man, and began beating him across the face with a hazel wand. Toonie thought surely this must be some carter or ploughman beating him to make him go faster; so he made haste to get on and be rid of the blows.

Then, all of a sudden, the little elderly man threw away his hazel stick, and fell down, clutching at Little Toonie's ankles, whining and praying him not to go on.

'Now that I have failed to keep you from coming,' he cried, 'my masters will put me to death for it! I am a dead man, I tell you, if you go another step!'

Toonie could not understand what the old fellow meant, and he could not speak to him. But the poor creature clung to his feet, holding them to prevent him from taking another step; so Toonie just stooped down, and (for he was so little and light) picked him up by the scruff, and carried him by his waistband, so that his arms and legs trailed together along the ground.

In the open moonlight ahead little people were all agog; bright dew-drops were shivering down like rain, where flying feet alighted — shot from bent grass-blades like arrows from a drawn bow. Tight, panting little bodies, of which one could count the ribs, and faces flushed with fiery green blood, sprang everywhere. But at Toonie's coming one cried up shriller than a bat; and at once rippling burrows went this way and that in the long grass, and stillness followed after.

The poor, dangling old man, whom Toonie was still carrying, wriggled and whined miserably, crying, 'Come back, masters, for it is no use — this one sees you! He has got past me and all my poor skill to stop him. Set me free, for you see I am too old to keep the door for you any longer!'

Out buzzed the fairies, hot and angry as a swarm of bees. They came and fastened upon the unhappy old man, and began pulling him. 'To the ant-hills!' they cried; 'off with him to the ant-hills!' But when they found that Toonie still held him, quickly they all let go.

One fairy, standing out from the rest, pulled off his cap and bowed low. 'What is your will, master mortal?' he inquired; 'for until you have taken your wish and gone, we are all slaves at your bidding.'

They all cringed round him, the cruel little people; but he answered nothing. The moonbeams came thick, laying their slender white palms graciously upon Toonie's head; and he, looking up, opened his mouth for a laugh that gave no sound.

'Ah, so! That is why — he is a mute!' cried the fairies.

Quickly one dipped his cap along the grass and brought it filled with dew. He sprang up, and poured it upon Toonie's tongue; and as the fairy dew touched it, 'Now speak!' they all cried in chorus, and fawned and cringed, waiting for him to give them a word.

Cudgelling his brain for what it all meant, he said, 'Tell me first what wish I may have.'

'Whatever you like to ask,' said they, 'for you have become one of our free men. Tell us your name?'

'I am called Little Toonie,' said he, 'the son of old Toonie that was lost.'

'Why, as I live and remember,' cried the little elderly man, 'old Toonie was me!' Then he threw himself grovelling at his son's feet, and began crying: 'Oh, be quick and take me away! Make them give me up to you: ask to have me! I am your poor, loving old father whom you never saw; all these years have I been looking and longing for you! Now take me away, for they are a proud, cruel people, as spiteful as they are small; and my back has been broken twenty years in their bondage.'

The fairies began to look blue, for they hate nothing so much as to give up one whom they have once held captive. 'We can give you gold,' said they, 'or precious stones, or the root of long living, or the waters of happiness, or the sap of youth, or the seed of plenty, or the blossom of beauty. Choose any of these, and we can give it you.'

The old man again caught hold of his son's feet. 'Don't choose these,' he whimpered, 'choose me!'

So, because he had a capful of moonshine in his head, and because the moonbeams were laying their white hands on his hair, he chose the weak, shrivelled old man, who crouched and clung to him, imploring not to be let go.

The fairies, for spite and anger, bestowed every one a parting pinch on their tumble-down old bondsman; then they handed him to his son, and swung back with careless light hearts to their revels.

As father and son went down the hill together, the old man whistled and piped like a bird. 'Why, why!' he said, 'you are a lad of strength and inches: with you to work and look after me, I can keep on to a merry old age! Ay, ay, I have had long to wait for it; but wisdom is justified in her children.'

Sabrina Warham   (1904)

Farmer Lorry has given grudging accommodation to his widowed sister, Mrs. Warham, at the Monastery Farm. But they live apart. Lorry has never forgiven his sister for having married above her class. Sabrina, who has come to stay with her mother, tries to break down the barrier; and one day, using her cousin David as a go-between, proposes an evening visit to her uncle.

OLD LORRY was prepared for her coming, a circumstance not likely to aid matters; for he was a broody one, a chewer of the cud of enmity, and in malice hard to be beaten. Crippled, not daring to move lest the twinges

44

of his malady should seize him, he had sat all day long in his chair by the fire fixing his mind to his purpose. Thus nine hours had been profitably spent, when Sabrina, holding the breath of her resolve, lifted the latch and entered.

At the far end of the chamber some half-dozen farm labourers sat smoking; an oaken screen dividing the room in half, lending a sort of privacy to the upper portion; against the partition stood a long dresser, upon which was set forth a goodly display of old pewter, the family plate of the establishment. Mrs. Willings, the mute, middle-aged house-keeper, a docile product of the farmer's domestic training, sat at mid-distance, and stitched. In a species of inner chamber formed by the broad ingle the farmer reclined alone. David was among the men; he came forward with a word of welcome when the opening door revealed their visitor.

Farmer Lorry turned his head stiffly and with precaution; blinking small eyes, he greeted his niece with sardonic courtesy.

'Oh, so you've come to call on us, have you? I'm sure we be much obliged to 'ee for the compliment. David, man, look' to your manners, and give your lady-cousin a chair!'

Sabrina was bent on resolute action to break down the barrier she disapproved.

'Give me a welcome first, uncle, so that I may feel I am not intruding,' she said hardily. 'I don't want to be looked on as a visitor, living in the house as I do now.'

'Ah, don't you now; don't you?' remarked the farmer, in mock cordial tones. 'Now, I call that friendly meant, I do! And what does your mother say to it, I wonder?'

'She has not said anything. Why should she?'

'Ah, she will when she hears of it, you be bound! You see, we don't make out for to think ourselves your mother's ek'als, or yours either; we recognize condescension when we see it. Still, if you will be pleased to sit down, I am pleased for 'ee to do so.'

Sabrina's colour was high. 'I came to find how you were, Uncle James,' she said, 'but I need not stay unless you wish.' Nevertheless, when David placed a seat for her she took it.

'Well,' replied Lorry, 'I be as you see me, no better and no worse. David, make up the fire!'

There for a time speech ended, while the younger Lorry gave a vigorous stir to the logs upon the hearth. The room was already too warm. He turned from his operations to inquire of Sabrina if her chair were placed as she would like it. She recognized gratefully the kind amends made by his tone for the old man's rudeness, and answering added —

'Do you use faggots here always? How brightly they burn!'

'*We* use faggots,' said the farmer, sticking to his device of carping comparison. 'Coals we keep for our parlour-boarders; they are only for the quality. Your mother ha'n't no complaint to make of 'em, I hope, young woman — lady, I should say.'

'Uncle James,' petitioned the girl, with grave earnestness, 'will you, please, try to remember what my name is, and call me by it?'

'Well, I've heard of it; but 'tis a great awk'ard mouthful, for plain folk to use: a real knock-me-down sort of a name, I call it.'

'Sabra makes it quite easy.'

'Za-a-bra!' drawled the old man, debasing the sound with slow relish. 'Why, surely that puts one in mind of they striped donkeys you see in travellers' menageries. Now, Zabby 'ud sound a deal better and more reasonable. I'll call 'ee Zabby with pleasure since 'tis to oblige 'ee — or Briny, if ye like that better.' Farmer Lorry accorded to the selected diminutives the lowest and most sordid rendering possible.

Sabrina gave a faint assent to the proposed usage.

Forthwith the farmer assumed a more cordial tone: the situation entirely suited his queer humour.

'Come,' said he, encouragingly, 'now we shall be getting on. Zabby'll do first rate. The fact is,' he continued, as though to explain past difficulties, 'I can't abide gentry, and I don't like mixing wi' 'em. Your mother, she got mixed up with gentry and ended by marrying one of 'em. What's it brought her to? Poverty and Popery, I say. What made her, come of a good Protestant stock, turn Papist? Having a gentleman for a husband, I say. Did being a gentleman make him keep his lawful wife? Did it?'

David thumped the fire, breaking the billets into fractions.

'Now, boy, boy!' cried the farmer, 'don't 'ee go wasting good fuel that way.'

Sabrina declined the diversion. 'Why are you saying these things now, uncle?' she inquired in even tones.

'Now? It's now that we are seeing the results of it all! Did it make him leave any provision for his family? Did it make him live decently, or die decently — being a gentleman, eh? I'm not for blaming *you*, Zabby,' went on the unbearable old man; 'it's not your fault you've got mixed up in it. But I'm just telling you what it is — a bad thing from the start. Don't you go trying to be a lady, Zabby; you'll only end as your mother has ended. Don't try it, I say!'

As though by this time he had earned some refreshment, he bade David draw some ale.

'I must try to believe that you mean kindly in saying these things,' said his niece, with rising anger.

'I don't mean kindly, and I don't mean unkindly,' answered the old curmudgeon. 'I only mean facts; you've got to stomach 'em some day, so it's better to know 'em now.'

'You tell me nothing that I am not aware of,' said Sabrina. 'I know everything already.'

'Oh, you do, do you?' said the farmer, queerly. 'You know that your father was a rogue, then?'

'I know that he did wrong things.'

'Did he ever do a right one?'

'He is dead,' said the girl, simply.

'Ay; and that was only half honest. Could he pay for his own coffin?'

Sabrina sat silent. But for her cousin David's sake she would now have gone, never to return; she was properly punished for having believed friendly terms possible.

The farmer said, after a pause to let his triumph sink in —

'Ah, if I'd only had the walloping of him when he was a boy. I don't turn out rogues, I don't, once I tackle 'em. That fellow over there now' — he pointed to his son — 'I had the making of him, he may thank his stars. Rogue was in him at one time, till I larruped it out of him.'

Farmer Lorry had a gross habit, arising from a vast sense of his own importance, of alluding to people in their presence as though they were absent or unconcerned: he was thus able to indulge his taste for back-biting in the very hearing of his victim. Protest was useless, while silence and submission were accepted as proof of the accusation. Under these attacks David had long since learned to sit unmoved: for passive endurance the meek housekeeper was his only possible rival. With Sabrina for audience and a certain recent recurrence to insubordination well in his mind, Farmer Lorry pursued his theme.

'Till I larruped it out of him,' he said, and pointed. 'Do you see that stick?' At a corner of the ingle lay a stout ash sapling, showing age and wear. 'There's the tool I turned him out with,' continued the old man, eloquent. 'And you may say it was hard work; why, so it was. And you may say, did I ever get any thanks for't? No, I didn't. But I've made my son what he ought to be, and he's no rogue; and maybe he'll thank his old father for it some day, though I may be in my grave then. Ay, you don't better the stick, I say; no other thrashing-machine ever came up to it. David, he looks at that and he remembers who it was once mastered him, and would still if 'twere needed. That's the truth, Zabby.' He added for a finish, nodding across the hearth to where his son sat passively regarding the flames. 'David there, he hears well enough what I tell 'ee; and he ha'n't got a word to say against it.'

Sabrina's patience had reached its limits: she rose abruptly.

'I hope you will be better in the morning, uncle,' she said, with cold civility, and passed out, giving but half a glance and a murmured good night to her cousin, who sat staring into the fire and making no sign. She was miserably conscious that her visit had been the occasion, if not the cause, of the indignity he had had to endure.

After she was gone David still sat staring and saying no word. He took up mechanically the staff of discipline lying near him, eyed its writhen stem, and the ferrule stumpy with long use. Extending it toward the fire, he began poking at the faggots; then, levering a log, he worked in the end, and there let it rest. Old Lorry, watching from his chair, cried peevishly —

'Now, boy, now, you are burning that ash stick!'

It was even so. A little tongue of flame lapped round the ferrule; in the centre it showed blue where the chemical action of heat on metal had begun.

David bent forward and stared into the fire, giving no sign, saying no word. He drove the stick a little further home, only a little further: inch by inch the fire crept along the wood.

Language not to be repeated came now from the farmer; his voice rose to a roar, wrath choked him; he broke into a whine wrung out by physical pain. The meek housekeeper came forward to learn what was the matter;

the men at the far end of the room stood awkward spectators of the scene. Farmer Lorry sat impotent, gripped hard by his malady in the rear: knives cut into him whenever he attempted to move.

David sat as one studiously absorbed, pushing the stick to the flame. Presently six or eight inches were gone: the ferrule dropped off, and lay a ghost of fire, blue amid the red ambers.

The farmer now called for others to lend aid.

'Take it off him, take it off him!' he cried.

The housekeeper, a mechanical messenger of peace, whose instinct was to obey, went up to David and touched the lapel of his coat.

'Go and sit down, Mrs. Willings,' said he; it was the only word he spoke through all that scene.

As one faithfully pursuing an experiment to its end, so David sat and watched impassively the burning of the rod which claimed to have made him a man. When the heat became too much for his hands, he thrust all that remained of the stump into the fire and rose quietly, as though the matter had thus reached final solution.

Not a man spoke in all that room: Mrs. Willings, for some queer reason of her own, sat and snivelled into a corner of her apron. Spent with rage, catching painfully at breath, the farmer sat in his chair speechless, eyeing his son. He looked now as though he were expecting a blow. When the hour struck and the farm labourers trooped off to their loft, David dismissed Mrs. Willings for the night and remained to lock up the house. Five minutes later he carried his father up to bed. The son was a man of few words, the father a man of many: yet a likeness between them showed now.

'Davy?' murmured the old man, in quavering tone, pitiful in its appeal: he said no more.

David answered him not a word.

The Cloak of Friendship . (1905)

THE HOUSE OF RIMMON

WHEN the final red blast of persecution had swept over the islands, leaving only the bare bones of the new Faith to bleach under the ashes of its temples, Koshi rose up out of his hiding, a lonely man.

He had been a priest of the old idol-worship, but his heart of perfect kindliness and charity had made him a mild convert to the better doctrine. Before the first trial of his convictions came, he could have sworn that none loved better, or would suffer more gladly to maintain, a creed based upon an ideal of world-wide compassion and charity. But at the first sight of a martyr's blood his courage had spilled out of him, and he prayed to his old gods to clear his wits of the new and perilous convictions that had mastered them.

In spite of his prayers, he remained an oozy unreclaimed swamp of remorse and Christian conviction. The heavy load of belief would not let him go; hiding from the voice of conscience that called him to a violent death, he became in time the one surviving unslaughtered Christian of his race.

It was a curious pang to him, with his inherited instincts of respect for family remains, that he dared not gather up the small bones of his own children and bury them. They had not paddled in the Rubicon, but had gone boldly in beyond their depth or his, away from the timorous wringing of his hands.

Gaunt with hunger, in an abasement of moral misery, he returned by stealth to the scorched scene of devastation which had once been his home; and was there presently found by the messengers of the Inquisition, beating out the old ritual for dear safety in front of his idol Rimmon, in the house which had before been the scene of his priestly vocation.

At the threshold, assuring himself of solitude, he had uttered his last prayer of integrity: 'When I bow myself in the House of Rimmon, the Lord pardon Thy servant in this thing!' He waited hoping for a sign of divine acquiescence; receiving none, he sighed heavily, and entering, bowed himself low. Rimmon was not his god's name originally: but, as a parable to his wretched soul, he so christened it, and began thenceforward to refit his abject life to the remembered ritual.

50

The prime movers of the predominant paganism, glutted with the blood of so many, viewed him askance, but let him be: priests of the old order were not so plentiful in the land that they could well spare him, an accredited ministrant in the ritual of the ancient worship.

Under the infliction of this obliquely directed worship, Rimmon sat placable — hands to lap, eyes moodily dropping: wondering apparently where had gone a missing fore-finger, the one lopping of his hard adamantine embodiment achieved by the fanaticism of the upstart faith during its temporary ascendancy.

Koshi, then, overborne by the paganism without, resumed his priestly office and appellation; but to his privacy, opening the secret thoughts of a heart convicted of spiritual leprosy, he styled himself by the name that seemed to go best with his return to superstition, nourishing some hopes of a final reconciliation and cleansing for his conscience, by bestowing on himself the name of Naaman.

He made it a signal of his abasement to be punctilious in all the observances his office required. Morning and evening he brought bread and fruit, and laid them at the foot of his idol; and as he waited for them to moulder and decay before partaking in a fasting spirit, all the while prayer to a denied Deity strove within him.

He was one whom accustomed ritual drew as a magnet the needle; scared, he found himself addressing refections of a Christian character to the imperturbable stone. In his released hours intelligence made him aware that the old superstitions were exploded for him for ever, that handhewn granite had its limitations excluding godhead; but when his body bowed, virtue or aspiration went out of him, he could not battle. Presently half involuntarily a transference took place: his shy cowardice caught at courage: with meek heterodoxy he attached divine attributes to Rimmon — and was off, in a very ecstasy of prayer.

Before long a strange uplifting took place in him. His face, no longer bowed under shadow of his cowl as he walked abroad, shone so that passers-by noticed it. People said the light of his god's countenance rested on Koshi; to one so favoured they brought their prayers.

Koshi prayed for them. Outwardly, to such as had contact with him, he was become a pattern of all lovableness. A benign atmosphere was settling down over the village, and beyond to a radius of which the House of Rimmon formed the centre. Prayer found answer. From day to day

Koshi's mere personal influence had more and more the weight of law-giving attached to it.

Something so beautiful and unquarrelsome infected the life of the local community, that the suspicion of a revival in Christianity brought about a pounding down of the Inquisitors. They found, on the contrary, the House of Rimmon exquisitely garnished, thronged devoutly on all high days with worshippers. Rimmon had never so flourished.

About this time there came a drought. Koshi, held down just then, on a sick-bed of fever, heard as his delirium passed away, the moans of a stricken multitude, sick people and much cattle. The heads of the community had been tenderly waiting on him, reserving for his use the only trickle of pure water that could be got. They were anxious for him to get well, loving him — also that he should go down to the House of Rimmon and, praying away the plague, get rain for them.

Koshi put off death, and rising up, a miracle of weakness, tottered to the House of Rimmon; there he prayed with closed doors. Many times through that day and the night following his feebleness made body and brain sink with exhaustion: but he would not let Rimmon's feet go.

Lifting up failing eyes, but with an unconquered spirit, under the arid blast of the second noon that smote in even to the darkness of that sanctuary, Koshi beheld with a squirm of horror the gentle, indolent palm of Rimmon go up and cross the air with a sign of blessing.

Outside came the crash of rain. Koshi lay bowed till the deluge washed in over the paved court, reaching his feet. The thanksgiving villagers, daring to break in after many hours, found him but one remove from a corpse. Borne back to his bed, all day he felt his feet kissed by a procession of pilgrims, and heard rain rushing: perpetually, to his mind's eye, drawn down by the hand of Rimmon lifted in the act of blessing.

His recovery, bringing him fearfully once more to the temple precincts, let him see Rimmon only as before, placid and indolent, with hands resting patiently in lap. But now his fame was established through all the country, and stretched from island to island.

Perpetual pilgrimages enriched the shrine; gold and jewellery were showered in refinement of the stern granite; mercenary appeals were made to the priest to secure the favourable ear of his god.

But Koshi, by no law forbidden from sharing in the god's prosperity, remained poor. Men, bewildered, cast about in their minds; and being

sure of Koshi's sanctity, came to hallow the eccentricity. He meanwhile
had ever before his gaze the wonder of Rimmon's uplifted hand. That
he had seen!

Before final old age took him, Koshi, dreamily pursuing the vision
which beckoned him, had re-established half the Christian virtues in an
unmeaning prominence. When his time grew short, beginning to have
vision of things definite and of near approach, he justified to himself the
use of a parable. Calling the chief magistrates of the archipelago together,
he told of a strange dream he had dreamed: — how, at the dead of night,
jealous of Rimmon's honours, all the other gods had risen up and come to
Rimmon's house, loading him with abuse and stripes. Rimmon, however, was too good to complain.

'It is but a dream!' he said, when they insisted on going to Rimmon's
house to make reparation to the god who had become so lovable in their
midst. They found his back of black granite grievously scarred, as though
outrageous whips of superhuman employ had been laid across it.

Amazed at the sight of that miracle, confirming his fable, Koshi caught
his breath and dreamed to greater effect.

Once more at dead of night the gods had come, and for fear and
jealousy made assault on one who, contrary to the godliness of paganism
made peace the halo of his abode. 'I dreamed,' cried Koshi, 'that they
hailed him as a malefactor to death, wounding his hands and feet!'

They all ran in gentle trepidation to the temple, and it was so: Rimmon's body had on it the sacred signs of martyrdom. Within twenty-
four hours Rimmon was the only idol of stone that stood up whole and
sound over the length and breadth of that land. At a single blow the
islanders had fallen back upon monotheism.

A mortal weakness of love took hold of Koshi; for three years he
laboured, instilling the love of Rimmon into the hearts of all. Now that
other gods were expelled, Rimmon was unfolding himself.

One day Koshi dreamed again, and said: 'Behold, in a while, a greater
than Rimmon draws nigh, before whom Rimmon himself must give
way and pass out of men's hearts.'

The people lifted up their voices and wailed at such tidings; they wanted
no greater god than this one, so beneficent to their needs. 'Rimmon himself,' said Koshi, 'will give the signal of his own departure, and stretch
out the hand of welcome.'

It was not long after this that, one day at sun-rising, the earth shook and trembled as Rimmon stood up on his feet, and going through the door of his temple, turned his face seawards.

Koshi lifted hands of thanksgiving. 'Look!' he cried, 'it is the beginning of the sign which I foretold: there he goes with the hand of welcome! All you who are able, rise up and follow to see him depart!'

At his word the people rose up with wailing to follow the footsteps of the departing deity. To this day those footsteps are seen in prints that point seaward and do not return. Only Koshi, the aged priest, remained alone to his inland seclusion.

Solemnly and thunderously Rimmon trod down a day's journey toward the coast. There came a ship over the sea's rim, outlandishly rigged; and Koshi, with seeing heart, knew that in it returned the compassionate Faith whose way he and Rimmon had prepared and made straight.

Rimmon came down to the water's edge, and stayed not his goings there; on he went into deeper and deeper flood to meet the nearing sail. First the sea took him by the foot, then by the knees, and then by the waist. 'The sign, the sign!' cried the multitude. 'Yonder goes Rimmon to bring us the sign we welcome!'

Soon the water had taken Rimmon so high as to his armpits; presently it took him by the throat. The ship was quite near; in the prow stood one holding a crozier, making sign of exorcism toward the formidable portent that approached. All the crew trembled and shrank at the sight, crying 'Slay him, or we perish!'

The Prelate cut the sign of the Cross despairingly in the biggest possible size. Rimmon bowed his head into the waves, and reached up a hand. A shout of applause and welcome sounded from the strand: he was seen no more. The ship and the croziered Pilot came on.

And meanwhile Koshi, knowing these things in a dream, rose up feebly from his bed, and going timidly to a place of ruins, gathered together the dust of certain small bones, and lay down with them in the House of Rimmon to die.

Prunella, or Love in a Dutch Garden   (1906)
    (In collaboration with H. Granville-Barker)

SCENE. *A garden enclosed by high hedges cut square. In the garden a statue of*
Love, with viol and bow, stands over a fountain. Through a hole in the
hedge PIERROT *enters and makes mischief.*

ACT I
(PIERROT'S PARABLE)

Asleep, on the edge of a town,
    Where the high-road ran by,
Stood a house with the blinds all drawn down,
    As if waiting to die.

And everything there was so straight,
    With high walls all about!
And a notice was up at the gate,
    That told Love to keep out.

But Love cannot read, — he is blind;
    So he came there one day,
And knocked; but the house was unkind,
    It turned him away!

But lo, when the gates were all closed,
    And the windows shut fast,
At night, while the householders dozed,
    Love entered at last.

ACT II
(PIERROT'S SERENADE)

How now, everywhere up in air stars stare:
    On the roof shines the moon.
Little bird in your nest, are you there?
    Up, song, to her chamber go: say low, 'Down below,
    Thy love begs a boon.'
Little bird in your nest, are you there?

Sleep, sleep, for Love's sake, let her wake!
    Say, 'Take no rest!'
Little bird, in your nest, are you there?
    Tame heart, take heat, go beat in the small sweet breast!
Little dove, bird of Love, are you there?

Hour of night, at her bower go beat: say,
    'Sweet, now rise!'
    Time flies! O Love, are you there?
Undo, and renew to the night the light of your bright blue eyes!
    For the man in the moon is here.
Do you hear? He is here!

The Chinese Lantern   (1908)
      (Produced at the Haymarket Theatre, June 1908)

In the studio of OLANGTSI, *Master of Arts, a large picture stands on a dais. Around it six or seven of the Master's pupil-apprentices squat painting. Outside street-cries are heard. Presently enters* JOSI-MOSI, *a rag-and-bone merchant.*

JOSI-MOSI Anything to shell to-day? Any bits, chips, scraps, rags, bones, old clothes? Not any? Mr. Olangtsi seems not at home.

NEW-LYN Well, if he is, you can't see him. You take your judicious hook!

JOSI Don't want to see him ... Shay! no honourable gentleman got nothing to — er — to — eh? Not got any old oil-skins, any old frames, any old lanterns, any old pictures not quite de fashion? ... Any old ...

HAN-KIN Here! What will indigent Avarice give me for that?

    (Offers damaged sign-board)

JOSI Well, if you wash to throw in a pair of old shoes to pay me for my trouble ... Yesh ... I'd take it.

HAN Humble but conscious Merit is much obliged. If it means no business, exalted Abasement had better clear out. There's work going on here — see?

JOSI Work?

HAN Yes, *work*, unpaid and over-time!

JOSI And all dat trouble over putting a bit of paint and paper togedder!

TEE-PEE Painting is a wonderful art, Mr. Josi-Mosi.

JOSI Ish it?

TEE-PEE A picture is a very wonderful thing.

JOSI Ish it?

TEE-PEE Yes ... sometimes ... That picture illustriously behind you now, — you know the story about that?

JOSI I knew dere wash a story: I never knew dat anybody believed it — except to keep up de price.

TEE-PEE Ah! you should get Tikipu to tell it you! He believes it ... don't you, Tiki?

TIKI-PU The Master himself tells it.

HITI-TITI The Master himself owns the picture, stupid! But go on! — I always like to hear it again.

JOSI Yesh, go on!

TIKI-PU You see, it was very long ago. It is easy not to believe what happened three hundred years ago.

JOSI Yesh — very eashy: I've found dat out. Go on!

TIKI-PU Wiowani, the great painter, when he painted that picture, was old and tired of life, and he longed for rest ... So he painted a little porch, and a garden; and in the porch just one spray of blossom in an old blue jar to remind him of youth, and an instrument of music to remind him of song, and overhead a lantern to give light when it grew dark ... And when the picture was done the Emperor himself came to look at it ... And, as he looked, he said: 'Oh, Wiowani, in there, it seems to me is rest! Would that you and I could go and live in a place like that for ever!'

And while he spoke the lantern began to glow.

Softly shedding its light on the floor below.

And the garden beyond grew dim, form within form;

But all the porch was brimming, and bright, and warm,

A home with its doors thrown wide for a well-loved guest;

And out of the dusk of the garden a wind came, blest

With the scent of flowers, all cool from the rising dew;

And lo, — in its depths at last, — there, born anew,

The picture passed, and was changed to a world of rest!

TEE-PEE (*derisively*) Oh, go on, Tiki-pu, go on, go on!

TIKI-PU Then, all at once, Wiowani reached a hand:
'Come,' he said, 'come with me! for this is the land
You seek, and thither I go!'
And into the picture he stept, and turning slow
Watched to see
Whether the Emperor would follow, or no.
Follow? Not he! — Not having the soul
Of a painter, how could he reach the goal?
So Wiowani went in by the door,
Stood, and beckoned, then turned about
And vanished away!
And the light of the lantern faded out
As fades a star at the dawn of day;
And the picture was only a picture once more!

JOSI Ugh!...It's a very intereshting shtory; but I don't happen to want to buy de picture — even with Mr. Wiowani thrown in.

HAN-KIN That's a stupid story, you know. What business has a picture with any perspective? You might as well talk of walking into a piece of music as walking into a picture!

(But later in the play somebody did walk into the picture, and walked out of it again. And that is what the play is about.)

Articles of Faith in the Freedom of Women　　　　　　　　　(1910)

THE SAND-CASTLE

A cogitating sage observed one day
Two children by the shore, intent on play —
A boy and girl: he with his sturdier hands
Had built his mate a castle in the sands,
And round about, to give an added grace,
Had reared a ring of towers, and in one place
A gate — intended not for use but show
Through which, in fancy, she might come — and go;

And here and there, on spire and parapet,
Were quaint and delicate devices set,
Which movement would disturb. So without stir,
Conscious that all this work was done for her,
The girl sat safe-immured; and for employ,
To keep her quiet, the calculating boy
Had brought her weeds and shells wherewith to dress
Her locks and make herself 'a great princess
Fit for a king'. Tempted such rank to claim,
With folded feet, domestically tame,
Resigned she sat and played the sedentary game.

The boy, thus disencumbered of his charge,
More freely moves, and roams the shore at large:
Lordly he struts, fantastically proud
He marks the advancing forms of wave and cloud;
Puffed to assume such foes against him hurled,
With straddled legs he challenges the world,
Then falls to action: — while attack postpones,
A chosen promontory he piles with stones
To right and left — quick batteries at command —
And here resolves to feign a desperate stand.

Then, seeing from afar a wistful eye
Watch his manœuvres, he makes haste to cry,
'Stay there, Princess — quit not that sheltered ground!
Monsters all mad to eat you here abound!
But my right arm is strong: not till I fall
Shall one of these assail your castle wall!'
Then conflict joins, seas mount, and far and wide
He flings his pebbles at the advancing tide.
Not once he misses: upward with a roar
Rises each wave, falls weltering in its gore,
And dying monsters grovel on the shore.

The approving sage observes the dauntless boy
Hurling defiance, facing odds with joy;

Too big already for his childish shoes,
Worlds he must have — to conquer or to lose.
But now, observing her dear lord hard-pressed,
His playmate quits her castellated nest;
Too high of heart to rest subordinate,
Lightly she tramples down her castle gate;
Two tottering towers fall to her flying heels;
War in her blood, deliriously she squeals,
And pounding hard, on limbs a little numb
From too long sitting, and with feet a-drum,
'Partner!' she cries, 'to share your fate I come!'

Straight the play ended, and real life began:
Dropping his hero's mask, the embryo man,
Turning upon her with indignant mien,
Cast to the winds his much-protected queen:
'Get out!' he cried, 'you leave my game alone! —
You've got your castle: go and play your own!
These are *my* stones, not your's. Besides, you know
As well as I do that a girl can't throw —
Not properly, so as to hurt or hit.
This is *real* fighting: you clear out of it,
Now, here, this instant! . . . If you don't obey,
The sea shall come and wash your tower away!'

She 'cleared': and straight, apparent to the glance,
The beach was shorn of all its bright romance:
The sea no more brought monsters up to land,
The towers were only bucketfuls of sand,
The warrior had his will — oh, empty joy! —
She was a girl again, and he a boy.
Forlorn he stood: his game — so proved the event —
Had all depended on the girl's consent:
Robbed of her countenance, he had no zest
To reinvoke those waves which rolled abreast;
Naught had he to defend, nor did she need
Defence of him, if envious pride decreed
She in his battles might not share and bleed.

The sage observed, and yet observed but half,
Nor saw in which direction went the laugh.
That night, when down the shore had ebbed the wave,
Lo! fort and castle shared a common grave;
Each reared on sand — the one so fairly decked,
The other ridged for war — alike lay wrecked:
At no man's bidding, with an equal sway
The tide had come and swept them both away.
The boy and girl, cross purposes forgot,
Slept reunited in their nursery cot;
But near at hand a midnight window blinked,
And there within — thesis to thesis linked —
The cogitating sage sat up and wrote
His tract, 'Why women should not have the vote.'
And this, ye gods, was all he had to say: —
'Yield up to woman what she claims to-day,
And seas will come and wash your forts away!'
O addle-pated sage, what fond invention!
The sea to your sham forts pays no attention.

The New Child's Guide to Knowledge (1911)
A Book of Poems and Moral Lessons for Old and Young

THE LOVE-POTION

In the household of Miss Barret,
Neat from basement up to garret,
Where Matilda got her training,
Ethics needed no explaining:
Having said a word in season,
Auntie never stooped to reason.

'Maud Matilda, take my counsel,
Feed your rabbit upon groundsel,
Give a bullfinch when he whistles
Hempseed, give a donkey thistles:

But oh, do not! — 'twould be ghastly! —
Feed a parrot upon parsley!

'Put no check on faithful Towzer's
Biting bits from beggars' trousers;
In the paddock where the colt is
Cast away your linseed poultice;
Give a donkey dock or carrot,
But not parsley to a parrot!'

Thus spoke Aunt to Maud Matilda;
And a curious longing filled her,
And a wonder what might follow
In that dark digestive hollow,
If she were to mix a little
Parsley with the parrot's victual.

Maud Matilda's common knowledge
Had not been acquired at college;
So from hints, conveying sparsely
What took place in beds of parsley,
Led by legendary history
Maud Matilda solved the mystery.

Putting two and two together,
Maud Matilda wondered whether,
From a spot so truly native,
Might not come the touch creative:
Fed on parsley, might not — may be —
Auntie's parrot have a baby?

Reader, if to this you're equal,
Please to mark the tragic sequel:
Watch Matilda, all a-flutter,
Cut a piece of bread-and-butter;
Watch the eager little hand which
Puts the parsley in the sandwich!

Sad it is how good intentions
Pave the way which no one mentions;
Sad that what our birth-rates thrive on
One bird cannot keep alive on:
Sadder still the parrot's language
When he'd swallowed down the sandwich!

With a wild and strange commotion
Through his system swept the potion;
Deaf to Aunt's devoted nursing,
Three hours later he died cursing;
Maud Matilda's Aunt, Miss Barret,
Lost her valuable parrot.

Reader, hear a word in season;
Never try to find a reason:
What your Aunt says — she has said it:
Swallow it, and give her credit —
Credit for quite good intentions
In a way which no one mentions.

Pains and Penalties   (1911)

THE DEFENCE OF QUEEN CAROLINE

ACT I

The scene is Queen Caroline's Villa at Leghorn. MR. VIZARD, *the Queen's legal agent, has come from England bringing news of the death of King George III; and of the action which the Government has taken to prevent the Queen from returning to England.*

CAROLINE So that is what your English Government is doing? ...
Have you any more news for me?
VIZARD Madam, I have ... On the day of the King's death, an agent of
the Government called upon your Majesty's Attorney, Mr. Brougham,
to put before him a proposition with regard to your Majesty ...
CAROLINE Yes, I am listening.

VIZARD Though informally presented, they undertake to be bound by it, in the event of your Majesty's acceptance. •

CAROLINE Well?

VIZARD Having in view the complete separation which has existed for so many years between yourself and His Majesty, the Government is prepared, so long as you, Madam, remain abroad, to secure to your Majesty a grant of £50,000 per annum, together with the full recognition of your Majesty's royal title in both Houses of Parliament.

CAROLINE (*with deliberation*) If I remain abroad?

VIZARD And in that event we are assured that your Majesty's *liberty* will in no way be — questioned — or inquired into.

CAROLINE And if I — do not — remain abroad?

VIZARD Then the grant will terminate, and Colonel Brown's operations will take effect . . . To be precise — a Bill of Pains and Penalties will be brought before Parliament, depriving your Majesty of all the emoluments, privileges, and honours of your Royal Title, and further pronouncing a dissolution of the union between yourself and His Majesty the King. That, Madam, is the alternative; and that is their offer.

CAROLINE And do you call that, my friend, a good offer?

VIZARD As to that no one but your Majesty can decide.

CAROLINE So! When they set spies — it was to frighten me?

VIZARD Perhaps only to incline your Majesty to their wishes.

CAROLINE I see . . . Have you more news still?

VIZARD Nothing, Madam, of equal consequence. I have said that on these terms your Majesty's title will be recognized in both Houses of Parliament. Elsewhere we are not offered the same satisfaction . . . On the day after the King's death an order was issued in Council making the necessary alterations in the public form of prayer for the King and for the Royal Family . . . I regret to have to inform your Majesty that under that order your Majesty's name has been omitted.

CAROLINE You mean that I am no longer to be prayed for?

VIZARD That, I regret to say, has been the decision.

CAROLINE That my name is no more to be heard anywhere in England? . . . So! . . . They think they can make of me 'that foreign woman'! Oldi! Oldi!

  (*Enter* OLDI)

OLDI Madam?

CAROLINE Come to me, quick! Where is Bergami? Where are all my friends? Tell them to come in!

VIZARD Madam! I implore your Majesty!

CAROLINE Do not implore me! I will not listen to you any more . . . I am Queen, and I will be obeyed!

> (*She strikes several times on the bell. While she is speaking servants enter, then* BERGAMI)

Oldi, do you hear what they have done? They have cut me out of their prayer-book. I am not to be prayed for any more! They are to take me out of their hearts — though I am alive!

VIZARD Madam! Madam!

CAROLINE . . . And why? Why? Because my husband has preferred living with other women: that is why! . . . *He* might go and kiss all his women. But I — I am not to kiss anybody! No! That is not allowed! . . . I am to live starved, with my heart all locked up — hungry, hungry! . . . Ah! mein Gott! I wonder I have not kissed everybody that was kind enough to come near me! . . . The first time that ever *he* came — that fine husband of mine — he held his nose at me, and cried: 'Brandy, brandy!' And for him it has been 'brandy, brandy' ever since! . . . All these years they have made *me* pay for *him*. *Now . . . he shall pay too!*

VIZARD Madam, I do entreat you!

CAROLINE Listen to me, everybody! I have done with being — patient now . . . They drove me out of the country with their proud ways; they would not look at me: . . . they put me on a man-of-war, and sent me away with a royal salute, because they were so glad to get rid of me. I wanted to have my child, but they took my child from me. In your laws the father may do anything — the child is his: it does not belong to the mother at all!

VIZARD Madam!

CAROLINE They made me forget her: when I wrote to her I got no answer: she was not allowed to write to me — I was only her mother! But *he* wrote: yes! — what was that to say? — 'Go and live your own life, and I will live mine!' A fine thing — that — to say to any woman!

VIZARD Ah! Madam, Madam!

CAROLINE And that is what he has done ever since . . . What business has he to ask *me anything — anything*! . . . I went away, I travelled: and wherever I went they told tales against me . . . My little daughter grew

E   65

up . . . When they married her, I was not to know! . . . And when she died, I was not to hear . . . When my little married daughter died in child-bed — it was only in the papers that I read the news . . . No one came to tell the mother that her child was dead . . . Oh! do you wonder that she died — afraid to become a mother in a country which takes from a mother all her natural right? And now to punish me, to keep me away, they have made of me that *thing* that is no longer to be prayed for! . . . But I will do something that they did not expect! I will go *back* to them! *Yes! I will go back, I will go back!*

· · · ·

CAROLINE Where is Bergami? Do not let him go till he has seen me . . . Send him to me.

(*Exit* OLDI: *the* QUEEN *sits waiting. Presently* BERGAMI *enters with hat and cloak*)

So you are going, Bergami?

BERGAMI Principessa, it is time: there are things which must needs be attended to.

CAROLINE I was not complaining. I am to be Queen now . . . It means that I must go back to England . . . You will remember your — Mistress, Bergami?

BERGAMI My devotion lies always at her feet.

CAROLINE And is that — all — you have to say?

BERGAMI Oh, Principessa, cara mia! How can I trust myself to speak?

CAROLINE You were not always so cautious, Bergami.

BERGAMI By experience one grows wise.

CAROLINE (*resignedly*) We will be wise, then, Bergami . . . So it is good-bye.

(*She offers him her hand.* BERGAMI *approaches and drops on one knee. As he is about to kiss, he turns her hand quickly and presses the palm to his lips. He goes out hastily.* CAROLINE *catches to her own lips the hand he has kissed. She totters and sways*)

CAROLINE Ah, Oldi, he has left me! And he has not said a word! . . . Oldi, Oldi, say that *you* were fond of me — that you did not deceive me, coming here to be my friend . . . No, no, don't kiss my hands! . . . Here! Oldi, here! (*They embrace.*) . . . I am not a bad woman, Oldi; — they may say what they like! . . . Ah, God, I shall go out of my mind, I think, losing all my friends in one day! . . . Your brother, he goes now for good and

66

all! And you, you, Oldi. — I cannot afford to keep friends any more . . . You will think of me sometimes, Oldi? All Europe will hear the news when I become Queen. And you — you will pray for me, will you not? The English, they will not pray for me any more: but the Italian people are more kind . . . There, go, Oldi! I tell you to go!

OLDI I am coming with you, Madam.

CAROLINE (*slowly and deliberately*) With a dead woman, Oldi, with a dead woman! . . . I think that this has been the last day of my life!

ACT III

A room in the Queen's House, St. James's Square. It is the evening of the eighteenth day of the second month of the Queen's Trial before the House of Lords.

SERVANT Please your Majesty, there is below someone who wishes to see your Majesty.

CAROLINE The name?

SERVANT He did not give any name, your Majesty — only that he had come from Italy upon your Majesty's service.

CAROLINE Let him come in.

(BERGAMI *enters, wrapped in a long cloak which half obscures his face, and which he throws back with a magnificent gesture. Caroline starts violently, her lips form his name inaudibly*)

CAROLINE My friend, why have you come here?

BERGAMI To prove to your Majesty my devotion.

CAROLINE I did not need proof.

BERGAMI Ah, Regina mia! is it forbidden that I should offer it?

(*She makes a gesture of warning*)

CAROLINE Why did you not first write to me?

BERGAMI Your Majesty's prudence forbade.

CAROLINE This is more dangerous!

BERGAMI For your Majesty's sake, I will dare everything.

CAROLINE Oh! . . . You mean you have come to show me that you are a brave man?

BERGAMI A faithful servant to my Queen — one who remembers and is grateful!

CAROLINE I would not have doubted you, Bergami.

BERGAMI Ah, most Gracious! is it not to you that I owe everything! There in Italy, this long while, every week has brought news of your Majesty surrounded by enemies, tried before judges, traduced by false witnesses, men whose characters I know — men whom I can prove to be thieves and liars — men who have only to see Bergami — (*He raises his voice proudly*).

CAROLINE Sh!

BERGAMI And they will tremble and turn pale! . . . That is why I — I — Bergami, have come to England — to offer myself a witness, and to lay all that I can tell at the feet of your Majesty.

CAROLINE You — a witness, Bergami? . . . What could you tell them that they would believe?

BERGAMI Of true service, of respect, of gratitude, of undying devotion!

CAROLINE Ah, that is right! That is so like you, Bergami! . . . You Italians, you are all just like little children; good children or bad children — that is the only difference! Bergami, stand there in the light, and let me look at you . . . You are still very handsome . . . You have come a long way?

BERGAMI From Barona, seven days and seven nights.

CAROLINE Caro amico! You gave yourself no rest: yet you do not seem tired.

BERGAMI My thoughts were always near your Majesty.

CAROLINE That was beautifully said, Bergami. Had you learned that by heart?

BERGAMI Col cuori — si, si! (*Lays his hand on his heart and kneels.*)

CAROLINE Yes, you are still very magnificent, Bergami! There is no one in England who is like you . . . (*She passes her hand over his head; he seizes and kisses it.*) Ah, well! it has done me good — just once to have seen you again! . . . From Barona, you say? Who is there with you now?

BERGAMI (*a little embarrassed*) Of my family, Principessa, I have with me my little daughter — Victorine.

CAROLINE Ah, the little Victorine! Tell me of her! How she must be grown!

BERGAMI She speaks often of your Majesty.

CAROLINE I shall not forget her: never! That little thing that slept in my arms as if she had been my own child — that cried so when I went and left her!

BERGAMI She cries after you sometimes still — just for a little.

CAROLINE Ah, it is good to be told that she cries after me still! When I came to England I gave up everything that made life sweet! . . . Perhaps I should not have come, Bergami, if only you had said to me 'Stay!'

BERGAMI Was it not your Majesty's own choice to return?

CAROLINE Ah, yes — that is how we have to choose, sometimes, against all that we wish deep down in our hearts . . . Well . . . I hope that you are happy, Bergami?

BERGAMI I have everything your Majesty has given me to make me so.

CAROLINE Then now you will return — you will go home.

BERGAMI When your Majesty no longer needs me.

CAROLINE You must go to-night, Bergami.

BERGAMI What does your Majesty mean? To-night?

CAROLINE Now, at once! Do not waste a moment, Bergami — If you wish to serve me — go!

BERGAMI Ah! now I see! You think that I am false? No! you do not trust me! That is plain!

CAROLINE I can trust you to be silent, my Bergami, but I cannot trust you so well if you begin making yourself talk . . . Oh, you have not been there! Never, never will they let you stop, if once you begin.

BERGAMI I know well, Madam, where to begin, and where also to end! That shall be seen!

CAROLINE Ah, talk not nonsense, my Bergami! I speak better than you know. For the witnesses at this trial they have two interpreters, yes: and when the two interpreters do not agree — then all the English Lords, who can speak no language but their own — that is one of the things they are proud of — they all vote that you are to mean as *they* choose — and not anything else! And in the House of Lords, my Bergami, the King has got his majority! — Oh, yes, he has his brothers there voting for him all day long! — yes, and the Archbishops of York and Canterbury both trying their hardest which of them can please him best, so that one of them may have the great honour to crown him at Westminster, presently! . . . Ah! What do you know about it?

BERGAMI I know only that I am true, and that your Majesty no longer trusts me!

CAROLINE Do you know, my friend, what cross-examination in an English Court of Law is like? . . . Then I will tell you! . . . They will ask you — do you remember going to bed on such and such a night five years ago? If you do not — then they say that you must have been drunk, not to remember it. And if you do — then they say that you must have been doing something most extraordinary to be able to remember it after all that time. Then they say — if you do not remember what you were doing — how do you remember that you ever went to bed at all? Then, if you say that you always go to bed, they will tell you of some night fifteen years ago when you did *not* go to bed: — so there you have been contradicted, and your evidence is no good ... Wait, wait! Oh, that is nothing! ... When they have got you to swear that you *did* go to bed — then they ask which side of the bed did you get into? — Oh! the left side, was it? Do you usually get in on the left side? If not, how did you come to get in on the left side on that occasion? Were you drunk? You swear that you were not — then you must have had a reason for getting in on the left side — no man, who is not drunk, gets into bed on the left side without a reason. And then — when they have so 'schwindled' you that you do not know whether you are on your head or your heels, they say suddenly: 'I put it to you that the reason you got into bed on the left side was because there was a — Well, a reason why you could not get in on the other side!' *That* is English law and justice, my Bergami. Can you stand a week of that on end — with the whole country howling round you, half of them cheering because you are such a brave liar, and the other half hooting you because you have told the truth — and an escort of sheriff's officers to bring the bits of you back to the witness-box every morning, if there is anything of you left? ... There, now I have told you — so you may know!

BERGAMI For your Majesty's sake I will face all dangers.

CAROLINE For my Majesty's sake, Bergami, you will put on a wig, a beard, and a false nose, wrap them up well, so that they shall not be seen, and run back to Dover — Dover was it that you came from? — then better go back by Bristol — to Bristol your very hardest; and not breathe one word of Italian till you are right over the sea and in your own blessed land again! ... You will do this for me, Bergami?

BERGAMI What? Your Majesty bids me disguise myself? — run as though I were afraid — make a mock of myself — wear a false nose!

CAROLINE Better a false nose than a false step, my good Bergami! Come, show what a fine pair of legs you have! Run! Run!

BERGAMI Basta! As your Majesty so wishes it — since your Majesty has no better use for me than that — Yes! I will go! (*He throws his cloak round him with an indignant gesture.*)

CAROLINE That is a good child, to be reasonable! Farewell, my friend! and take care of yourself. Do not be too brave till you are safe home again! Wrap yourself up well!

BERGAMI Addio, Madame!

CAROLINE Addio, caro amico! (*Exit* BERGAMI in *wrath.*) There goes a true friend, that I have had to say 'No' to! Oh, what a thing it is to be a Queen.

John of Jingalo The Story of a Monarch in Difficulties (1912)

JOHN OF JINGALO had been in harness all his life: he had never known freedom, never been left to find his own feet, never been taught to think for himself except upon conventional lines; and these had kept him from ever putting into practice the rudimental self-promptings which sometimes troubled him. He had been elaborately instructed, but not educated; his own individual character, that is to say, had not been allowed to open out; but a sort of traditional character had been slowly squeezed into him in order to fit him for that conventional acceptance of a variety of ancient institutions (some mouldering, some still vigorous) which, by a certain official and ruling class of monetarily interested persons, was considered to be the correct constitutional attitude. Monarchy, that is to say, had been interpreted to him by those who sucked the greatest amount of social prestige and material benefit from its present conditions as a 'going concern'; and in that imposed interpretation deportment came first, initiative last, and originality nowhere at all. . . .

He had been trained, for review purposes and for the final privilege of carrying a cocked hat as well as a crown upon his coffin, in a profession which he would never be allowed to practise; and, having been 'brought out' with much show and parade at an early age, had been introduced to a vast number of very important people, and dragged through a long series of social functions, which, however crowded, gave always a free floor for his feet to walk on, and never presented a single back to his view. At these functions thousands of brilliant and distinguished people had bowed their well-stored brains within a few inches of his face, had exchanged with their monarch a few words of studied politeness and compliment, now and then had even laid themselves out to amuse him, but never once had they imparted to his mind an arresting or a commanding thought, never once endeavoured to change any single judgment that had ever been formed for him. . . .

In addition he had been trained, on strictly impartial and non-committal lines, to take an interest in politics; to have within certain narrow and prescribed limits an open mind — one, that is to say, with its orifice comfortably adapted to the stuffing process practised on kings by the great ones of the official world; and when his mind would not open in certain required directions, well, after all, it did not much matter, since in the end it made no practical difference.

Under these circumstances he would have been a mere social and official automaton had not certain defects of his character saved him. Though timid, he was impulsive; he was also a little irritable, rather suspicious, and indomitably fussy in response to the call of duty. Temper, fuss, and curiosity saved him from boredom; he was conscientiously industrious, and though there was much that he did not understand, he managed to be interested in nearly everything.

In the fiftieth year of his age this monarch, amiable, affable, and of a thoroughly deserving domestic character, was destined to be thrust into a seething whirlpool of political intrigue, in which, for the first time, his conscience was to be seriously troubled over the part he was asked to play. And while that wakening of his conscience was to cause him a vast amount of trouble, it was to have as enlarging and educative an effect upon his character as her first love-affair has upon a young girl. From this moment, in fact, you are to see a shell-bound tortoise blossom into a species of fretful porcupine, his shell splintering itself into points and erecting them with blundering effectiveness against his enemies. And you shall see by what unconscious and subterranean ways history gets made and written.

. . . . . .

The sentence which had attracted the King's attention, coming as it did from the newspaper on whose opinions he most frequently relied, ran thus —

'In this developing crisis the Nation looks with complete and loyal assurance to him who alone stands high and independent above all parties, confident that when the time for a final decision has arrived he will so act, within the recognized limits of the Royal Prerogative, as to add a fresh lustre and a renewed significance to that supreme symbol and safeguard of the popular will which, under Divine Providence, still crowns our constitutional edifice.'

The King read it three times over. He read it both standing and sitting: and read in whatever attitude it certainly sounded well. As a peroration its rhythm and flow were admirable, as a means of keeping up the courage and confidence of readers who placed their reliance upon literary style nothing could be better; but what, by all that was constitutional, did it mean? — or rather, how did it mean that he, the high and independent one, was to do it? Point by point its sentiments were unexceptionable; but what it actually pointed to he did not know. 'Add lustre?' Why, yes, certainly. But was not that what he was already doing day by day on the continuous deposit system, even as the oyster within its shell deposits lustre upon the pearls which a sort of hereditary disease has placed within its keeping? 'Renewed significance?' But in what respect had the significance of the royal office become obscured? Was anything that he did insignificant? 'Symbol and safeguard of the popular will?' Yes: if his Coronation oath meant anything. But how was he, symbol and safeguard and all the rest of it, to find out what the popular will really was? No man in all the Kingdom was so much cut off from living contact with the popular will as was he!

The King was in his study, the room in which most of the routine work of his daily life was accomplished — a large square chamber with three windows to one side looking out across a well-timbered park toward a distant group of towers. But for those towers, so civic in their character, it might well have been taken for a country view; scarcely a roof was visible. . . .

. . . He walked to a window and stood looking out into the soft sunlit air, slightly misty in quality, which lay over the distances of his capital. Away behind those trees, beneath those towers, sending towards him a ceaseless reverberation of bells, wheels, street cries, and all the countless noises of city life, went a vast and teeming population of men and women, already far advanced on the round of their daily toil. He was in their midst, but not one of them could he see; not one of them did he really know as man to man. Everything that he learned about their lives came to him at second or at third hand; nor did actual contact bring him any closer, for wherever he moved among them they knew who he was and behaved accordingly. For twenty-five years he had not walked in a single one of those streets, the nearest of which lay within a stone's throw of his palace. As a youth, before his father came to the throne, he had sometimes gone about, with or without companions, just like an ordinary person, taking his chance of being recognized: it had not mattered then. But now it could not be done: people did not expect it of him; his Ministers would have regarded it as a dangerous and expensive habit, requiring at least a trebling of the detective service, and even then there would have been apprehension and uncertainty. He was King; and though, whatever might happen to him, his place would be automatically filled, and government go on just as before, yet, as a national symbol, his life was too valuable to be risked; and so on ascending the throne he had been forced, as his father before him, to resign his personal liberty and cease to go out in the happy, unpremeditated fashion of earlier days.

He had long since got over the curious home-sickness which this separation had at first caused him, and as an opening to personal enjoyment the impulse for freedom had long since died within him. But his heart still vaguely hungered for the people who called him their King; and looking out into the pale sunshine that was now thinly buttering the surface of his prosperous capital, and listening to the perpetual tick and hum of its busy life, he knew that for him it was and must remain, except in an official sense, an unknown territory. And yet out there, in that territory which he was unable to explore, the thing that is called 'the popular will' lived and moved and had its being! Dimly he dreamed of what it might be — a thing of substance and form; but there was none to interpret to him his dream — except upon official lines.

Before his eyes, a salient object in the heavens surpassing the stony eminences which surrounded it, rose the tall spire of the twin Houses of Parliament. Upon its top swung a gilded weathercock; while about a portion of its base stood a maze of scaffolding, the façade of the building having during the last few months been under repair. There seemed, however, for the moment to be no workmen upon it. Presently, as he gazed vacantly and without intent, something that moved upon the upper masonry engaged his attention. Slowly along its profile, out of all those hidden millions below, one of his subjects, a single and minute representative of the popular will, emerged cautiously into view.

The King was gifted with good sight; and though the figure appeared but as a tiny speck, it was unmistakably that of a man bearing a burden upon his back and ascending steadily towards the highest point of all. In a word it was a steeplejack. As the name passed through the King's mind it evoked recollection; and he said to himself again, 'I wonder whether they call *me* Jack — I wonder.'

With a curious increase of interest and fellow-feeling he watched the distant figure mounting to its airy perch. And as he did so a yet further similitude and parable flashed through his mind. For the man's presence at that dizzy height he knew that the Board of Public Works was responsible: as a single item in the general expenditure, the weathercock of the Palace of Legislature had had voted to it a new coat of gilt, and this steeplejack was now engaged in putting it on. He was there, in the words of a certain morning journal, 'to add fresh lustre to that supreme symbol of the popular will which crowned the constitutional edifice.'

As the words with their caressing rhythm flowed across the King's brain he discerned the full significance of the scene which was being enacted before him. This weathercock — the highest point of the constitutional edifice — requiring to be touched up afresh for the public eye — was truly symbolical of the crown in its relation to the popular will; twisting this way and that, responsive to and interpretive of outside forces, it had no will of its own at all, and yet to do its work it must blaze resplendently and be lifted high, and to be put in working trim and kept with lustre untarnished it required at certain intervals the attentions of a steeplejack — one accustomed to being in high places, accustomed to isolation and loneliness, accustomed to bearing a burden upon his back before the eyes of all: one whose functions were rather like his own.

He saw that the steeplejack had now reached the point where his work was waiting for him, work that required nerve and courage. He wondered whether it were highly paid; he wondered also by what means the man slung himself into position, and by what process the gold had to be applied so that it would stick. Perhaps he only polished up what was already there, coated and covered from view by the grime of modern industry. If so, how did he scrape off the dirt without also scraping off the gold? Perhaps, on the other hand, all the old gold had to come off before new gold could be put on. He wondered whether the man ever forgot his perilous position, whether habit did not make him sometimes careless, whether he ever felt giddy, and how far the exploit was really attended by danger to one possessed of skill and a cool head; and as he thought, putting himself in the man's place, his hands grew sympathetically moist.

Well, he was wasting time, he must really get to his own work now; that secretary would be wondering what had become of him. He glanced away over the distant roofs that here and there emerged above the trees, and then for a last look back again. And as he did so all at once he started and uttered an acute exclamation of distress. A dark speck had suddenly detached itself from the ball upon which the vane stood, and could now be seen glissading with horrible swiftness down the slope of the spire. It fell into the scaffolding, zigzagged from point to point, and disappeared. There could be no mistake about it, it was the man himself who had fallen: that single and minute expression of the popular will had passed for ever from view; and the smooth and equable hum of the unseen millions below went steadily on.

The Royal Runaway A sequel to *John of Jingalo*   (1914)

CHAPTER V

THE KING RUNS

THE train, when at last it came and caught him up to cushioned seclusion, carried him once more within sight of Castle Royal, behind which at that moment a fullish moon was rising. On its topmost rotundity, so like a military drum in its proportions, the Royal standard still waved, announcing a monarch in residence.

How empty of the truth that flourish! And how characteristic of the whole order of things which now escaped him, that for many weeks to follow that same lie continued to nail its colours to the mast and spread them with feeble flutter to the wind.

His last sight of those ancestral turrets, whereto the cross-currents of conspiracy, usurpation, and rebellion had carried his forefathers, was thus symbolically crowned; and for many days thereafter the vision stayed, of a flag that waved derisively to departing monarchy.

'I do just as well without you!' it seemed to say; 'so long as I wag, titular monarchy can go on.'

The King took the opportunity which solitude in a first-class railway carriage afforded him, to sort into the carpet-bag all the jewels which formed part of the Spinach-Pinchbeck inheritance. This early dividing of the sheep from the goats gave him a quieter and more assured conscience: he had no intention of running away with anything that did not belong to him.

At the junction he changed into a corridor train and was pleased to find that in the forward portion dinner was about to be served. He had learned, even thus early, that there was some incongruity between first-class passengers in fur-lined overcoats, and carpet-bags. Porters had smiled at the resolute hold he had kept on his new belonging; and so, on the arrival of his train, he retired to a back part of it, and there, hiding the bag under his seat, sat with face dipped low into the open sheets of an evening journal.

He was still very nervous about being recognized; every fresh encounter filled him with spasms of alarm, but left him with new assurance, his incognito still intact. To the service-waiter he had confided a wish for a table to himself, and when the man returned with summons to the feast he found himself personally conducted with an assiduity of attention that left nothing to be desired.

As the meal drew near to its end polite inquiry reached him as to his destination: in a few minutes the train would again be stopping; was he intending to change? But the destination he had chosen was much further away — Hamswerp, that great inland port upon the frontiers of Jingalo, to which through the neutralized waters of a neighbouring State came all the sea-borne trade of the Kingdom. Thence through a hundred miles of estuary went liners to all parts of the world; thence he had no doubt some ship would bear him without delay to the arms of his beloved Charlotte.

Thus booked to so distant a point upon the route he finished his meal without haste, sipped his curaçao and smoked a cigar. When this was done he bestowed upon the astonished and gratified waiter a coin that sought no change, and proceeded to his carriage in the rear.

Half-way along the corridor he found that his course was blocked by a door bearing the legend 'Guard only'. He knocked, and the guard opened with a polite face of inquiry.

'I want to get back to my carriage,' said the King.

'There's no carriage behind this,' answered the man.

'Oh, but surely!'

'No, sir, we dropped our three rear carriages at the last stop.'

The King took the blow with surprising equanimity.

How rapidly he was learning things!

'What has become of them?' he inquired.

'They've gone north,' explained the guard. Then seeing this passenger's look of mild perplexity, 'I hope you didn't leave any luggage there, sir,' he said.

The King paused. 'Well, as a matter of fact, I did; but it is really of no consequence.'

'You can send a wire up the line, sir, at the next stop,' said the man. Again the King paused to consider matters.

'I don't think I need trouble you,' he said at last. 'After all it wasn't exactly mine.'

The man looked at him queerly. 'Well, sir, of course, that's your affair,' said he; 'but you didn't set out to lose it, I suppose?'

'Oh, dear me, no!' replied the King. 'All I mean is that it may just as well wait; — nothing perishable about it, you know.' And to avoid more questions he turned away and resumed solitude in another compartment.

Thus early, then, had he and the Spinach-Pinchbeck heirlooms parted company: pure accident had relieved him of an embarrassment. But now it struck him for the first time that he was leaving traces which might hereafter prove troublesome. This highly coloured carpet-bag with its tell-tale contents would be all too easy a means of identification upon inquiry; everybody would remember and would describe him: before he was out of the kingdom he would be tracked.

And if so, would they haul him back again? He had a suspicion that it was entirely contrary to the law for a constitutional monarch to quit his dominions without the consent of his Ministers. He knew that queen bees were not allowed to, except when mating, and that James II and Louis XVI had both got into trouble from making too free with themselves and endeavouring to escape from their own jurisdiction. They had been seized and brought back again prisoners.

The idea of any such compulsion sent a flush of heat to the King's brain; sooner than submit to it he would throw himself from the railway carriage; and having a curiously graphic and investigating mind, he let down the window and looked out to see what sort of ground he was likely to fall on. Beneath his eye, streaked with light from the roof-lamps of the carriages, galloped a low sloping bank clothed with heather and brushwood — as suitable a provision for desperate escape as he could have wished for. Suddenly, with a flick, a stone arch crossed his line of vision. 'I should have been dead!' meditated the monarch, a little startled: there was more danger in jumping out of carriage windows than he had foreseen.

He leaned back, and for a few moments luxuriated mildly in the vision of his battered body thus broken in a last desperate attempt to win free-dom. No King would have died like that before; and how Max would have admired! Then, reminding himself that all such imaginings were a mere foolish indulgence, he drew up the window again and settled down comfortably in his corner for an after-dinner nap.

He slept longer and more soundly than he would have thought possible under such conditions. When he came to himself again the train was travelling at a gentle speed over a wide sea of metal-rails, dotted with signal-boxes, and lighted by the steely glare of electric arc-lamps. A continuous jolting over points, and a complaining squeal uttered by the engine at intervals, told that they were negotiating the entrance of a great terminus. This was Hamswerp.

The train slid to its platform and stopped; all the carriage doors were opened by sidling porters, and the King got out. It was now nearly half-past eleven; the platform seethed with people. An hotel-porter, with red band to his cap, came touting: the King passed him by, noting, how-ever, the name of his establishment. 'King's Hotel — very suitable, I am sure!' was his mental comment.

Anxious by unobserved ways to disconnect himself from the carpet-bag with its crimson-rose cover and compromising contents, he avoided the cab-stand which stood ranged against him, and mingling with the com-mon herd passed out into the street.

When clear of the station premises he inquired for the King's Hotel;

and receiving directions arrived five minutes later at a large and palatial establishment nominally his own.

Upon crossing the threshold he was received with multiple attentions; porter and page-boy passed him to the inquiry bureau, where his modest request for a self-contained suite of rooms was met in a manner which at once showed a raised sense of his importance.

'You have luggage, sir,' inquired the clerk deferentially.

'No, I have not,' replied the King. 'I happened to lose it in the train.'

There was a moment of delicate hesitation; the man subtly inspected his visitor. 'In that case, sir,' said he, 'we usually ask for a deposit.'

'Oh, certainly,' assented his Majesty, and the clerk's manner became reassured.

The King had already sorted his late Queen's petty cash into various pockets. 'Will you have gold or notes?' he inquired. Gold was chosen.

'A mere form, sir,' explained the clerk respectfully, 'but we have to keep to our rules. Will you kindly sign the book?' He turned a large ledger as he spoke; and the King was already in the act of mechanically complying before he came to himself. He dared not stop.

The fatal thing had been done; there on the hotel-book page was 'John R.' staring him in the face, and the clerk was watching him.

It was in these moments of danger that the monarch always showed at his best; he had done it, and it could not be undone. Without any appreciable pause he added the word 'King'.

'And that's the truth, at any rate,' he said to himself.

'John R. King,' it was absolutely true, and it told nothing.

CHAPTER VI

THE KING GOES SHOPPING

Across the pavement he looked in and saw other customers being served. From these he gathered that it was not necessary to take off his hat: that was knowledge gained, it gave him ground to go upon.

Nerving himself for the adventure he pushed open the swing-door and entered.

Immediately a young man came softly stepping towards him, and received him with a fawning condescension so precisely after the manner of Court-functionaries that for a moment his heart stuck into his throat; he saw himself discovered.

But no, this was the mere ritual of trade; for in a country where trade is all-important we treat our customers as in the past we treated kings.

'I want clothes,' said his Majesty in answer to an inquiry.

An interrogative catalogue of articles brought definition to his desire. 'Yes, shirts. And collars,' he added.

He was conducted to a counter, where the inquiry was repeated. 'I want collars,' said his Majesty.

The shopman glanced at his throat for information as to pattern. 'Yes, sir; what size?'

The King missed the point. He had never in his life worn collars marked with a size. 'About the same size I am wearing,' said he.

The man looked at him a little curiously. 'Seventeens, I should think, sir,' he remarked after a brief scrutiny.

The King accepted the man's word for it and took two dozen. Then he asked for shirts.

'Sixteen, sir, or sixteen and a half?' came the inquiry.

'I think two dozen would be better,' said his Majesty, much puzzled to know what use half a shirt could be. Presently as he watched the shirts being sorted out he realized that they would take up rather too much space in the portmanteau. 'I think I had better have only a dozen at present,' he said.

The shopman sought to tempt him with a special reduction; by taking two dozen he would save fourpence halfpenny; but the King remained firm. 'One dozen will be sufficient.' Then he asked for ties.

The shopman glanced again. 'Black, sir?' he inquired sympathetically.

'No,' said the King, 'not black: something rather less noticeable. I will have grey.'

He bought a dozen of those: they would not take up so much room as the shirts. Of handkerchiefs he required six dozen, for he felt upon him the beginnings of a cold. He took one of them, put it into his pocket, and began to feel clean again.

After that he reverted to single dozens. His new stock of garments mounted up on the counter beside him, making a pile of goodly size. He crowned his purchases with a white bath-towel dressing-gown — the sort of garment which, had it been intended for lady's wear, would have had the epithet 'very chaste' attached to it. On men's toilettes such moral compliments are not bestowed.

'And the next article?' inquired the shopman insinuatingly.

'That is all,' replied the King with so quiet a decision that no pressure was put upon him to buy more.

'Where may I have the pleasure of sending them?' queried the man as he made out the list.

'I have a portmanteau outside,' said the King. 'If you will be good enough to have it brought in and pack it for me, I shall be much obliged.'

The shopman was all complaisance, and the Commissionaire was called.

Then came the adding up of the bill. It amounted to £19 3s. 11d. The King put down a £10 and two £5 notes.

'Sign!' cried the man with startling suddenness, in a loud almost threatening tone.

The King was much taken aback by this abrupt change of manner.

'What do I sign?' he inquired. But already the thing was being done, and he saw that he had made a mistake.

Then he received a handful of change, graceful bows from the assistant and shop-walker, and preceded by the Commissionaire bearing his well-laden portmanteau, passed out to the waiting cab.

As soon as his back was turned, the shopman's manner changed: he grinned.

'Rum customer,' he remarked genially: 'bought everything by the dozen. Sort of a Duke, I should think; been out on the loose somewhere and lost his luggage. Looks as if he'd never done shopping for himself before. And — did you see?'

'See what?'

'Took off his hat to me as he went.'

'So he did to me,' said the shop-walker. 'Yes, there is something funny about him.'

Thus, without intending it, the King was making himself remembered wherever he went.

St. Francis Poverello (1918)

THE influence of St. Francis is the most illimitable and incalculable spiritual event which has befallen the world since the beginning of the Christian era. Perhaps this is only another way of saying that his life is the most Christian thing which Christianity has yet produced.

Why of all the saints does he stand so much alone? What is it that differentiates him from the rest? We hear his name used to indicate a certain attitude towards life that men have discerned more plainly in him than in others. But what exactly is that attitude? Can it be defined, or is it only to be felt, spiritually sensed, but not to be reasoned about?

In the main it was a rediscovery of human nature — a rediscovery based on a belief and trust in its underlying goodness. Throughout the Dark Ages, after the Church had fought down paganism, man had been taught that his tendency was to do evil. Francis set himself, on the contrary, to show man that his tendency was to do good; and for the simple and sufficient reason that, in the direction of good, human joy awaited him. Good and joy were, for St. Francis, interchangeable terms; and as, in the process of creation, God viewing His work each day had seen that it was good, it followed necessarily that the whole creation was an act of joy, and must so be viewed by man before he could become sacramentally at one with the mind of His Creator. Since, then, God enjoyed the world, man must enjoy it also; and the way was easy; he had only to be himself, to be good. But the pattern of all goodness was Christ; and the astounding paradox before which Francis stood eternally amazed was that when Joy came visibly to earth, man, blind to its true meaning, had slain it. Afterwards he had come to know what he had done; but in the mystery of that wounding there had come to the world a new sacrament; and man must receive back into his heart the Passion of His Lord, in order to realize and make once more his own the joy which behind the veil of sin lay everywhere.

Thus in maimed form and through much suffering, Francis, while he strove to embody Christ, strove also to embody joy. Behind all contrary appearances Christ and joy were truly and indivisibly one. That is the explanation of him and of his creed. 'This', he seems to say to his fellow-men, 'is the instantaneous cure of all ill, all grief, all sin. Do you suffer pain, or injury, or wrong? You bear it more easily by smiling on it than

83

by weeping. Are you humbled to the dust? Remember that brother dust is God's making, and you sit the equal of kings. Do men meditate violence or mischief against you? Then be much more than forgiving; consent so swiftly and heartily to the trespass they intend that you undo the mischief ere it is begun. Like a lover or a host ready with welcome, you run to meet them, making them virtuous before they are aware! They come to wrong you? You thank them for doing you a favour. They seek to defraud you? They enable you to bestow on them a gift. They mock and rail against you? It is a kind showing of faults you might otherwise have forgot. They take from you your dearest possession? They give you the freedom that poverty alone can bring.

Is all this a foolishness of mockery and of make-believe? By no means: for if you so deal with it human nature responds, meets you half-way, becomes — perhaps to its own surprise — the great miracle.

Thus with the touch of a child St. Francis shows how on earth man may enter into heaven. You cannot reason with him for he is above reason; you cannot prevent him, for he is there before you; you cannot be angry with him, for your anger has nothing on which to strike. Reducing every evil motion to impotence he throws you back on yourself, and makes you realize with a shock that you are good — that good has only to be presented to you unconditionally and you recognize it as your birthright — a thing of which, so long defrauded, you now become repossessed. Human nature is the great miracle, for it is the image of God.

The Sheepfold The story of a shepherdess and her sheep, and   (1918)
how she lost them

BOOK III: HER MISSION

CHAPTER V

THE HILL OF DIFFICULTIES

THE 'Mother' was no scholar: she took the Scriptures very literally, but, with a shrewd eye for her texts, applied them to practical ends. When problems troubled her she turned to 'the Book' as her guide: opened it almost at random and let her eye travel till it found something to rest on. 'I will make him a ruler among the princes' was the guidance which this method provided in respect of a man whose infirmity of purpose had caused her well-nigh to despair of him. She gave him a post of trust and authority, and he became a reformed character. Simple souls beholding that transformation regarded it as a miraculous performance.

By the guidance of Scripture also, a natural feature of the landscape became elevated into a symbol, and helped Jane through many difficulties. Above the settlement rose a small steep hill, conical and bare; the house lay almost under its shade, level fields stretching beyond. Thither, for lack of loftier elevations, Jane lifted up her eyes to fetch strength, and on occasion directed to it the feet of her followers when they seemed to need guidance. She taught them that sanity might be found there.

One small instance will serve: two of the community, for reasons important only to themselves, thirsted for each other's blood. Being an ill-matched pair, the fight with fists sought by the one was sedulously avoided by the other. For this reason he went armed, letting his rival know of it; whenever they encountered out came the knife. Baulked by the pacific intervention of others, the feud infected their brains. One day Jane found them at grips, saw real danger threatening, and sprang between. The man for the fair fight, which he was so sure of winning, regarded himself as the injured party.

Jane did not parley: bidding the armed man wait below, she led the burlier of the two up the Hill of Difficulties. All the way he talked volubly, stating his case. She let him wag on.

The ascent gained, they turned about, and gazing down had a pleasant bird's-eye view of the adversary, faithful to his post, steadfastly eyeing them.

'Shake your fist at him,' said Jane.

The deed was done; a shaken fist gave response from below.

'Do it again!' And once more like followed like.

After a third shaking of fists — 'He's got his dirty knife out!' complained her companion.

'Spit at him!' said Jane.

The man paused, doubtful whither she was leading him. 'He won't see that,' he objected.

'All the better for you: it gives you the pull. Spit away!'

The pause extended. 'I wun't,' he protested. 'You do make I feel a fool.'

'So you've got to it, have you?' said Jane. 'Kiss your hand to him — he's a fool too.'

She signalled the other up to them; he came slowly. 'Bill says he's a fool,' she announced; 'what are you?'

'I'm only standing for my rights to be left alone,' said the new arrival obstinately.

'Well,' said Jane, 'you can have 'em if you'll pay for 'em. You can't get nothing worth having in this wicked world without paying for it. You've only to let Bill knock you down once, and he'll let you alone for ever after. Won't you, Bill?'

This was not exactly what Bill meant, though it was the end he sought.

'I want to show as I'm the better man,' he said with dogged reasonableness.

'So you are, if you only mean flesh and bone,' replied Jane. 'Any one can see that. If you wasn't, what's he carrying his butcher's knife for?'

'Because he's dirt: that's what he is!'

'Sam,' said Jane, 'you give me that knife.'

He surrendered it obediently. 'There!' she pointed: 'he ain't dirt now. Be a man, Sam, let him hit yer: it's only once!'

Sam looked at her, bewildered, helpless, imploringly: she had taken his knife off him. Then he braced himself, drew in a breath, tightened his lips and shut his eyes.

Jane steadied her voice to say, 'There, Bill, your man's waiting; knock him down!'

Bill faced the situation in dull perplexity, but could not carry on. 'Why'd I want to hit a thing like him?' he said at last.

'Why should you?' agreed Jane. 'Or him a thing like you? There's no beauty as I see to choose between you. Well? You don't seem so keen after all. Open your eyes, Sam, he ain't going to hurt you.'

'But we bain't friends!' said Bill vengefully, his moral feelings unappeased.

'No?' She paused a moment. 'Now look here! If you won't take your own way, will you take mine?'

Their eyes gave assent. Jane restored to Sam his lost property.

'Just you two exchange knives then! Sam has got the bigger one and knows it; that's where he had the pull of *you*. Men can't help being fools, but they can help being bloody fools. Come on, Samuel, there ain't to be no hewing of Agag to-day.'

Thus bidden, Sam made the required sacrifice.

'Now Bill,' said Jane, 'show yourself the better man! Take Sam on your back and carry him down home; he's feeling faint.'

They obeyed as though they had been little children. The community watched their descent from that mount of transfiguration with feelings almost of awe. Surely, for such mothering of grown men to be possible, a walking miracle had come among them!

'And we'll all have jam for tea,' said Jane in conclusion. 'The Devil's done for himself! Sam and Bill have found they can't do without each other.'

That was a fact; Sam and Bill became bosom friends.

For always, then and after, Jane had the wit to perceive that simple souls need ritual; and the camp never lacked its daily parable while she was in it.

When the community desired a new song that they might sing, Jane wrote this for them:

> Man's a fool! From all his thievings
> God gets left, and God's the leavings.
> Bread of life be in the baking:
> Man's the meal, and God's the making.
> On the fire which hath no dying,
> Man's the fat, and God's the frying.
>
> When we toil for friend and neighbour,
> Giving service, God is labour.
> In the joy, which cometh after
> Honest labour, God is laughter.
> And when cares have ceased to cumber
> Brain and body, God is slumber.

Choosing a cheerful tune to fit the words, the congregation sang, 'Man's a fool!' with great heartiness and conviction. Jane joyed to hear them. 'If those as wastes time calling 'emselves miserable sinners would only shorten it to fools,' she remarked, 'they'd get a deal nearer home, and do 'emselves more good. It's the truer word anyway.'

But though the Mother loved laughter, believing it a cure for nine-tenths of man's ills, she could be solemn also. One day there fell on the community a shadow of evil so black Jane could not laugh about it. It was the darker being unrevealed: it recurred, and still its origin was not traced.

But Jane's remedy was not to question or search by material ways; nor was the culprit called on to confess to deeds done in the dark. But at the falling-in of night she called her flock together, and numbered them, and led them to the Lord's showing a way of her own. Solemnly up the Hill of Difficulties they went, Jane leading them, and silently stationed under a moonless heaven of stars, stood out the hours till dawn.

One that was there tells of it. "Twas the only time I ever see Mother Jane with tears in her eyes, when she called us in and told us what was among us. Then she took us up to the hill, and we all waited for the Lord's showing: and nobody wasn't to speak. We'd stood there a whole hour before Mother Jane first said the word: it came so sudden some of us almost cried out. "Make me a clean heart, O God, and renew a right spirit within me!" That was all she said. Two hours later she said it again; and then, when we was all standing about ready to drop, she said it a third time. We was all crying then, we couldn't help. But when the light came it showed the granting of her prayer, and the one as hadn't got the right heart had gone. He never came back either: but don't you doubt, if he had Jane would have taken him. For she'd a great faith in her. Aye, there isn't a doubt we did well along of 'er.'

Ploughshare and Pruning-hook Ten Lectures on Social Subjects   (1919)

CONSCIOUS AND UNCONSCIOUS IMMORTALITY

BECAUSE the bee and the ant live unconscious of their impending doom, are we, therefore, to regard them as a hoodwinked race, set to labour at the dictates of the Creative capitalist on terms which contain in them no adequate reward? Suppose, for a moment, that revelation could descend upon ants' nest and hive, and tell these workers that beyond death the future held for them no store — that their immortality was the immortality not of individual but of race; and suppose that thereupon they all struck and went forth to die each singly in their own way — would that moral emblem impress us, do you think, as a thing worthy of imitation or of praise?

And surely it is the same with man. Individualism, separatism, self-obsessionism, though still present in the phenomena of existence, are more and more subject to qualifications from which they cannot escape. Even the most evil form of individualism has to be parasitic or predatory; it cannot exist alone; even against its will it becomes conditioned by other lives. And the communal sense of man, implicit within the innumerable forms of life through which he has evolved, will continue to lay its hold on the parasitic and the predatory, and will do so quite effectively on the basis of an evolutionary past, the tendencies of which were established before theological definitions came to give them impulse and strength.

Is it not almost ludicrous to suggest that that communal instinct will cease to play, if the hope of individual reward after death is withdrawn from the human race? Will man — because he is nobler than the beast, because at his best he does things more altruistic, more self-sacrificing, more self-forgetting, more self-transcending than any of these — do less nobly because he envisages destiny, which (if he sees it as destiny) he will see as the logical outcome of evolutionary law?

It is possible, it is even probable, that all phases of theological thought have had their use in giving direction and stimulus to the human brain; but if they have done nothing but stimulate rebellion against obscurantist authority they have had value of a positive kind. But we may go even further than this, for 'everything possible to be believed', says Blake, 'is an image of truth'. And under many a concept, distorted by ignorance or guile, has lain a germ of the true life which draws man on to communal ends. In time that germ puts off the husk that seemed once (perhaps in some cases actually was) the protective armoury through which alone it could survive for the use of a later day. But though old reasons have been shed, the essential value has not changed; and often it is less by logic and reason than by the strong and subtle links of association that we preserve what is good of past credulities.

The doctrine of conscious immortality, however much belittled by its appeal to selfish individualism, has done a work for the human race. It has held the germ of an ideal for unity which is receiving a more universal interpretation to-day than the earlier theologians would ever have allowed, or than man, in his then stage of development, could have thought it worth while to hand on to his intellectual heirs. Perhaps only because he conceived it in just such a form have its values been preserved.

I am reminded in this connection of the method by which the wild swine of the New Forest were taught to obey the voice of the horn by means of which the swine-herd called them back each night from their free roaming in the forest. The way he did it was this. Having first formed his herd, some four or five hundred strong, he penned them in a narrow space where water and warm shelter were to be found; and there, in the allotted enclosure, according them no liberty, he fed them daily to the sound of the horn. Food and music became a sort of celestial harmony to pig's brain — when they heard the one, good reason was given them for expecting the other.

Presently, in a well-fed condition, they were set free to roam; and being full and satisfied they did not roam far; and at night the horn sounded them back to an ample meal, and continued to sound while again they ate and were satisfied.

So at last, by association, the horn came to have such a beneficent meaning that the mere sound of it sufficed to bring them back at nightfall to their appointed place of rest. They might roam for miles and miles during the day, but night and the sound of the horn brought them all back safe to fold. And when the habit had become established, they did not cease to return even though the swine-herd no longer supplied the food which had first given music its charm to those savage breasts.

And, similarly, I doubt not, that, though all hope of material profit or reward be withdrawn from man's mind, that call of the horn which he has heard of old will still bring his spirit to the resting-place at the appointed time; nor will he wish either to shorten his days or debase his pleasures because the horn has ceased to provide the meal which it once taught him to expect.

.   .   .   .

But — whether life thus rises by unknown law to further ends, or whether it passes out, like the life of leaves, into the general decay with which autumn each year fertilizes the bed of mother earth — of one thing I would ask you to be confident — that the bandying of words and theories, and the discussion, tending this way or that, of man's destiny after death, are not in any way likely to alter or to undo those forward-driving forces and communal desires with which, from an inheritance of so many millions of years, the life of humanity has become endowed. The will to live will still lift up the race and carry it forward to new ends, whether man thinks he sees in death the end of his personal existence, or only a new and better beginning. And whether he claims or resigns that prospect of reward he will never be able to rid himself of the sense which revives after all failures and crimes, that man is his brother-man — or be able to refrain at his best from laying down his life, without calculation of personal benefit to himself, so that others may live.

Little Plays of St. Francis (First Series)   (1921)

THE BUILDERS

The first meeting of FRANCIS *and* JUNIPER. *For the rebuilding of St. Damien's* JUNIPER *has brought a barrow-load of stone.* FRANCIS *comes down the ladder and sees* JUNIPER *entering with his fourth stone. He stops and stares at* FRANCIS.

FRANCES Brother, where do these come from?

JUNIPER It's my own house I'm pulling down — to get rid of the rats.

FRANCIS You brought stone yesterday.

JUNIPER Ah, for Dom Silvestro that was. You said you could do with more, but hadn't the money.

FRANCIS I still have not the money, Brother.

JUNIPER No more have I. But I've the stone. There's another for you.

FRANCIS You have a beautiful face, Brother. What is your name?

JUNIPER I — beautiful? Had God made all the world like me, you'd run away from it. Name? — Juniper.

FRANCIS A good name: one of God's planting, for it bears fruit.

JUNIPER Juniper, the fool, I am. — There's another for you. — That's what everybody calls me, who knows. And there's not a bigger fool in this world.

FRANCIS Thank God for that, Brother. A good fool is a great work of mercy.

JUNIPER For why, then?

FRANCIS God hath saved him without making him wise.

JUNIPER Wise? Oh! had He made me wise, I should have died scratching my head over it. Here's another for you.

FRANCIS Put them down outside, Brother. So much carrying tires you.

JUNIPER And who am I that's not to be tired? What else was I made for?

FRANCIS To give joy in Heaven.

JUNIPER The Lord help 'em if they are waiting to get it out of *me*!

FRANCIS Why? Are you not a stone-mason?

JUNIPER No, Master! I'm doing this for play. A cobbler is my trade.

FRANCIS Well — a cobbler, then. Who gives more joy than a cobbler? He is the means by which we go, making the way easy; he saves us from stones and thorns, from the fangs of serpents, and from frost-bite. By his aid we make long journeys, seeing the world, and the wonder of it: Rome, and the Holy Land, and churches where Priests say Mass: to cities also, and men's houses, making us become friends. Thus are we brought together in understanding and fellowship, which from the beginning was God's will concerning us. See, then, how good and joyful a thing it is to be a cobbler! And he that gives joy on earth gives joy in Heaven.

BROTHER WOLF

FRANCIS, *taking* JUNIPER *with him, has gone out, at the risk of his life, to meet* LUPO *and his robber-band. In the end he wins* LUPO *to forgive Assisi the wrong she has done him.*

LUPO Thou man of wonder! Who art thou?

FRANCIS I am the little fool of Assisi, the Poverello; hast thou not heard tell of him? Men laugh when they speak of me.

LUPO From Assisi art thou?

FRANCIS She was my mother; I was born there.

LUPO She was mine — and she cast me out! In the place of justice she denied me; in my own house she robbed me; in the market she mocked me; in the street she stoned me; she cursed me, she hated me, she sought me that she might slay me. And now shall I let vengeance go?

FRANCIS Take thy vengeance, Brother, and do this. Be thou kind to her!

LUPO I? — Kind!

FRANCIS O Brother, stand by my side, and look upon this city! Is she not fair? See her face, how it turns to thee in the light of the sun! Behold her towers like watchmen upon the walls, and her roofs like wings to cover her, and her windows like eyes. She hath ears also, and hands, and feet, Brother; and therewithal she hath a heart. And in her heart standeth the fear of thee. Down below are streets, and doors, and a market-place, and homes both for rich and poor. And these be full of the music of men's voices and the laughter of children, of tears also, and cries of sorrow and anger. But it is not sorrow or anger which giveth beauty to her face, or strength unto her towers. And the fear of thee that is in her heart bringeth no happiness.

Come, Brother, let thy heart go down with me into yonder city. Here is a house where a mother suckles her babe; and the child knoweth her, though he understandeth not. Here is a house where a young man bringeth his bride. He closeth the door, he turneth, he kisseth her. Sweet is the taste of love upon their lips. Here is a house where a man lies dying: he hath been strong, but now he is feeble and weak. Many things did he with his body, Brother; often he did ill, sometimes he did well. Now cometh death, and he understandeth not; yet the good that he did comforteth him. Yea, because he had love and not hatred within his heart, therefore he is not solitary.

(FRANCIS *lays his hand on* LUPO's *breast*)

Ah, Brother, what is this that moveth *thy* heart, so that it leapeth? Listen, I will tell thee. A man stood once and looked upon a city; grievously had she sinned. And by his side stood the angel of God that was come to destroy it. So he said to the angel, 'If there be found in this city fifty righteous, wilt thou not spare it for fifty's sake?' And he answered, 'I will spare it for fifty'. Then he said, 'If there lack five of the fifty?' 'I will not destroy it for lack of five.' 'If there be forty?' 'I will not destroy it for lack of ten.' 'If there be thirty?' 'Nay.' 'If there be twenty?' The angel said, 'I will not destroy it for twenty's sake.'

And he said, 'Oh, let not my Lord be angry, and I will speak but this once. Peradventure there shall be ten found there?' And he said, 'I will not destroy it for ten's sake.' Brother Wolf, thou art a sinner, as I also am a sinner. Wilt thou, having so many sins to thy charge, be less merciful than God that is without sin?

(LUPO *buries his face in his hands. From a distance comes the chiming of bells*)

JUNIPER It is the bells, Father!

FRANCIS Yes, 'tis the bells of Assisi that thou hearest. They are ringing for thee. Come, and I will show thee twenty in that city, yea, forty, yea, fifty, yea an hundred that shall be glad, when thou hast taken from their hearts the fear they have of thee . . . Brother Wolf.

(LUPO, *with a sob, reaches out his hand to* FRANCIS)

LUPO I am blind, Father; lead me . . . My life is in thy hands. I will go down with thee! Yes, I will go down.

JUNIPER (*rapt in ecstasy*) O Father, I was a fool! For when I came here, I was afraid.

(FRANCIS, *leading* LUPO *by the hand, starts to go.* JUNIPER *with a face of beaming contentment follows. The bells say everything*).

Angels and Ministers   (1921)

THE QUEEN: GOD BLESS HER!
(1876)

The QUEEN *discusses with* LORD BEACONSFIELD *the War between Turkey and Russia.*

THE QUEEN But do you think, Lord Beaconsfield, that the Turks are going to be beaten?

BEACONSFIELD The Turks *are* beaten, Madam . . . But England will never be beaten. We shall dictate terms — moderating the demands of Russia; and under your Majesty's protection the throne of the Kaliphat will be safe — once more. That, Madam, is the key to our Eastern policy: a grateful Kaliphat, claiming allegiance from the whole Mahomedan world, bound to us by instincts of self-preservation — and we hold henceforth the gorgeous East in fee with redoubled security. His power may be a declining power; but ours remains. Some day, who knows? Egypt, possibly even Syria, Arabia, may be our destined reward.

> (*Like a cat over a bowl of cream, England's Majesty sits lapping all this up. But, when he has done, her comment is shrewd and to the point*)

THE QUEEN The French won't like that!

BEACONSFIELD They won't, Madam, they won't. But has it ever been England's policy, Madam, to mind what the French don't like?

THE QUEEN (*with relish*) No, it never has been, has it? Ah! you are the true statesman, Lord Beaconsfield. Mr. Gladstone never talked to me like that.

HIS FAVOURITE FLOWER
(1881)

LORD BEACONSFIELD — *with his feet drawn up for death* — *has a prophetic nightmare, which his physician* (DR. KIDD), *who was the first English doctor to take a scientific interest in dreams, explains on pre-Freudian lines.*

DOCTOR Medical science is beginning to say 'Yes'; that in sleep the subconscious mind has its reactions.

BEACONSFIELD Well, I wonder how my 'subconscious mind' got hold of primroses.

DOCTOR Primroses? Did they form a feature in your dream?

BEACONSFIELD A feature? No. The whole place was alive with them! As the victim of inebriety sees snakes, I saw primroses. They were everywhere: they fawned on me in wreaths and festoons; swarmed over me like parasites; flew at me like flies; till it seemed that the whole world had conspired to suffocate me under a sulphurous canopy of those detestable little atoms. Can you imagine the horror of it, Doctor, to a sane — a hitherto sane mind like mine? . . . For I assure you that the horror I then conceived for those pale botanical specimens in their pestiferous and increscent abundance, exceeded what words can describe. I have felt spiritually devastated ever since.

Dethronements Imaginary Portraits of Political Characters, (1922)
done in Dialogue

THE KING-MAKER
Brighton — October 1891

A week before his death PARNELL *foretells to his Wife the future liberation of Ireland.*

KATHARINE It *has* happened, you know, sometimes, that love and politics haven't quite gone together . . . Still, you love — Ireland.

PARNELL Not as she is to-day — so narrow and jealous, so stupid, so blind! Has she anything alive in her now worth saving? That Ireland has got to die; and, though it doesn't sound like it, this is the death-rattle beginning. Ireland is going to fail, and deserves to fail. But another Ireland won't fail. She's learning her lesson — or *will* learn it, in the grave. Something like this was bound to come; but if it were to come again twenty years on, it wouldn't count. She'd know better.

KATHARINE Twenty years! We shall be an old couple by then.

PARNELL In the life of a nation twenty years is nothing. No. Ireland was shaped for failure: she has it in her. It has got to come out. Subjection, oppression, starvation, haven't taught her enough: she must face betrayal too, and of the most mischievous kind — the betrayal of well-meaning fools. After that, paralysis, loss of confidence, loss of will, loss of faith — in false leaders. Then she'll begin to learn.

KATHARINE Do you mean that everything *has* failed now?

PARNELL Yes; if *I* fail. I'm not thinking of myself as indispensable: it's the principle. That's what I've been trying to make them understand. But they won't, they won't! Independence, defiance — they don't see it as a principle, only as an expedient. They may make it a cry, they may feel it as their right; but when to insist on it looks like losing a point in the game — then they give up the principle, to become parasites! That's what is happening now. It's the slave in the blood coming out — the crisis of the disease. That's why I'm fighting it: and will, to the death! And when — when we are dead — some day: she'll come to her senses again — and see! Then — this will have helped.

THE MAN OF BUSINESS

Highbury, Edgbaston — August 1913

CHAMBERLAIN Sometimes the political world has no use for statesmen — except to down them. Sometimes it prefers politicians, and perhaps rightly. Every age makes its own peculiar requirements; and those who find out when the political line is the better one to follow, are the successful ones. You and I have been — politicians; let's be honest and own it. And now my particular politics are over. Circumstances have emptied me out. That's different from mere failure. Great statesmen have been failures; we've seen them go down, you and I — too big, too far-seeing for their day. But they went down *full*, with all the weight of their great convictions and principles still to their credit. I'm empty. Time has played me out. That's the difference.

DISTINGUISHED VISITOR I am confident that history will give a different verdict . . . What more can one do than direct it for the generation in which one lives? That, it seems to me, is our main responsibility.

CHAMBERLAIN Well, that's what you and I have done. How? Mainly by pulling down bigger men than ourselves. Randolph, Parnell, Gladstone — we got the better of them, didn't we? Have you never wondered why men of genius get sent into the world — only to be defeated? Gladstone was a bigger man than the whole lot of us; but we pulled him down — and I enjoyed doing it. Parnell, for all his limitations, was a great man. Well, we got him down too. And I confess that gave me satisfaction. You helped to pull Randolph down; but you didn't enjoy doing it. That's where you and I were different. .

. . . . .

Parnell, how he tried all his life to make a speech and couldn't. But what he said didn't matter — there was the man! What a force he might have been — was! What a Samson, when he pulled the whole Irish Party down — got them all on top of him to pull with him. What d'you think he was doing then? Trying to give his Irish nation a soul! It looked like pride, pique, mere wanton destruction; but it was a great idea. And if ever they rise to it — if ever the whole Irish nation puts its back to the wall as Parnell wanted it to do then — shakes off dependence, alliance, conciliation, compromise, it may beat us yet! They were afraid of

G 97

defeat. That's why we won. A cause or a nation that fears no defeat —
nor any number of them — that's what wins in the long run. But does
any such nation — any such cause exist? I'm not sure. . . .

THE INSTRUMENT
Washington — March 4th, 1921

It is the day of the installation of the new President. WOODROW WILSON
explains to his friend and secretary, MR. TUMULTY, *how he failed to win
the Peace.*

EX-PRES. I went over to Paris thinking to save the Peace: there came a
point when I thought it was saved: it would have been had the Senate
backed me — it could have been done then. But when I put the case to
which already we stood pledged, I convinced nobody. They did not want
justice to be done.

TUMULTY But you had a great following, Governor. You had a
wonderful reception when you got to Paris.

EX-PRES. Yes: in London too. It seemed then as if people were only
waiting to be led. But I'm talking of the politicians now. There was no
room for conviction there; each must stick to his brief. That's what
wrecked us. Not one — not one could I get to own that the right thing
was the wise thing to do: that to be just and fear not was the real policy
which would have saved Europe — and the world . . . Look at it now!
Step by step, their failure is coming home to them; but still it is only as
failure that they see it — mere human inability to surmount insuperable
difficulties: the greed, the folly, the injustice, the blindness, the cruelty of
it they don't see. And the people don't teach it them. They can't. No
nation — no victorious nation — has gotten it at heart to say, 'We, too,
have sinned'. Lest such a thing should ever be said or thought, one of the
terms of peace was to hand over all the blame; so, when the enemy signed
the receipt of it, the rest were acquitted. And in that solemn farce the
Allies found satisfaction! What a picture for posterity! And when they
point and laugh, I shall be there with the rest. It's our self-righteousness
has undone us, Tumulty; it's that which has made us blind and hard —
and dishonest: for there has been dishonesty too. Because we were exact-
ing reparations for a great wrong, we didn't mind being unjust to the

wrongdoer. And so, in Paris, we spent months, arguing, prevaricating, manoeuvring, so as to pretend that none had had any share in bringing the evil about. When I spoke for considerate justice, there was no living force behind me in that council of the Nations. They wanted their revenge, and now they've got it: and look what it's costing them! . . .

No, they wouldn't believe me when I said that to be revengeful would cost more than to be forgiving. And still they won't believe that the trouble they are now in comes — not from the destructiveness of the War, but from their own destruction of the Peace. I had the truth in me; but I failed. I was a voice crying into the void — a President without a people to back me: a dictator — of words! And they knew that my time was short, and that I had no power of appeal — because the heart of my people was not with me! If they had any doubt before, the vote of the Senate told them. . . .

TUMULTY . . . You must have got a pretty deep-down insight into character, Governor, when you came to the top of things over there, to the top people, I mean.

EX-PRES. Yes, it was very interesting, when one got accustomed to it: highly selected humanity, representative of things — it was afraid of. There daily sat four of us — if one counts heads only; but we were, in fact, six, or seven, or eight characters. And the characters sprang up and choked us. Patriots, statesmen? oh, yes! but also 'careerists'. Men whose future depends on the popular vote can't always be themselves — at least, it seemed not; for we should then have ceased to be 'representative', and it was as representatives that we had come. And so one would sit and listen, and watch — one person, and two characters. Lloyd George, when his imagination was not swamped in self-satisfaction, was quite evangelical to listen to — sometimes. But there he was representative — not of principles, nor of those visionary sparks which he struck so easily and threw off like matches, but of a successful election cry for 'hanging the Kaiser' and 'making Germany pay'. And having got his majority, he and his majority had become one. But for that, he might — he just might . . . yet who can tell? That tied him. I was alone. . . .

That was my plight, while there in Paris we held high court, and banqueted, and drank healths from dead men's skulls. Did nobody guess — outside — what was going on? I gave one signal that I thought was plain enough, when I sent for the *George Washington* to bring me home again.

But, though I listened for it then, there seemed no response ... And then, rather than let me so go and spoil the general effect (the one power still left to me!), they began to make concessions — concessions which, I see now, didn't amount to much; and so they persuaded me, and I stayed on, and signed my failure with the rest ... Tumulty, when I faced failure, when I knew that I had failed — Yes; don't trouble to contradict me. I know, dear friend, I know that you don't agree; and, God bless you! I also know why ... When I knew *that*, after the whole thing was over, and I was out again and free, do you suppose I wasn't tempted to go out and cry the truth (as some were expecting and wishing for it to be cried) in the ears of the whole world? — let all know that I *had* failed, and so — that way at least — separate myself from the Evil Thing which there sat smiling at itself in its Hall of Mirrors — seeing no frustrate ghosts, no death's heads at that feast, as I saw them? ... I came out a haunted man — All the more because those I was amongst didn't believe in ghosts — not then. People who have been overwhelmingly victorious in a great war find that difficult. But they will — some day.

TUMULTY Well, Governor, and supposing you had yielded to this 'Temptation', as you call it, what's the proposition?

EX-PRES. This ... I had one power — one weapon, still left to me unimpaired: to speak the truth, the whole truth, and nothing but the truth, so help me God! And the proposition is just this: whether to be stark honest, even against the apparent interests of the very cause you are out to plead, is not in the long run the surest way — if it be of God — to help it make good: whether defeat, with the whole truth told, isn't better than defeat hidden away and disowned, in the hope that something may yet come of it. You may get a truer judgment that way in the end; though at the time it may seem otherwise. Yes, I *was* tempted to cry it aloud — to make a clean breast of it — to say, 'We, the Governments of the People, the Democracies, the Free Nations of the world, have failed — have lost the peace which we could have won, because we would not give up the things which we loved so much better — profit, revenge, our own too good opinion of ourselves, our own self-righteous judgment of others.' ... I was tempted to it; and yet it has been charged against me that I would not admit failure because I wanted to save my face.

TUMULTY You have never been much scared by what people *said*, Governor. That didn't count, I reckon.

EX-PRES. No, Tumulty; but this did — that where all seemed dark, I still saw light. Down there, among the wreckage, something was left — an instrument of which I thought I saw the full future possibility more clearly than others. I believe I do still. And my main thought then was — how best to secure that one thing to which, half blindly, they had agreed. To win that, I was willing to give up my soul.

TUMULTY It's the Covenant, you mean, Governor?

EX-PRES. Yes, the Covenant! That at least was won — seemed won — whatever else was lost. Some of them were willing to let me have it only because they themselves believed it would prove useless — just to save my face for all I had to give up in exchange. And so I — let them 'save my face' for me; let them think that it was so — just to give this one thing its chance. And so, for that, and for that alone, I bound myself to the Treaty — stood pledged to do my utmost to see it through: a different thing, that, from telling the truth. Was I wrong, Tumulty — was I wrong? . . .

TUMULTY (*expanding himself*) No man who believes in America as much as I do will ever say you were wrong, Governor.

EX-PRES. But when America stood out — when the Senate refused to ratify — then I *was* wrong. For then, what I had backed — all that remained then — was a thing of shreds and patches. Nobody can think worse of the Treaty than I do with America out of it, with the Covenant left the one-sided and precarious thing it is now. Had we only been in it — the rest wouldn't have mattered. Call it a dung-heap, if you like; yet out of it would have sprung life. It may still; but I shan't see it, Tumulty; and that vision, which was then so clear, has become a doubt. Was I wrong — was I wrong to pretend that I had won anything worth winning? Would it not have been better to say 'I have failed'?

TUMULTY Chief, I think you did right. But I still feel I'm up a back street. How could things have come to fail as much as they did? After all, it was a just war.

EX-PRES. Tumulty, I have been asking myself whether there can be such a thing as a 'just war'. There can be — please God! — a just *cause* for war. When one sees great injustice done, sees it backed by the power of a blindly militarized nation, marching confidently to victory, then, if justice has any place in the affairs of men, there is sometimes just cause for war. But can there be — a just war? I mean — when the will to war takes hold of a people — does it remain the same people? Does war in its hands remain an instrument that can be justly used? Can it be waged justly? Can it be won justly? Can it, having been won, make a just peace? No! Something happens: there comes a change; war in a people's mind drives justice out ... Can soldiers fight without 'seeing red' — can a nation? Not when nations have to fight on the tremendous scale of modern war. Then they are like those monstrous mechanisms of long-range destructiveness, which we so falsely call 'weapons of precision', but which are in fact so horribly unprecise that, once let loose, we cannot know what lives of harmlessness, of innocence, of virtue, they are going to destroy. You find your range, you fix your elevation, you touch a button: you hear your gun go off. And over there, among the unarmed — the weak, the defenceless, the infirm — it has done — what? Singled out for destruction what life or lives; ten, twenty, a hundred? — you do not know. So with nations, when once they have gone to war; their imprecision becomes — horrible; though the cause of your war may be just ... What I've been realizing these last two years is a terrible thing. You go to war, you get up to it from your knees — God driving you to it — unable, yes, unable to do else. Your will is to do right, your cause is just, you are a united nation, a people convinced, glad, selfless, with hearts heroic and clean. And then war takes hold of it, and it all changes under your eyes; you see the heart of your people becoming fouled, getting hard, self-righteous, revengeful. Your cause remains, in theory, what it was at the beginning; but it all goes to the Devil. And the Devil makes on it a pile that he can make no otherwise — because of the virtue that is in it, the love, the beauty, the heroism, the giving-up of so much that man's heart desires. That's where he scores! Look at all that valiance, that beauty of life gone out to perish for a cause it knows to be right; think of the generosity of that giving by the young men; think of the faithful courage of the women who steel themselves to let them go; think of the increase of spirit and selflessness which everywhere rises to meet the claim. All over the land which goes to war that is happening (and in the enemy's land it is the same), making war a sacred and holy thing. And having got it so sanctified, then the Devil can do with it almost what he likes. That's what he has done, Tumulty. If angels led horses by the bridle at the Marne (as a pious legend tells), at Versailles the Devil had his muzzled oxen treading out the corn. And of those — I was one! Yes; war muzzles you. You cannot tell the truth; if you did, it wouldn't be believed. And so, finally, comes peace; and over that, too, the Devil runs up his flag — cross-bones and a skull.

TUMULTY (*struggling in the narrow path between wrong and right*) But what else, Governor, is your remedy? We had to go to war; we were left with no choice in the matter.

EX-PRES. No, we *had* no choice. And what others had any choice? — What people, I mean? But that is what everyone — once we were at war — refused to remember. And so we cried '*Lusitania!*' against thousands of men who had no choice in the matter at all. Remedy? There's only one. Somehow we must get men to believe that Christ wasn't a mad idealist when He preached His Sermon on the Mount; that what He showed for the world's salvation then was not a sign only, but the very Instrument itself. We've got to make men see that there's something in human nature waiting to respond to a new law. There are two things breeding in the world — love and hatred; breeding the one against the other. And there's fear making hatred breed fast, and there's fear making love breed slow. Even as things now are, it has managed — it has just managed to keep pace; but only just. If men were not afraid — Love would win.

That, I've come to see, is the simple remedy; but it's going to be the hardest thing to teach — because all the world is so much afraid.

False Premises　　　　　　　　　　　　　　　　　　　(1922)
　　　Five One Act Plays

THE HOUSE FAIRY

The HOUSE FAIRY *tells her own story to the* CHILD

CHILD Have you ever seen a fairy, Granny?
GRANNY (*in a soft whimsy tone*) Yes.
CHILD What was it like?
GRANNY Very like you and me, my dear. Folk might often meet a fairy, and not know.

Eh, but there was a fairy once — different from the rest: liked to be along o' the common folk, she did; watch 'em at their work, see 'em making the bread, milking the cows, skimming the cream; liked to hearken to their voices, calling their children to bed, talking in the ingle o' nights, making plans for the morrow, learning to know the thoughts of each other's hearts. And along of that — because she'd the friendly mind, she didn't care to go riding the wind with the rest. For they be merry and gay, they be; but they haven't got thoughts in their hearts like you and me. One day . . .

CHILD Go on, Granny, I'm listening.

GRANNY One day she came to a house where children were crying — father and mother dead, and no one to fend for them. Eh! little things, little things, they was; and no sooner had she pushed open the door and looked in than she forgot all about being a fairy. In she went — lived with 'em — made it her home.

CHILD Did they know she was a fairy, Granny?

GRANNY Nay, nay, they were all too little and young to know anything, except to be glad someone was come to look after 'em. But when the fairies found out, they were angry, and came to fetch her away: but she wouldn't go — told 'em she meant to stay and see to the children's needs. 'You'll find it a hard life,' said they. 'Maybe I shall,' said she. 'In a year's time,' they said, 'you'll be wanting to come back, and then we won't have you. If you won't come back now,' they said, 'you've got to stay — fifty years! Sure, and you'll have had enough of it then!' 'Eh, maybe I shall,' she said; so they left her to try. Fifty years. She never saw 'em again.

(*But at the end of the fifty years they come for her, and she has to go*).

Echo de Paris   (1923)

The scene is the outside of a Paris restaurant in 1899.

R.R. My dear Oscar, why cannot a Scotsman be a genius as comfortably as any one else?

OSCAR WILDE. I ought to have said 'artist': I mean artist. It is much easier for a Scotsman to be a genius than to be an artist. Mr. Gladstone, I believe, claimed to be a Scotsman whenever he stood for a Scottish constituency, or spoke to a Scottish audience. The butter-Scotch flavour of it makes me believe it was true. There was no art in that; and yet how truly typical! It was always so successful. . . .

Because, Robbie — to return to your question — your Scotsman believes only in success. How can a man, who regards success as the goal of life, be a true artist? God saved the genius of Robert Burns to poetry by driving him through drink to failure. Think what an appalling figure in literature a successful Burns would have been! He was already trying to write poems in polite English, which was about as ludicrous as for a polite Englishman to try to write poetry in the dialect of Burns. Riotous living and dying saved him from that last degradation of smug prosperity which threatened him.

L.H. But do you mean no artists are successful?

OSCAR WILDE Incidentally; never intentionally. If they are, they remain incomplete. The artist's mission is to live the complete life: success, as an episode (which is all it can be); failure, as the real, the final end. Death, analysed to its resultant atoms — what is it but the vindication of failure: the getting rid for ever of powers, desires, appetites, which have been a lifelong embarrassment? The poet's noblest verse, the dramatist's greatest scene deal always with death; because the highest function of the artist is to make perceived the beauty of failure.

R.R. But have Scotsmen of genius been any more successful, in a worldly sense, than others? I seem to remember a few who failed rather handsomely.

OSCAR WILDE Possibly. Providence is sometimes kinder to us than we are to ourselves. But never was there a Scotsman of genius who survived his youth, who was not fatally compromised by his nationality. To fail and die young is the only hope for a Scotsman who wishes to remain an artist. When, at the end of the eighteenth century, Scotland produced her second great writer of genius, she inspired him to a terrible betrayal (for which the tradespeople of literature still praise him) — to break his art on the wheel of commercial rectitude, to write books which became worse and worse, in order to satisfy his creditors! In Dante's *Purgatorio* there is nothing to equal the horror of it. But he succeeded; and Scotland, in consequence, is proud of him. I see by your faces that you all know the man I mean: one does not have to name him. Think of unhappy Sir Walter, writing his transcendent pot-boilers for no other reason than to wipe out bankruptcy! Bankruptcy, that beneficent fairy, who presents to all who trust her with their insolvency, five, ten, fifteen, sometimes even nineteen shillings in the pound of what they owe to their creditors — to those usurious ones whose extortionate demands, recognized in other branches of the law, here get turned down. How much did she give me, Robbie?

R.R. An extension of time, Oscar. She hasn't done with you yet.

OSCAR WILDE No; she does not dismiss the lover from her embraces while she has any hope of securing the restoration of his balance, or of discovering some deeper stain in his character. What touching devotion! She is the romantic figure of the money-market. But I believe — or at least I tell myself — that fewer Scotsmen go bankrupt than any other nationality. It is not, however, merely monetary success which seduces them; success, in all its aspects, has for them a baleful attraction. They succumb to it intellectually, morally, spiritually. On that Carlyle wrecked his chances of producing a permanent work of art greater than his *French Revolution*.

ALL Carlyle?

OSCAR WILDE I surprise you? Is that because we all know that Carlyle remained poor? So do misers. Carlyle was the greatest intellectual miser of the nineteenth century. In his prime he wrote his greatest book — the history of a failure — the *French Revolution*. The time came when, with all his powers matured, he stood equipped for the writing of his supreme masterpiece. There was no need to look far afield for a subject: it stood obvious awaiting him. After his *French Revolution* he should have written the life of Napoleon — the greatest success, the greatest failure that the world has ever known. He would have done it magnificently. What a spectacle for the world: the Man of Destiny receiving from the son of humble Scottish peasants his right measure of immortality! But because Carlyle was a Scotsman, he would not take for his hero the man whose life ended in failure: he could not bring himself to face the *debacle* of Waterloo, the enduring ignominy and defeat of St. Helena. Had he been true to his art, he would have realized that St. Helena was the greatest theme of all — for an artist, the most completely significant in the whole of modern history. But because he had the soul of a Scotsman, because he worshipped success, he looked for his hero, and found him in that most mean and despicable character, Frederick the Great: a man to whom Heaven had given the powers of a supreme genius, and Hell the soul of a commercial traveller with that unavailing itch for cultural gentility which Voltaire has exposed for us. On that mean theme he wrote his most voluminous work, and became, in the process, that skeleton in Mrs. Carlyle's cupboard which the world now knows.

Trimblerigg A Book of Revelation (1924)

At the age of twelve MR. TRIMBLERIGG *feels called to the ministry.*

THUS early did the conversion of souls enter into the life and calculations of Mr. Trimblerigg. A striking justification of his chosen calling followed immediately, when, without in the least intending it, he converted an almost lost soul in a single day — the soul of an Uncle, James Hubback by name, the only uncle upon his mother's side left over from a large family — who while still clinging to the outward respectability of a Free Church minister, had taken secretly to drink.

Mr. Trimblerigg had been born and brought up in a household where the idea that spirits were anything to drink had never been allowed to enter his head. He only knew of spirit as of something that would catch fire and boil a kettle, or embrace death in a bottle and preserve it from decay. These aspects of its beneficence he had gathered first in the back kitchen of his own home, and secondly in the natural history department of the County Museum, to which as a Sunday-school treat he had been taken. Returning therefrom, he had been bitten for a short while with a desire to catch, kill, and preserve frogs, bats, beetles, snakes, and other low forms of existence, and make a museum of his own — his originality at that time being mainly imitative. To this end he clamoured to his mother to release his saved pennies which she held in safe keeping for him, in order that he might buy spirit for collecting purposes; and so pestered her that at last she promised that, if for a beginning he could find an adder, he should have a bottle of spirit to keep it in.

Close upon that his Uncle James arrived for a stay made sadly indefinite by the low water in which he found himself. He still wore his clerical garb but was without cure of souls: Bethel and he had become separated, and his family in consequence was not pleased with him. Nevertheless as a foretaste of reformation he wore a blue ribbon, and was prevented thereby from letting himself be seen on licensed premises; while a totally abstaining household, and a village with only one inn which had been warned not to serve him, and no shop that sold liquor, seemed to provide a safe environment for convalescence.

It is at this point that Mr. Trimblerigg steps in. One day, taking down a book from the shelf in the little study, he discovered behind it a small square bottle of spirits: he did not have to taste or smell it — the label 'old brandy' was enough; and supposing in his innocence the word 'old' to indicate that it had passed its best use, at once his volatile mind was seized with the notion that here was a mother's surprise waiting for him, and that he had only to provide the adder for the bottle and its contents to become his. And so with that calculated larkishness which made him do audacious things that when done had to be swallowed, he determined to give his mother a surprise in return.

Going off in search of his adder and failing to get it himself, he gave another boy a penny for finding him a dead one. An hour later the adder was inside the brandy bottle behind the books; and an hour after that his Uncle James had achieved complete and lifelong conversion to total abstinence.

The denouement presented itself to Mr. Trimblerigg at first with a shock of disappointment in the form of smashed glass, and his dead adder lying in a spent pool of brandy on the study floor; and only gradually did it dawn upon him after a cautious survey of the domestic situation that this was not, as he had at first feared, his mother's angry rejection of the surprise he had prepared for her: on the contrary she was pleased with him. His uncle, he learned, was upstairs lying down, without appetite either for tea or supper. Mr. Trimblerigg heard him moaning in the night, and he came down to breakfast the next day a changed character. Within a year he had secured reinstatement in the ministry, and was become a shining light on the temperance platform, telling with great fervour anecdotes which gave hope. There was, however, one story of a drunkard's reformation which he never told: perhaps because, on after-reflection, though he had accepted their testimony against him, he could not really believe his eyes; perhaps because there are certain experiences which remain too deep and sacred and mysterious ever to be told.

But to Mr. Trimblerigg the glory of what he had done was in a while made plain. More than ever, it showed him destined for the ministry; it also gave colour to his future ministrations, opening his mind in the direction of a certain school of thought in which presently he became an adept. 'The Kingdom of Heaven is taken by tricks', became the subconscious foundation of his belief; and when he entered the pulpit at the age of twenty-one, he was by calculative instinct that curious combination of the tipster, the thimblerigger, and the prophet, the man of vision and the man of lies, which drew to itself the adoration of one half and the detestation of the other half of the Free United Evangelical Connection, eventually dividing that great body into two unequal portions, and driving its soul into a limbo of spiritual frustration and ineffectiveness till it found itself again under new names.

Odd Pairs   (1925)

THE TWO WIDOWS OF CHADSEY

AFTER three years of wedded rule, Jane presented her husband with a son, to her own intense satisfaction. In those early days of maternity, when she carried the small Jim in her arms, her face softened and seemed to acquire a new light. I have seen Jane Waldron in wrath, and I have seen her nursing her young, and on each occasion I thought she had beauty. You could not define it: it was soul not flesh that stood out before you, making the rugged surface on which it rested appear comely: sunlight on stone, you might say, for her face did not move, and I never saw her smile in all the years I knew her.

Now whether that aspect of her struck the jealous eyes of the woman she had supplanted, or whether it was that the other having no child felt injured by the comparison, I cannot doubt (in view of subsequent events) that from this time Susan Bannier began definitely plotting to undermine a happiness that she envied.

I have told you that Tom came of a not too steady family; but under Jane's management he fell submissively in to the groove set for him. He brought her his week's wages regularly, and out of them she gave him fourpence a night to spend up at the inn.

All this was private between them, and even between them was hardly put into words: it was an understood thing that at half-past nine he was to come home. Now and then, for an event, he was unpunctual in his return: she had her word ready for him then. Tom, simple shy chap, took it as right payment, and did not complain. His dread was to be pointed at publicly as a man without freedom, henpecked — he that had been a gay young cockerel in his bachelor days; so, for a manifesto, he took now and then more margin than his wife allowed, and bore what followed with an easy mind, since for so small a payment he kept up the appearance necessary for his self-respect.

Susan Bannier was probably by this time remote enough from his thoughts; she had risen above his head, had married a man of substance, wore a green silk dress on Sundays, and only descended to the bar-parlour on great occasions. Truth to say, her looks were going off in the opposite direction to Jane's: while the one thinned and became metallic to look on, the other filled out and frowsed. Yet she had a taking way that appealed to some men; not least, perhaps, to her old lover when she tried it on him once more. Think charitably of her now, as she lies there!

A temporary indisposition of her husband's was Susan's first excuse for making a regular appearance behind the bar. When he returned to his work she had already accustomed his guests to her presence; and the inn did no worse business because of that.

I gather that at that time she used to take rather less than small notice of her old flame: she would sit in her corner doing ornamental needle-work, so finding it easy to be either absorbed in her material, or join in the conversation that went on round her. Tom might talk — for he was reckoned good company in those days — then would Susan be silent; others might follow, Susan would throw in her word. 'Twas so naturally done that probably none but Tom Waldron himself took note of it.

One night there happened to be a lull in the round of talk: Susan looked up suddenly and addressed Tom direct. 'Tom Waldron,' says she, 'do you know that 'tis after half-past nine?'

Tom did know well enough; half-past nine was 'about his time', so he would have said; but to-night was one of his choice nights off, one of his methodically planned days of independence when he intended to go home late and get a scolding. Susan's remark (for she had her eye on things) came like an arrow at the joints of his harness.

Tom, sly to encounter and turn the shaft, owned that he had been looking at the clock, for clocks did vary so; he believed this at the Buck's

Head, was a good six minutes faster than his own; maybe she did that to get rid of them betimes. Well, he would trouble her for another half-pint, and then he would take her time in his head and carry it home to compare. So the matter passed: Tom just a little too explanatory and diffuse for the air of ease he wished to assume; for his eye had been running anxiously to the clock, as his way was when calculating how much over-time he should take.

But the thing stuck in his mind; his habits had become too regular for safety. Bowing his head to the storm that greeted him on his return, he was yet meekly resolving that he must incur the like in yet greater proportion the next night as well.

The next night Susan Bannier's eye went to the clock: her tongue struck the hour. 'Tom Waldron,' says she, ''tis after half-past nine'.

'So it is by your clock, Mrs. Bannier,' he replies, smooth as can be; 'by mine 'twill be five minutes more, so I reckon. We baint so particular as to time when we're here, be we, neighbours?'

'Oh! I thought half-past nine was your time for getting home,' she answered with a touch of significance in her tone.

'Well, so it is generally,' he replied, and stayed on till ten. He left owing for an extra pint, explaining that he would pay for it on the morrow.

On the morrow no Tom came. Poor Jane had made a beginning of the end, and had cut off supplies. The next day was Saturday.

Tom, they say, was in great form that night at the Buck's Head, singing and joking and standing treat all round. On Saturday night, in the natural course, more liquor flowed than on other nights, wages being then fresh in pocket. Things, therefore, were fairly well on, when at about half-past nine the door opens and Jane Waldron enters.

You would be thinking, perhaps, from what you already know about her, that Jane's method was that of the high hand and the stretched out arm, and that she would have plucked forth her man as a brand from the burning before all eyes, careless save to declare her own authority.

That it was not so done gives to my mind a double pathos to the event. Stubborn of will as she was by nature, the poor soul had already recognized her mistake, and was seeking by all means in her power to repair it. She had, I believe, until that night, never set foot in the place to which she allowed her husband to come nightly; and her appearance now caused an arrest of all talk and laughter about the room. Men looked on with an unquiet suspicion that something was to happen in disturbance of the general ease.

The sudden hush of voices made, I doubt not, the ordeal of speech more difficult for her. She stood in the doorway, supporting in both hands a heavy bundle, 'terribly strained-looking', an eye-witness told me afterwards, as her eye searched round the room. Then sudden and brisk, 'Ah, Tom,' she called out, getting sight of her man, 'I hoped as I should catch 'e before 'e started home! This weight's near breaking my back: I should have took the perambulator for it, but I forgot. Do 'e come now, and carry it for me.'

Tom had by this time plenty of drink inside him, but he was not what is locally reckoned as drunk: 'just a bit merry' was the definition of him up to this point. He got up steadily enough, showing no ill-humour or unreadiness at the request: thought, likely enough, that here was a good opportunity for peace to be re-established. He went across to his wife, to relieve her of her burden.

A voice said, 'I was just going to tell you, Tom Waldron, that it was half-past nine.'

Then, it would seem, that all at once he became conscious of eyes set on him, of ears listening, and that he stood a marked man in the midst of his small world, put to the test, about to be exposed and brought to derision. He took up his pint-pot and slung it across to the slab whence the liquor was served, and spoke out that all should hear him.

'I'll trouble you for another pint, m'm,' was his word. And Susan Bannier smiled.

Tom turned to his wife; putting on a hearty air, he cried, 'Come, Jenny, you have a drink too before we go home! Just you put that truck down.' And he began fumbling in the small leather money-bag he carried, for the requisite coin.

His wife stood hesitating at the door for one brief instant; then crossed the room quickly, and in hot wrath clawed bag and all out of his hand. There was no longer any disguise of her meaning then.

'Now come on with you!' she cried, loud enough for all to hear.

Tom's face put on a stubborn look. 'All in good time,' he says. 'We'll have our drink first, you and I.'

'Not a drop!' cries Jane, and has the money in her pocket that all may see whose word is law.

Cosy of speech, as if wishing to allay the trouble that has arisen, 'It will be all right: you can owe for it,' says Susan Bannier: and, suiting action to word, fills up the pewter.

Tom, with a fending hand, as though expecting his wife to make assault on the interdicted draught, lifts the pot, and waxing bold of tongue, 'Susie,' he cries, 'here's to you! Don't Tom Waldron me no more! I was Tom to 'e once.' Speech went under to beer.

'Now, Jenny, there's for you!' he says after a full draught, setting down the pewter before his wife. Furious, and with sudden hand, Jane seized it and sent the contents flying into Susan Bannier's face. 'You jade!' she cried. General uproar drowned what else she had to say.

Lookers-on came to intervene, for it looked as though further violence threatened. Yet all made way for her quickly when, with a blazing face, she turned and strode out of the door. Only then did men breathe freely again, for in wrath, Jane Waldron was the strong man of them all. 'All lit up, she looked,' was the report given me by one who had been there. I saw that same look myself later, though she was of cooler blood then.

The Death of Socrates   (1925)
  [A paraphrase from *Plato's Dialogues*, the *Crito*, and the *Phaedo*, with additions: adapted for the stage]

The scene is the prison-house, where XANTIPPE *has come with her two children to say goodbye to* SOCRATES.

SOCRATES Indeed, wife, my death and the manner of it are rather fortunate to you than otherwise. For I have many friends who think they owe me a kindness, and they will take care of both you and my children better than I should have done.

XANTIPPE But that will never be the same!

SOCRATES No, my dear; nor should I have been the same to-morrow as I was yesterday.

XANTIPPE Oh, how can I bear to think of it! Strangers!

SOCRATES You used to complain, my dear wife, that I was so much a stranger — always gadding about. And even when I was at home you used to say you could never understand me. You will understand these better.

H   113

XANTIPPE I won't! I won't! I don't want to understand them. I never have understood anything — how I ever came to marry you: how we ever came to have children!

SOCRATES No, my dear; that is indeed a great mystery. But on that matter you understand as much as I do: more — for in the process of gestation a woman's experience goes further than a man's. It means more to her.

XANTIPPE It means nothing! Only pain, pain, pain!

SOCRATES Well, pain is a teacher. And you have endured more of his teaching than I have. You used to say I didn't respect you. But I do, my dear, in those matters where you have had more experience. Also our children love you better than they love me. That is your right, and where you have the advantage.

XANTIPPE What advantage now, when every one will point at them and say their father was a criminal?

SOCRATES No, my dear; not a criminal, only a dangerous man.

XANTIPPE Yes; I say a criminal.

SOCRATES Indeed, I think, had you been on the jury you would have voted for my death. Well, wife, at last I am going to please you; for I could have escaped death had I accepted a certain offer that was made to me.

XANTIPPE You never had any sense — that I could discover!

SOCRATES Then, my dear, I will reveal it to you now. In all our life together have I ever reproached you?

XANTIPPE You never had any cause!

SOCRATES Or beaten you — believing I had cause?

XANTIPPE (*grudgingly*) You have not beaten me.

SOCRATES Then, in either case, that was sensible of me; for either you were blameless, or else you were unteachable. Choose which of the two explanations you prefer; but in either case grant that I showed sense.

XANTIPPE Socrates, you are heartless!

SOCRATES My dear wife, you will soon have to go; and I wish to send you away satisfied. How much better for you to go feeling that I have got what I deserved, than that I was the victim of injustice! For a man so evil as to be heartless, my penalty is a light one. Go, then, my dear; and let your complaint continue to be that I never knew how good a wife Heaven had bestowed on me.

XANTIPPE You never did!

SOCRATES As I say, my dear.

XANTIPPE Never!

SOCRATES Never. So now I am going to ask you to do me a kindness: These two of our children are still young; and though they hear us now, they understand little of what we are saying, and will remember less. But it will, on the whole, be to their happiness if they are allowed to think that I was a good father to them, or at least not so bad as you yourself held me to be. And as my friends, in whose charge I leave you, will often tell them that I was not altogether unworthy to be their father, I ask you then to keep silence about the faults which you saw in me — the more so as then they will have ceased to cause you annoyance.

I judge by your silence (that rare gift which you have so seldom bestowed on me) that my request is granted. Believe me, I am grateful. And now, wife, since all unpleasantness between us is so soon to be over, and in order that our last moments together may be as happy as possible, I wish to praise you for the part you played in the life we have shared. Though I may have seemed indifferent and unresponsive to your care for me, I have not been unobservant. I have marked your industry and thrift; also your ingenuity in contriving to make much of the little with which I provided you. Your management has been wonderful. I know, too, with what joy you constantly got the better of a bargain — wherein no trader that I ever met could stand against you. You kept a clean house, and made servants obedient; and if any of them were able to rob you I never knew of it. Therefore to me it remains true that as you, who had the care of my money, were never robbed, I was never defrauded. Nor did you ever complain of having children, in spite of the pain that it caused you; and though you sometimes complained of having a husband, I know you would have complained much more had you been forced to bear children to one who was not your husband. For all these things I commend you as a good helpmate; and in leaving to you the care of my children, I do so with confidence that your good qualities will not be less when I am gone than they were when you had the additional trouble of me. Farewell, Xantippe! If the consciousness of virtue can keep anyone happy, your lot will never be a miserable one.

The last words of SOCRATES *to* CRITO *and his Disciples, before the Jailor enters with the poison.*

CRITO Socrates, have you any further commands — about your children, or any other service we can do for you?

SOCRATES Only take care of yourselves, Crito. Doing that, you will be rendering me and mine a service, whether you promise it or no. But I do not ask for promises.

CRITO We will do our best, Socrates . . . And how shall we bury you?

SOCRATES How you like, Crito. But first you must catch me; and make sure that I do not run away . . . See how he opens his eyes! I cannot make Crito believe that I am still the talking Socrates; he fancies I am the the other — the dead body — which I shall presently be leaving behind me. And he asks how he is to bury me.

And though I have been talking at such length, comforting you and myself with the assurance that, when I have drunk the poison, I shall not remain here, but shall go to a better place, my words have had no effect upon Crito. Therefore, what I have failed to do you must do for me, and convince Crito, when I am gone, that it is not me but only a body that remains. And do not let him cry out when he sees it being buried, or burned, as though it were hurting me. For it won't, Crito.

So be of good cheer, dear friends; and when you are burying the body say: 'This is only the body.' And with that do as custom ordains, or whatever else you think best.

Of Aucassin and Nicolette   (1925)
     (A translation in prose and verse from the old French) together
     with The Story of Amabel and Amoris

THE STORY OF AMABEL AND AMORIS

AMORIS *has been sent to the Holy Well to be washed of his love for* AMABEL, *the goat-girl.*

> Amoris with love for load
> Setteth forth upon his road;
> And to Heaven he makes his vow,
> As he goes to wash him now:

If from him the holy well
Washes thought of Amabel,
Or do make him hold amiss
All the beauty and the bliss
Of her body's comeliness:
Then for prayer or praise will he
Nevermore bend down the knee,
Nor with life nor love agree,
　　　Nor Heaven see!

And Amoris went on till he came near to the holy well. And many pilgrims and lepers and lame men were coming that way also, meaning to be cured of their ills. But Amoris was the only one among them that went hoping not to be cured. And when he was come to the door of the church wherein the holy well lay, he saw there a cripple on two wooden legs and crutches standing. And the cripple went not in with the rest, but stood asking for alms. Then said Amoris to him: 'Brother, why do you stand asking alms, when there is here a holy well which cures all maladies, if so be one has the will to be healed? Maybe if you went in, God would grant you no longer to be lame.'

The man said: 'Fair brother, ten years since I came here a cripple in one leg only; one was of wood, but the other was of flesh and sound. And when I went down into the well I prayed that my legs might be restored to me as much a pair as God could make them. So I prayed, and coming up out of the water I found I had two wooden legs instead of one! God be praised! That was a great miracle, was it not? So I stand here and ask alms, and increase men's faith when they hear my story.'

When Amoris heard that, he was quite glad, and gave the man full twenty pieces of silver. 'Certes,' said he, 'I hold this for a good omen! Now when I take my malady — even my love for Amabel — down to the water and bid it drink there and be healed, I trust God will increase it to me as he did the wooden legs of this poor cripple!'

Therewith went he in; and all round he saw upon the walls the signs of those that before him had been healed. There was no malady under the sun but had been healed there one day or another. So without more ado he prays God and all the saints to succour him, and goes down into the water, with his heart full of sickness for Amabel, his dear delight, whom he remembered so well.

> Blithely to the water went
> Amoris, the well-content;
> Like a bird that goes to fish,
> Down he ducked to win his wish.
> God and all the saints he prays:
> 'Rather let me end my days
> Captive in a dungeon cell,
> Than lose love of Amabel!
> But if God will bring us fast
> Unto lovers' ends at last,
> Gladly here I render Him
> All I have of life or limb:
> Use of tongue whereby I talk,
> Use of feet whereon I walk,
> Use of hands wherewith I fight,
> Use of eyes which bring me sight,
> Use of me and all my might,
> So I come to earn aright
> > My dear delight!'

The Comments of Juniper   (1926)

THE LAST COMMENT

As JUNIPER *lies dying there comes to him a vision of Judgment, and from the Seat of Judgment comes a* VOICE.

VOICE What hast thou done with they life, Brother?

JUNIPER I don't know, Father . . . Nothing, Father.

VOICE Nothing?

JUNIPER Nothing well enough that I ought to have done, Father. Many things well enough that I shouldn't have done.

VOICE How 'well' — things that you should not?

JUNIPER Well enough to please the Devil, Father.

VOICE Many have complained of thee.

JUNIPER The Lord help, heal, and keep them all from the hurt I've done to them!

VOICE Doubt not He will, Brother; the better if thou art now penitent.

JUNIPER Sure, I'm penitent for everything. I'd be penitent of being born; but God won't let me. It would be wrong, wouldn't it, Father? . . . And besides . . .

VOICE Yea, speak!

JUNIPER If I hadn't been born, I shouldn't have known the little Father.

VOICE The little Father was not God, Brother. Thou wast born to know and worship God — not man, His creature.

JUNIPER I should never have come to know Him, but for the little Father.

VOICE Why? Wast thou blind?

JUNIPER No; only a fool, Father. But *he* loved, he knew, he made me understand.

.   VOICE Is that all thou canst say for thyself? If not, speak on!

JUNIPER I've no more, Father.

VOICE If any other hath charge or accusation to bring, let him speak now!

A MAN'S VOICE Father, I was naked in sin; this man clothed me. I used him roughly; he thanked me. I robbed him; he was grateful to me.

VOICE Any other?

A WOMAN'S VOICE Father, my husband was in prison for theft; we were starving. This man, having nothing of his own, went to the altar, and, to his own hurt, took alms from God to satisfy our need.

VOICE Any other?

VOICE OF ELIAS Father, this man feared me: I had authority; binding him to obedience; I was cruel to him, despising his foolishness. But when I myself became an outcast, then he forgave, then he prayed for me; and, serving me without fear, won for me pardon, penance, reconciliation.

VOICE Is there any other?

VOICE OF FRANCIS Father, when God in His mercy made man, He made few wise, but many foolish. Then sent He His Son, our Lord Jesus Christ,

to be understood of fools better than of wise men. So, when He called me
also to His service, the better to understand Christ and His Love for all,
He gave me this fool for example and guide, for rest, and for refreshment.
And because of him, in dark nights I found my way, and on long journeys
failed not: so lived — he helping me!

VOICE That is past, Brother. What use hast thou for him now, when
all journeys are over, and nights ended? Tell it, so that he may hear!

VOICE OF FRANCIS O little sheep, hear my voice, make haste and come
to me! Yea, on holy obedience, I bid thee come!

JUNIPER Name of Jesus! . . . Little Father!

Ironical Tales   (1926)

BLIND KNOWLEDGE

A SAINT, wishing to live the perfect life, started to pray. He prayed for
nothing but to know God; and at this prayer continued without inter-
mission for some fifty years. All that time he prayed, and God never once
heard him.

Now, it happened about that time, when fifty years had passed, that a
poor woman died whose life had been no better than it should be. One
day, looking through the window of his oratory, she had seen the Saint
upon his knees; and beholding him so rapt from the world, so untor-
mented by the things which tormented her, she had conceived a great
love for him, different in kind from all the other loves which had emptied
her life of happiness. After that it became her rest and consolation to look
in at him every day. 'If only,' she said to herself, 'he would turn and take
notice that I exist, and pray for me — then I might cease to be a sinner.'

But he never did. Occupied in praying that he might know God, he
knew nothing of his fellow-men, and cared less. Pounding the steep
ascent to Heaven, he left the pence lying behind him.

When the woman died, expecting to be in Hell, she found instead that
her thread of a soul had become joined, entangled, nay, almost woven
into a piece with the outer hem of God's raiment. There it hung, very
much afraid, fearing that it was all a mistake, touching His Feet, saying
nothing.

God became aware of her; He took her up — drew her out, as it were — without in any way disentangling her from the weft, and examined her. Searched by the All-seeing Eye, she told her story; and thus it was, for the first time, that God heard tell of the Saint. 'He never spoke to me,' she said, 'never looked at me, did not know that I existed.'

'Nor did I know it of him,' replied God.

'He was always praying to you,' she said.

'I never heard him. Indeed, I only know of him through you.'

'Then how did you know of *me*?' she asked.

'Through your love for him.'

Contented, she returned to her place at God's Feet, while He, descending through great depths and by difficult ways, sought out the Saint.

The Saint, as always, was babbling his prayer, when the Light Celestial shone in on him.

'What is that you are saying?' inquired the Divine Presence.

The Saint, hearing a voice, replied, 'I am praying that I may know God.'

'He doesn't understand a word of it.'

'How do you know? You are not God.'

'Why am I not God?'

'Because you have a voice which I can hear with my ears; and you have a light which I can see with my eyes. But these are deceptions of the senses.'

'I perceive,' said God, 'that you are praying to know the unknowable. But it is only by praying through that which you know that you come nearer to God.'

'You must be the Devil,' said the Saint, 'for you are talking heresy.'

'I always do,' said God, 'it is only so that I can make men understand me. Here is heresy for you, my son, which you have been avoiding all your life, therefore have lost your way. Listen!

'Without your senses, you cannot love; and without Love you cannot know God. I sent Love into the world that men might know it, and that through it they might know Me, and I them. For it is only through Love that God and man can know each other. I only knew of you, through a soul that loved you. Had you loved her, or some other, I should have known you sooner.'

By these words the Saint was first amazed, then troubled, then humbled. 'Who was she, Lord?' he asked.

'A sinner, one of many. You did not know she existed, nor did you care. But she knew that you existed; and *she* cared.

'And that is how I have come to know, my son, that you are anything — except a foolish noise!'

JOY IN HEAVEN

THE old clown, past his work and against doctor's orders, was performing his last stunt. Thousands watched and applauded. Light-headed, exhausted, he turned and tumbled like one inspired.

Death held up the hoop of strained paper, through which he could not see the change which was there awaiting him: held it up over his head, for a higher leap than he had ever leapt before. Gathering his failing faculties for a last effort, up he went in a spin, twizzled through it, and entered Heaven.

The sudden and unexpected sight of that imperishable world was too much for him. 'O Hell!' he cried, and whisked back again.

From the murmurous pity of the spectators they carried him behind the scenes. There he lay with dazed eyes, gasping feebly, trying to explain:

'Jumped farther than I knew, that time!' he whispered painfully. 'Got into the wrong hole. How? — I don't know . . . Queer place! . . . Took a look, and came out again.'

'What was queer about it?' inquired Harlequin, in a friendly attempt to make conversation for a mind that wandered.

'Nothing — except me. Queer place for *me*, I meant. I was the only queer thing in it.' His face grew haggard with the horror of that strange loneliness wherein he had found himself.

'They all looked at me — and nobody laughed!' he said.

'Maybe you didn't give them time,' said Harlequin. 'People are slow sometimes to see a joke.'

'But they saw *me*,' said the old clown. 'They saw *me*, and they didn't laugh.'

He shuddered both at the memory, and at the prospect. 'Just fancy!' he whispered: 'Suppose! . . . Wouldn't it be — Hell?'

But that instinctive revulsion from the inevitable was useless. Though for a moment the shock of it had sent him back, life could no longer contain him. And so presently entered, with mission to fulfil (it being against all rules for any that once set foot in Heaven to drop out again), and compassed about in a soft glow of delicately reflected lights, not Death this time, but his own Guardian Angel.

In his hand he carried a large luminous hoop, with a hole in the middle just big enough for a man's head. Waving it with inviting gesture before the dying eyes, 'You must come back,' said the angel.

The familiar hoop-like shape with its strange radiance attracted the old clown's curiosity. 'What's that?' he inquired feebly.

'That is your halo, which has been waiting for you,' said the angel. 'Put it on!'

Apprehensively, but meekly, the old clown obeyed. Then without any further struggle, led gently by the hand, he passed elsewhere.

As they entered the celestial regions, the angel, his mission accomplished, making respectful obeisance to the glorious company there expectantly assembled, said, merely by way of explanation, 'Here we are again!'

And suddenly, at that familiar word, life, courage, spirit, and confidence came back into the old clown with a rush. It seemed to him that he was in his old world again: that life had a meaning still. Inspiration tingled from his head to his heels; joy came back to them like wings.

Taking off his halo, he tumbled through it, looping the loop as only a clown can — not once nor twice only, but twenty, thirty times. And as he did so — to its eternal credit be it spoken — how Heaven laughed!

Uncle Tom Pudd   (1927)
    A Biographical Romance, of which his niece, Miss Miriam Foley,
    is the narrator

I

'THE best bargain I ever made in my life,' he said, 'was when I sold the only pair of trousers I then possessed for three pounds, and got a better pair in exchange the same day.'

He glimmered; the hook of narrative (provocation in its first statement) hung waiting for the fish to bite. There was the usual cunning flutter of the eyelids, as though he was appraising how much that day I was prepared to swallow.

Wishing to be entertained, I looked as gullible as I could; and forthwith he started.

'It was one of those periods in its neglect of me,' he began, 'over which the family likes to draw a veil. It had left me in such destitute circumstances, that I was travelling not only without a suit-case but without a ticket: in America one does it on the buffers, on the backs of the cars; in England you can do it on the backs of those other buffers — the collectors. So far I had evaded the collectors on their regulation rounds; but routes have their moments of difficulty where, if there are no empty first-class compartments, one has to be strategic. D'you know, my dear, that English railway-officials are so class-conscious that they will look under the seat of an empty third-class carriage, but not under a first? It's extraordinary; but years of experience, in both, have taught me that it is true. Well, on this occasion I had found the necessary empty first; but the merging moment had not yet arrived, when at a small wayside station the train was unexpectedly stopped, not according to schedule, and into my compartment mounted a large stout gentleman in broadcloth, gold watch-chain across his central deity, and carrying an attaché-case. The train, as I learned later, had been specially stopped for him.

'We had hardly started again when, with a twist and busy twiddle of hands, he began brushing himself. "Great Heavens!" he suddenly exclaimed, "I've been sitting on an ant's nest!"

'I suppose, with so good a suit, it seemed a story that needed explanation. He explained: he had dismissed his car, and awaiting the train's arrival had sat down on the bank of the road, preferring it to the station. Now — up to his waist — they were all over him. He brushed and beat himself. They came running across to me; as fast as I could I sent them to a better world.

' "Do you mind," he said at last, "if I take off my trousers and shake them out of the window?"

' "Take off everything, if you like," I said. He limited himself, however, to the essential. But he made a mistake. I suppose it was because I was seated on the getting-in side that he went over to the other. That act of modesty was fatal. No, my dear, don't look alarmed; I did not throw him out of the window for the sake of his trousers, nor did I find that three pounds in the pocket of them. He let down the glass, hung out his trousers, and proceeded to shake. What happened to the ants I don't know; in the size of the catastrophe that followed, we forgot all about them. It was only the trousers on which, for my sake, Providence had fixed its intentions. An express train, bound for Bristol, whisked them out of his hands. I had never heard a man shriek before — not like that. Prosperous broadcloth raped of its respectability: lost virginity was nothing to it. There, in the vacuous railway-carriage he turned, and saw all the world staring at him. Not I, my dear; I looked out of the window at the uncertain weather, cows, swallows, telegraph wires — anything to divert my attention; but even then a premonition stole up my legs, of what was going to be required of them. A religious man off his balance directs his prayers to strange addresses; "Good God," he cried, "have you a pair of trousers you can lend me?" Replying to that flattering invocation, I might have said, that, as such, I did not wear trousers; but, speaking as a mere human, I said I only had those which I had on. It seemed then for him that the world had ended, and that suicide was the only course left. I rescued him from despair by telling him that for three pounds he might have mine. So great was his distress, the price did not seem to him a tight one; but the fit, when he came to put them on, was. However, he managed it: the buttons and the button-holes met and clung together like Tennyson and the larger hope; for a time, at all events, they would not give way. He explained that he was a surgeon called urgently, at short notice, to perform an operation of the appendix. I wonder how he performed it after that agitating experience. His hand was still shaking when it shook mine; we parted at the next stopping-place, and I have never seen or heard from him since. The incident, no doubt, is one that he would rather forget.'

My uncle artfully stopped his narrative, lit his pipe, and began ruminatively smoking.

'You aren't going to leave the story there, are you?' I queried. 'What became of you?'

'Well, my dear,' he said, 'here I am; and, as you see, I have managed to get another pair of trousers. What more do you want to know?'

'How you got to your journey's end.'

'That,' he replied, 'was no difficulty at all. Money had come, enabling

me to pay my fare — that part of it, at least, which I could not avoid paying; and as for my state of undress — well, in exchange for my trousers, he
had left me his story; and as luck would have it a wire had come up the
line: had any gentleman lost a pair of trousers which by description he
could identify? If so the Bristol express was willing to return them.

'I was able to describe them well; I said, also, that they probably had
ants on them. That clinched the matter; a friendly station-master locked
me up in a waiting-room with a fire, and a rug to wrap round me; and
three hours later, steeped in the romance of their further adventure, I
received a very good pair of trousers which, though not mine, I felt that
I had fully earned. Their story came with them.

'They had, it appeared, flown in through the window of a first-class
carriage, and alighting in the astonished lap of a maiden lady, sitting solitary, had scared her well out of her wits: a mere cenotaph, so to speak, of
that intrusive male whom the lone travelling female so fears. But even its
ghost so frightened her that she pulled the connecting cord, and brought
Bristol's expectations to a standstill.

'She must surely, I think, in the interval, have repented the deed; for
was ever so compromising a situation, or one more difficult to explain?
Joseph's coat in the hands of Potiphar's wife was nothing to it. A gentleman's trousers do not, in the eyes of the law, without corroborative
evidence, fly in through a train-window travelling at express speed; the
body has also to be accounted for: where was it? No doubt that was being
asked at Bristol when my friendly station-master's inquiry came down the
line and released her from custody.

'The trousers I had so well identified were handed to me on arrival
without question, and the misfit was not observed. I pawned them the
next day, and bought others more suitable; that is to say, I bought first
and pawned afterwards. And isn't the world a wonderful place, my dear?
How often, from that day on, must not three people — perfect strangers to
each other — have had mutual thoughts of quite exceptional interest,
wondering where in the world, and how, and when next, and if ever: and
a pair of trousers the centre of it all? Yes; I often think of her, my dear, as
the "not impossible she" of my alter ego. For had I myself flown in through
that window instead of my trousers — as they became — I might have
married her instead of your aunt Judy.'

And then as he spoke, the mere mention of Aunt Judith caused the hypothetical romance to extend itself, and the date to shift into a decade later. 'To be sure,' he went on, 'I was married to your aunt Judy already, though never in the position, with her, of flying in through the window without the rest of me. But she didn't then know where I was, or what name I was travelling under; and so circumstanced, I might easily have forgotten that I was married, and if one could prove absolute forgetfulness, would it be bigamy in the legal sense at all? Surely no; but — as when you kill a person by accident — only misadventure.'

'There is yet another possibility,' I suggested. 'You may have met this lady, and talked to her, and never known, in this uncommunicable world, that she was actually the lady of your dreams. It might even have been *me* — now for the first time hearing your end of an unexplained incident.'

'Oh, no, my dear!' he said, fixing me with a rogue's eye. '*You* wouldn't have pulled the communication cord.'

11

It is an interesting fact that, by having no morals of his own, my uncle frequently tested mine. We haven't yet learned to make a proper ethical use of our criminals; we ought to keep one in every school-room as a working example. My uncle — bless him! — gave me more conscience in a month than five years of governesses in my childhood had done. At school, of course, one learns to be social, but too conservatively. Of that also he was a corrective. There were few things he touched, in the moral world, that he did not — at least slightly — unhinge. Perhaps he also unhinged my mind; living with him certainly made a difference.

When he and the 'Urge and the Uplift' met again, there was more stroking of the keys and hand-holding; and after she had gone I said something. At once new insight into life was offered me; and it came as though sure of my approval: 'Yes, it's very pathetic, my dear; there are whole neighbourhoods where women simply want to have their hands held for them — nothing else. Poor starved human nature, and nobody to understand it! Now that's what I do: it's the only sort of knowledge I lay claim to — a knowledge of human nature. And then — see where it lands you — if, for instance, your aunt Judy comes to hear of it! Down at Pudbury, now, we have a Maria Jones and a Martha Priestly —

127

perfectly respectable characters, both of them; but both wanting badly to have their hands held, and so respectable that they daren't ask anyone to do it for them — till I happened to come along and discern their symptoms. I was only home for a short time, so that hurried matters, and produced complications, as you shall hear. The fact that I, an elderly man, arranged for the double event to take place all in one evening, when your aunt Judy was away for a day, proves how innocent, how respectable it all was — or was to have been. And so, from nine to ten, I sat under a haycock holding poor Maria Jones by the hand; and I meant to sit under another haycock from ten to eleven, holding Martha Priestly's hand. But women are so unpunctual in their appointments, except when it's the palmist, and then the unpunctuality is always his: in a professional palmist's ante-chamber you find them waiting six deep. For my palmistry Maria Jones was late, and Martha Priestly was early; the consequence was that they both took the matter — which on my part was purely impersonal — personally; and where I had only intended compassionate allowance and kindness, tongues were loosed, and noses put out of joint, and faces scratched; and I had to come away.

'Now you, my dear, understand all this, and can sympathize; but your aunt Judy wouldn't. She never wants to have her hand held — 'tisn't in her: temperamentally she is a tin-tack virgin, and why she married me or anybody — '

He let the subject go — sat meditative, then said, 'Why do we call people 'cats' when we *like* cats?'

And I knew he was thinking still of my aunt Judith.

Thus, under his guidance, my new moral training went on; and while over a good many moral questions, which I had thought fixed beyond controversy, he gave me an unsettled mind — over others, his departure from what I considered decency shocked and angered me.

It was not, I daresay, over these particular matters that my aunt had found him 'impossible' — very likely she had not even discovered them; but they formed a basis of impossibility in his character which I found it hard to get over. Later, upon my second trial of him, these two fell into place; and I made a sort of allowance for them — gave them, that is to say, leave of absence. But it was a blow — a hurt to one's class-pride, I suppose — to find that he had practically no sense of honour. On my first discovery of it I sent him away for it, as you shall hear; but before any serious manifestation, it had already begun to peep out, causing me one day to inquire in irritated bewilderment whether he had no moral attitude about anything.

He wasn't in least put out by my annoyance; it seemed rather to amuse him; he became obligingly explanatory; and, as usual, my aunt Judith served as a peg for his apologies — the moral emblem, in opposition to which all things were lawful.

'Moral attitudes,' he said, 'are only physical; if we were invisible we should have no morals at all. You can't feel indignation lying on your back with your mouth open — try it, and you will see. I used to believe in prayer, because I thought it was impossible to be angry while you were on your knees saying them. But your aunt Judy taught me better. She took me to church with her, and said the general confession, loud, so that I might hear it, and know that she meant *me*. And the tone of voice she used was not the tone of voice she would have used about herself. That's why I left off going to church: she cured me of it. Prayer to her means a brass trumpet — a ram's horn, at the blast of which the walls of Jericho must fall flat. Well, so far as this Jericho is concerned, they don't; they merely run away.

'And yet, I suppose, I did once believe in prayer, as forty years ago — a younger son, with no choice between that and the colonies — I was ordained into the Church. But if anything of that sort was left — she finished it for me. There are people, you know — she's one — who like miracles and answer to prayer for themselves; but if it happens to anyone else, it's only a coincidence. Now I remember when we were at Wynmouth, she and I — I suppose it was on our honeymoon — for it's only at Pudbury we've ever been together since; there's an island there where one can bathe without machines; and there, on that island, something did happen which might have made me recover my faith if your aunt would only have allowed; but no — Providence, if it exists, belongs to her alone.

'Well, I will tell you what happened. It is an island of peculiar sanctity; and of course, leaving your aunt out, that might have accounted for it. Some years ago it became the abode of a community of "Anglican Benedictines" — as they called themselves — but now reconciled to Rome, driven thereto by the scandalous disqualification from office of their Father Abbot, who used to celebrate Palm Sunday by riding round the

island on a white ass escorted by choir-boys; they, to make it go, beating
it with palm-branches from behind and holding out carrots to it in front.
And then the awful thing happened: the donkey ran down into the sea
carrying him with it, like Europa and her bull, and gave the Abbot a drown-
ducking from which he can't properly be said to have survived, for in the
process of resuscitation he was found to be a woman.

'Well, that is not my story, though — if portents and wonders affect
a locality — it may help to account for it. My story comes from the fact
that, during our stay at Wynmouth, I used to go over to the island in
order to bathe without encumbrance of any kind; and one particular
morning your aunt had given me three pounds to pay some account that
was owing in the town, and I had put it in my pocket-book. I lay on the
shore for two or three hours, read, smoked, and bathed; when I came
back for lunch, pocket-book and pounds were missing.

'Your aunt, careful soul, asked for the the receipted bill, so I had to
own up. I don't think she believed me — she thought I had embezzled it;
and so it was merely as a punishment that she insisted on my going back to
the island directly lunch was over (a lobster lunch, my dear, and a very hot
day; think of it!) to look for the missing articles. Quite an absurd thing
to do; for the tide there is tremendous, nearly twenty-four feet, I believe.
I had bathed while it was going down; it was now coming up, and I had
to row hard against it. I was very hot and cross; and I asked God to let
the day perish wherein your aunt Judy was born. That, however, was
merely incidental and — by the way — a prayer that wasn't answered;
though another, as I was presently to learn, was.

'So I landed on the island, very forlorn and hopeless, and I wandered
along the watery strand like Robinson Crusoe looking for the footprint of
his man Friday. And there, just on the edge of the wave, I found it —
only the footprint, though: my pocket-book, lying open, with the in-
coming sea-ripples turning over its pages, and the three pounds gone.

'I picked it up, too wet and dishevelled for further use, merely as a
proof that I had really been. And then, my dear — now are you going to
believe? — then, lightly riding the waves, like Britannia on her trident or
a witch on her broomstick, one of my lost Bradburys came floating towards me open-armed. I rescued it. Providence drew me on. On the
next wave behold another; clearly wonders were happening. I stood and
gazed; but though I accepted the benefaction in simple faith, I didn't and

I hadn't prayed about it. And then — you may believe me or not — on the next wave a third Bradbury came curtseying and fawning to my feet.

'You might think that was the end; but no! Scarcely had I restored the three lost pounds to my person, when the portent of a fourth Bradbury jigged coquettishly into view, like Ariel on a dolphin's back — or Puck, which was it? But that's only from Shakespeare; this was from a higher source still. I took it, I did not know how it could be mine, but as Heaven had sent it, it seemed to come within the ten commandments all right. And so I went back to your aunt Judy — very pleased with Heaven for returning me so high a rate of interest on a two-hours' loan, but wondering whether I would tell her anything about number four, for fear that she should claim it.

'However, I told her all about the other three; and "Wasn't it luck?" I said. No, it wasn't luck, it appears, at all; it was your aunt. Suddenly she became Sunday: "It didn't occur to you, I suppose," she said, "that I had made it a subject for prayer?" You see, she believes in what she calls "intervention"; that, when we've scrambled our eggs, God unscrambles them for us again. So she'd been praying, it seems. What a spectacle on the moral plane for those situated so as to behold it! — me, the culprit, rowing and sweating on a vain errand, not believing in it; and your aunt at my back, praying angrily; and God, apparently not angry, answering her prayer! But she hadn't prayed — I didn't believe it! She had sat there believing that I had stolen it; so I wasn't even to have the credit of finding it.

'As prayer had been mentioned, I claimed my share of it; and I told her about number four: her prayer, I suggested, had secured the return of three pounds, and mine a pound extra. She told me not to be blasphemous; and for fear I should have any faith left in the efficacy of *my* prayer, proceeded to insist and explain how it must have been owing to my carelessness, and because I had an extra pound left over from somewhere, which I had concealed and forgotten.

'And I suppose that is the more likely explanation. But why — if the return of three pounds was a miraculous answer to prayer — she shouldn't go the whole hog, and accept the increase as well, I can't think. Why must she have her own pocket edition of Heaven, and deny me mine? But that's your aunt all over: our minds don't run on the same lines, we hardly live in the same world. I wish we didn't. She was as cross for the rest of that day as if I had lost the money for good and all; and I believe what annoyed her most was seeing me spend — I bought some good cigars with it — that pound which Heaven had sent me.'

Ways and Means (1928)
    (Five One Act Plays of Village Characters)

A MINT OF MONEY

Two men have come to rob an old miser of his hoard. They have hunted for the money, and can't find it.

JIM Mate, he's playing for time, he is! He's got something up his dirty sleeve. Now then, where's that gold?

OLD MAN I haven't got no gold. I told yer that when yer began.

BILL You told us better since: five hundred pounds, yer said.

OLD MAN Ah! mebbe. It'll take ye all night to count it though. You think I be a fool: Eh? So I would be if I was to keep gold here — a lonely place like this — so as any could come and rob me. Eh! Eh! I'm fond o' money; but I ain't a fool, not like that.

JIM Here! We've had enough o' yer talk. Have done! Where's the money?

OLD MAN The money? Ah! now you're talking sense. It's down in the floor under that chest . . . It's going to be a sad shock for yer. I warn yer o' that.

    (*The two men go and lift the chest, disclosing a large hole. Bringing the lamp they peer down into it. The* OLD MAN *chuckles delightedly*)
        Heh, heh! Heh, heh, heh, heh, heh!

BILL What ha' ye got it in coppers for, you dirty scut?

OLD MAN So as nobody shouldn't take it away, not without a cart — and a man to spade it up for 'em. Yepennies, yepennies every one! I give ye a hundred each: I told yer that. I've been waiting for this to happen, twenty year.

BILL (*taking him by the nape and shaking him*) Ah, you — dirty old thief, you!

OLD MAN (*squealing*) Ay! ay! ay! ay!

(BILL *flings him roughly away; but the* OLD MAN *recovering his feet continues to have his say*)

If you'd killed me then, you'd a' been sorry for it. Eh, you would! Without a cart it wouldn't 'a been worth doing. How'd ye go for to spend five hundred pounds all in yepennies, eh? — without being found out? Go on! Fill your pockets o' yepennies: I can't say fairer than that. Four hundred and eighty yepennies to a pound; I give yer a hundred each, as I said; and mind you count 'em so as to be sure I ain't cheating yer. Yepennies be plaguy things to count when you've got to be quick. And you'd better look sharp now, sonnies; that's the carrier's cart coming along. He brings me his yepennies; and I change 'em for him. Heh, heh, heh! Heh, heh!

(*Sure enough, the sound of the carrier's bell is heard coming along the road; reason for* JIM *and* BILL *to make haste*)

JIM   I've half a mind to throttle you now — you blinking old fool!

OLD MAN   Ah! I've been too clever for you, that means. Twenty years I've been waiting for this to happen: twenty years! There was a woman, once, used to spy under her bed every night to see if there was a man; and one day she found 'un. 'Why I've been looking for you forty years,' says she; 'and here you be at last!' Eh, you may call me miser, if you like; so I be! But it wasn't only the money as I counted on. I've always had in mind how this might happen, if fools like you was to come. And now it has!

(*Outside one hears the carrier's cart coming to a halt. Exit* JIM *and* BILL *hurriedly. The* OLD MAN *is still laughing when the curtain falls*).

The Life of H.R.H. The Duke of Flamborough   A Footnote to   (1928)
                                               History

The supposed Life of a nineteenth-century Royal Character, written by his valet, Mr. Benjamin Bunny.

HIS BIRTH CERTIFICATE

AUGUSTUS WILLIAM CARL JOSEPH EMMANUEL, the only son of his princely parents the Duke and Duchess of Flamborough, was born at the castle of Steinburg on the Rhine, on a 25th day of March early in the nineteenth century; and, for the first two months of his existence, was, in a prospective sense, the most important person in the world then living.

For those two months he had — or his parents had for him — the very highest expectations, though mingled with a dash of doubt. The succession to the throne of his fathers, but not of his race, was just then in an exiguous and withering condition. Like a ripe heifer turned loose into a field of oxen, the royal inheritance had unseasonably hung fire for a number of years; during that time hope of posterity had either been lacking or had died young.

The oxen — brothers and uncles — had been capable of much in the past, but now, apparently, were not to be relied on, though German brides of a child-bearing type had been found for them; and though as a final duty to king and country six out of eight had settled down to the dull doom of matrimony, only two of these gave any sign of useful and practical results.

Of these the first and the most forward, by the grace of his good wife, Princess Wilhelmina Caroline of Thurm-Turingen, was H.R.H. second Duke of Flamborough, and, in the line of succession to the throne of his father (now so near his demise), fourth among eight brothers, all, in the reputable sense, childless — without heirs, that is to say.

A little behind in acceptance of matrimony had come number three, the Duke of Bendigo; but he dying soon after, and his wife not in her first youth by any means, there had remained a doubt. This doubt, however, was now resolving itself — hopefully for the House of Bendigo, less hopefully for the House of Flamborough, which in its own interests wished things, very naturally, to be otherwise.

Nevertheless, in an almost neck and neck race of wife versus widow, wife won; and for two months, H.R.H. Augustus William Carl Joseph Emmanuel lived, moved, and had his being as a prospective monarch whose rights, temporarily at an rate, there was none to dispute.

That being so, his birth had of necessity to be very circumspectly attended; for just as, here in England, we still search the cellars of our House of Commons for a possible Guy Fawkes at each opening of Parliament, so, when an heir is born to any European throne, a similar search or watch is instituted against any possible repetition of the 'Warming-pan Plot', which having been invented in one country may actually happen in another.

And so, some days or weeks before his expected arrival, there came very importantly from oversea, with signed and sealed credentials, plenipotentiaries and experts — not in the art of midwifery, but in the law and constitutional practice of monarchical primogeniture — to attend, watch, certify, and register the event with such thoroughness that no question of it could ever thereafter arise. Though fools might rush in unavoidably in the course of nature, warming-pans must be constitutionally kept out, or at least carefully examined as to their contents before introduction for bed-warming purposes could be allowed.

The plenipotentiaries were — that one of the Royal Dukes whose interest in the succession came next; Lord Sago, Ambassador to the Rhineland, specially appointed for the time, and the Right Hon. John Montague Rice, Writer to the Signet and Privy Councillor. By these, with signatures appended, the following safeguarding document was issued upon the day of birth:

'We the undersigned (names and dignities here follow), specially instructed to attend the Confinement of H.R.H. the Duchess of Flamborough, do hereby solemnly declare that, having been apprised by H.R.H. the Duke of Flamborough, at a quarter past one of the clock on the morning of March 25th in the year of our Lord 18 —, that Her Royal Highness's labour pains had commenced, we did straightway together, each in the other's presence, and of intent purpose, all being in our right minds, repair forthwith to the room adjoining that in which Her Royal Highness was to be delivered, the door between these two rooms remaining open during the whole of our attendance; and that having been previously informed by His Royal Highness that Her Royal Highness would be confined in HER Bedroom up one pair of stairs, and that free access must remain from that room to HER Dressing-room immediately contiguous thereto, and these rooms having been previously shown to one of us — the Right Hon. John Montague Rice, the seal of the said John Montague Rice was affixed (so as to close it) to the outside and keyhole of the outward door of the said Dressing-room, under the directions of H.R.H. the Duke of Flamborough — He having locked the said door, and given the said key thereof to the said Right Hon. John Montague Rice, so that no communication with the Bedroom could thereafter take place from without but under our eyes, we remaining in the room adjoining the Bedroom, through which all persons entering the Bedroom must pass; that on arrival we found Her Royal Highness in the genuine experience of Her labour pains, and that sharp labour pains continued till ten minutes past two o'clock of the morning aforesaid, when Her Royal Highness was safely delivered of a male Child, whose sex we determined by actual inspection; and that said Child was alive and of sound health and limb at the said hour, and so continues to be at the time when, together, and each in the other's presence, we make this declaration affirming it to be true, and hereto affix our signatures in proof and witness thereof.'

Cornered Poets　　　　　　　　　　　　　　　　　　　(1929)

THE MESSENGERS
(1803)

BLAKE *has been commissioned by* WILLIAM HAYLEY *to decorate his library with portraits, of certain great historical characters. Conceived imaginatively, Mr. Hayley does not find them very like their originals. 'A portrait should be a portrait,' he says. And now he is questioning the portrait of Newton.*

HAYLEY But Newton, my dear sir, Newton was a great scientist.

BLAKE Newton would have had no science had he depended on it. All that he discovered was by imagination. But, in order to convince blockheads, he had to put it mathematically — otherwise they would not have believed him. Newton never talks mathematics to me: he knows better. If he did, I should paint him with his face to the wall.

HAYLEY Really, Mr. Blake, you surprise me! With his face to the wall? That would be a very curious portrait: the back of a man's head — most original!

BLAKE Sometimes the back of a man's head tells more than his face — is the most truthful thing about him. Only yesterday Voltaire came and asked that he might sit to me.

HAYLEY Voltaire? But Voltaire is dead, my dear sir!

BLAKE The vegetable Voltaire is dead, sir; but his spectre — the most powerful part of him — is as much alive as ever it was. I found him sitting in the closet, sir.

HAYLEY My dear Mr. Blake, how very awkward!

BLAKE Not at all sir. I got him out without any difficulty. He wanted to sit to me, I refused to do him such honour. 'Your face,' I said, 'does not please me.' At that he made a characteristically ribald remark, and presented me with a different part of his person. Then I perceived on the back of his head a large wart. It had the complete face of Rousseau upon it; so if I give you the back of Voltaire's head, you will have Rousseau's face to admire as well.

THE CUTTY STOOL
(1784)

BURNS *has been on the Cutty Stool at Mauchline Kirk, doing public penance for one of his numerous falls from grace. Now — the ordeal over — he is talking to the brother of his partner in guilt, who brings word to him that mother and child are doing well.*

BURNS Is't a fine bairn?

ANDREW It's yer ain image, Robbie.

BURNS Then it maun be! (*He sits thinking; then — his voice changing to tenderness*) Puir brat! Puir wee innocent brat! Where did the making o' bastards come in, A wonder? A lang time after the making o' mon, sae A reckon. An' that's the ditch yer holy anes will never get ower.

ANDREW What's that ye say?

BURNS If ye put a nightcap on top o' a hill, will that send it to sleep — or a volcano, either? Or if ye put a piece o' sticking-plaster over the mouth of a river, will that stop the tide running? There's a mon been inventing a steam-engine, A'm telt; a very simple true thing, by the sound o' it. Ye fit a cap to its nozzle, an' screw doon till it bursts; or if it disna burst, it gets up an' does something. That's human nature, Andy. It's a great discovery; an' when men an' ministers hae got that intil their heids, it'll help 'em tae mak a better warld than they do noo. . . .

But O God, the grief, the trouble o' it! The black doubt whether ye're onything but a speck o' dust picked up oot o' the ground an' blown — blown onywhere till it just falls back again, dust into dust! . . . God! . . . Look at me! Look at these hands — a' the movements, an' the strings in them; an' the shape, an' the strength, an' the knowledge in them o' a' the things they've learned doing, an' loved doing! See the subtlety o' it a'; an' this tae be only dust! An' that — only a bit o' me! What are they for? The steering a plough, or the driving o' horses? the holding o' a pen? the handling o' a woman's hair, let doon i' the dark tae cover yer eyes frae the stars? Or just the putting o' food into yer mouth, or the tipping up o' a pewter-pot?

. . . .

Do ony o' us ken wha we really are? . . . A wish A did. Am A onything but a puir weak mon that happens wad ha' done better no' tae be born? Onything but a loose crazy loon making rhymes tae tickle the lugs o' the tipplers o' a' the taverns — an' a few lasses, maybe, that had better no' listen tae 'em? Will A ever be remembered after A'm gone? What's he that's got haud o' me — here inside? Is it God, or Deil? If it's God, why are we always fechting — Him an' me? If it's the Deil — how is it A hae sich love in me that A'm neebor to whatever has life in it? The Deil loves naething, except tae torture it. A love aeverything. An' oh, mon! what an agony's the flesh that ye canna' tak the whole warl' in yer arms, an' care for it like as if ye were its ain feyther: fend it frae harm, hush it, warm it, sing tae it till it sleeps! . . . The warld'll end some day. Will there be ony singing in it then? Will it gae up wi' a merry noise, tae the sound o' the trump? Eh! maybe, when a' folk are deid in it, there'll be ae wee lark singing up in the clouds — tae itsel', or tae its mate, maybe; or just a sparrow chirping on an auld tumbled-in roof where once was a warm hearth, an' a licht, an' the sound o' bairn's voices.

. . . .

THE FIRELIGHTERS

(March 6th, 1835)

JOHN STUART MILL, *accompanied by his Egeria,* MRS. TAYLOR, *has spent three mortal hours explaining volubly to* CARLYLE *how the manuscript of his* History of the French Revolution *came to be used by a maid servant for the lighting of fires. And now they have gone; and* CARLYLE *and his* WIFE *are left alone together. As* CARLYLE *walks back to his place, she hears the groaning sigh which the presence of his visitors has restrained. She looks up as he passes her chair.*

MRS. CARLYLE Aren't you going to kiss me, Tom?

CARLYLE (*as he does so*) That's kind of ye!

MRS. CARLYLE My dear, it isn't *kind*! It's a 'thank God!' for getting rid of them. What use to us could they be? This is for you and me, and no one else in the world: you and me *together*. He at his bleatings, and I — shut up in a box with no lid to it — not able to give you word or sign how my heart was breaking for you — couldn't come near you! Oh, my dear, my dear!

CARLYLE You think I didn't know that, without any flag-wagging to tell me?

MRS. CARLYLE There are some things a body starves if it can't say. We weren't given our senses and affections never to show them.

CARLYLE Aye; but *there's* always the danger.

MRS. CARLYLE There isn't any — now *they've* gone!

CARLYLE Aye, gone! Mercy has come to us at last!

MRS. CARLYLE And quite time it did, to save the wits of one of us! Here have we been sitting like a pair of pin-cushions for him to jab words into! Words, words! Saying the same thing over and over again — no beginning and no end to it!

CARLYLE Aye; a sore visitation this — to both of us. What's it to prove?

MRS. CARLYLE That you can be great over it.

CARLYLE Oh, if only I had the faith for it! Would God that I had the faith! . . . But I haven't.

MRS. CARLYLE I'll have the faith for it, if you'll have the courage, Carlyle. Aye, you are hurt and sore wounded; but you've been a hero.

CARLYLE What have I done, woman, to be called a hero?

MRS. CARLYLE That you didn't kill him! And you didn't skin him, either!

CARLYLE No need; you did that for me.

MRS. CARLYLE If he'd as many skins as a cat has lives, I'd have liked to have all of them! What did he sit there for, talking, talking? Why — when he'd given you the plain facts of it couldn't he go?

CARLYLE He wanted sympathy.

MRS. CARLYLE And you gave it him! My dear, you were wonderful; but it nearly killed me. There was I crying my inside eyes out, tender as a lamb-cutlet — for *you*, my dear; and — for *him*? wanting to jump up and scream 'You blind fool, for God's sake, get out!' It almost pulled me to pieces, that did! Carlyle, don't harden yourself now, there's no need for it. I'm not wanting sympathy, I'm wanting the man's blood!

CARLYLE Aye, like ye would! But what for, if you had it?

MRS. CARLYLE Just to know that he *hadn't* it. Bleed a man, and he's harmless — comparatively — for the time being, at any rate! But oh, my dear, my dear! all your work — those months while I've watched and waited, and you've grunted and grumbled at yourself, and said you'd put the whole thing in the fire, if you could have your wish, and begin again! And now it's come — happened; and you see what a dear fool you were — and always will be; for you'll never alter. All your life you are going to be miserable, grinding out things the world will remember you by, and doing it like a dog scratching out fleas all the time! And I've got to kennel with you while you are doing it! Don't harden yourself to *me*, Tom! Talk to me! I said I didn't want sympathy; it's a lie! I do; I need comforting. If you don't comfort me, I shall go out and murder the first man or woman I meet — as a substitute for the one that's escaped me.

CARLYLE D'you want that poor girl's blood too, she that did it?

MRS. CARLYLE She? That girl? I don't believe a word of it! 'Twas that woman, with her six feet of virtue reaching to the skies!

CARLYLE Tut, tut! Ye're mad on that woman.

MRS. CARLYLE She's mad on herself. That's what's wrong with her: a self-worshipping goddess, she is! So much worship he's poured over her, she's caught it from him! Did you see her sitting there — lapping up the situation, and enjoying it — thinking how dramatic it all was! — like a crocodile drinking milk! How do we know that she didn't give the Irishwoman the papers herself?

CARLYLE Aye; when ye've no facts — the next best thing is to shape them to your ain liking.

MRS. CARLYLE One fact's plain enough anyway! She's jealous of you for daring to be a greater writer than that tame cat of hers. And don't forget, Mr. Carlyle, he'd started on the same thing himself, and gave it up when he heard you were doing it: which did show he'd some sense at any rate.

CARLYLE Aye; and was kind over it, too. Handed me on his books and materials. Ye mustn't forget that.

MRS. CARLYLE *She* didn't think it kind of him. She's had it against you ever since. And it's my belief, Carlyle, that if she *knew* of his having your manuscript (which of course she did) she'd never rest until she got hold of it. And then who knows *what* she wouldn't do?

CARLYLE Ye'd better sit down and write a play of it. Eh! women are strange creatures, and fine fighters — left to themselves! If they hadn't man to tame them, 'twould be a bloody world, I'm thinking. So she did it, eh?

MRS. CARLYLE She saw that it *was* done, I'll be bound! There's a girl that can't read; and fires always being lighted; and what he writes goes into them — after it's been printed — 'Always make a point — do in future make a point of *that*, Mr. Carlyle!' — And what's easier for that woman than to make an altar of his rubbish, and put you for a victim on top of it?

CARLYLE Aye, Jane, my lass — now you are enjoying yourself! Go on!

MRS. CARLYLE I enjoy finding the truth about people, and telling it. Show me the outside of a thing, and I'll tell you its character, if it's got any. It wasn't for your outside, Tom, that I took *you*. And though your inside's not so attractive either, I've never repented. It's never struck me to say that we are happy together; but if anything were to put us apart, I'd scream down Heaven with curses on those that did it. Now; do you believe me?

(*He sits inscrutable: and she continues*)

What's happened now was to *me* as much as to you, every bit. I've got to have six months' worse growlings because of it: and maybe, all the time, not a word of kindness shall I get from you. And I'll not ask it; it's the price I pay for having you. So, if you wouldn't mind, Mr. Carlyle, just for once — before you begin beating me again — if you wouldn't mind letting me have the assurance — from something you say now, or do — that the beatings I get do *you* good anyway! I'm not going to flatter you by pretending that they do *me* any! It only just happens that to-night I want a word of comfort and reassurance, from the only being who can give it to me — that I am not useless, though I may no longer be ornamental.

(*After enjoying the somewhat prolonged silence that ensues, she says*)

I'm waiting, Mr. Carlyle.

CARLYLE Maybe if I gave it you, it 'ud spoil you.

MRS. CARLYLE We'll risk it.

CARLYLE I don't like risks: I've got the Scot in me.

MRS. CARLYLE Then you don't like me: for I'm the biggest risk you ever took in your life.

CARLYLE (*admiringly*) Eh, that's true! The woman has got me.

MRS. CARLYLE Have I? I'm not so sure of it. Have you got *me*?

CARLYLE If I hadn't . . . Yes: ye can take this to your comfort, if it's any comfort to ye! . . . If I hadn't *you* —

> (*So far he gets but no further; and after giving his pause its measure, she speaks again*)

MRS. CARLYLE It's hard to get out, isn't it? — that without me would make any difference big enough to find a word for. Never mind: try! You needn't say it in terms of affection. Just state the fact.

CARLYLE Aye: there ye go! I could have sworn to it. Always shall I have ye interrupting me just when I've a thing to say that, maybe, was worth saying! Eh, where have I put my pipe?

MRS. CARLYLE It's in your own hand.

> (*He proceeds slowly to fill it, but does not light it*)

CARLYLE What was I to tell you? You want me to exaggerate? I'll not. Put it this way, and let that content ye — That if I hadn't you, here, always troubling me, that burnt sacrifice would never get itself written again. But it's going to be.

MRS. CARLYLE. Yes; and a work for two of us — don't make a mistake about that! It's not going to make me happy, Mr. Carlyle; six months of growlings and complaints never did that for a woman. But it's going to make me proud of you.

CARLYLE Aye: a proud day for both of us — this, first and last!

MRS. CARLYLE That we ever let those two go out alive? I'm not so Christian.

CARLYLE No: but ye've that in you that makes up for it . . . (*Then as he slowly rises*) So, now I'm going to bed. Good night to ye, lass.

MRS. CARLYLE Good night, Tom.

> (*He moves to the door, then comes back and lays a hand on her*)

CARLYLE Eh; if it's understanding you want, I was the right man for you.

> (*Having said that he goes. She stands looking after him till the door shuts: then it opens again, and a head comes in*)

CARLYLE Ye'll see I'm called the right time to-morrow — early?

MRS. CARLYLE I'll see you called, Tom, the right time every day, till the Day of Judgment.

CARLYLE She was late one day — so there now!

(*And this time he really has gone. With a jerk of the head* MRS. CAR-LYLE's *face takes on its normal expression once more. 'Carlyle's himself again!' it seems to say. The expression is not exactly a happy one, but there's humour in it: she is conscious that* THOMAS CARLYLE *is her man, and that no one else in the world would get within miles of managing him as she does.*)

SAL VOLATILE
(1670)

Before her final retirement to a life of virtue, NINON DE LANCLOS *discourses to the last of her many lovers of faith and morals.*

NINON I recall the story of Ignatius Loyola and the young man, to whom he was spiritual director, who loved too well one that had entered into the bonds of matrimony . . . To Ignatius, his friend and director, this young man had confided that on certain nights, in the husband's absence, he went regularly where he should not. And after many exhortations to penitence, and many failures to amend, he ceased at last to trouble his spiritual father's ear with a tale which had become monotonous.

Now it so happened that his way to bliss lay over river, by a bridge; and it was winter. One night, as he crossed, he heard a voice from the water calling him by name; and looking down, saw the head of Ignatius sticking up like a fish, neck deep, teeth chattering, and the voice of imposed conscience cried, 'My son, where are you going?' Honestly he confessed the truth, but was not for turning back: he was promised, the lady was expecting him. Then said Ignatius, 'I shall wait here till you return'. From that fishy answer he fled in horror; but it was useless, the fish had already swallowed him: consciousness of his beloved director, waiting neck-deep in icy water, robbed him of felicity. Torch extinguished, he returned, and gave himself up to a captivity from which he was never able after to escape.

There is an example of religion for you! — unconscionable, possessive, tyrannous to attain its end. What have you to say?

SÉVIGNÉ Only that apparently it was successful.

NINON As a rape, Monsieur, is sometimes successful. But this violation — not of the body but of the soul — this trading upon the generous instincts of his friend — was, surely, a darker deed. For here was a secret told in confession; and if what the Church claims for confession be true, it should never have gone further. But it did. Ignatius, the spiritual director, betrayed the secret to Ignatius, the busybody, the meddler; and devised the betrayal so subtly, with so poignant a persecution of his own flesh, that the baseness of the deed escaped the notice of its victim.

Turn Again Tales   (1930)

RIGHT-ABOUT-FACE

ONCE upon a time there lived a man and his wife who had been married for fifty years, and were therefore no longer young. But that seemed to matter little; all their neighbours, looking at them, declared them to be the happiest couple ever known, and when asked for the reason would recall how the wife had a fairy Godmother. 'No doubt,' they said, 'it was her gift to the two upon their wedding-day that has kept them happy.'

But as a matter of fact the fairy Godmother had given no present at all, but only a promise. 'My child,' she said to the young bride on the day of her marriage, 'it is my intention that you should be happy; but fairy gifts are often dangerous. So now go your way and fear nothing; but when you cease to be happy send for me; then, perhaps, I may be able to do you some good.'

And so the fairy departed; and the bride went on her way; and now she had been married for fifty years, and had never sent for her fairy Godmother.

You might almost think she had forgotten her; but, anyhow, one day the fairy Godmother came to the door and, without knocking, looked in; and there sat the old wife polishing the family pewter so bright that she could see her own face in it quite plainly. And to be sure, just then it was her very own face that she was looking at.

She gazed at it for a long time, then she shook her head sadly. 'No, no,' she said, 'you are not so fair as you used to be, so don't try to think it!'

And just at that moment she saw her fairy Godmother standing in the doorway, and suddenly she remembered everything, and with a loud cry she dropped the pewter plate and ran as fast as her old legs would carry her, and, flinging herself into the fairy's arms, she laid her head upon the magical heart and burst into tears.

'So you've come at last! So you've come at last!' she cried. 'I thought you never would!'

'You never sent for me!' said the fairy. 'If you wanted me so much, why did you not do so?'

The other looked at her with dim eyes. 'I put it off,' she said.

'For long?'

'For years.'

The fairy smiled, for she understood the ways of human hearts. 'I suppose, then,' said she, 'that it began the very day after we parted?' And the wife owned that it was so.

'And why did you not send for me?'

'Because I was ashamed. I had no reason to give; only that I was not quite so happy as I had meant to be.'

'And now?' inquired the fairy?

'Ah, now there *is* a reason!' So, in the home of fifty years, they sat down side by side, and the old wife told of all the sorrow that was in her heart.

'You see,' she said, 'it is like this: I love my man and he loves me; but to him I'm only a sort of nine parts out of ten. There's one part of his heart that doesn't belong to me, that he takes away and keeps all to himself. And what that other part is I cannot guess, but I shall never be happy till I know.'

'And when you know,' said the fairy, 'what then?'

'Then I know I shall be miserable,' answered the old wife sadly. 'And then you must fulfil your promise, and make me happy again.'

'I never promised that,' said the fairy. 'I only said that I would try to do you good. But tell me first, how are you so sure that one part of your husband's heart does not belong to you?'

'By this,' said the wife. 'Day by day we live together, and I see him contented in all I do for him; contented to hear me as I speak; contented to sit and watch me when I am silent at my needle or at my spinning-wheel. And then a day comes and I know he is not contented any more;

K   145

and without saying a word to me, he gets up and goes away; and though
he is not long gone, and though he always kisses me tenderly when he
returns and is content once more, yet I know there is just a part of him
that doesn't belong to me; and that is the part, I think, that I would give
up all the other parts to possess.'

'Well,' said the fairy, 'if that is your mind in the matter, it is easily
done. If you choose to give up all those nine parts that you possess and
take only the one that is denied you, I can give you your wish. Is that
what you mean?'

But at that the old wife grew frightened. 'No, no,' she said, 'let me
know first what the secret thing is that draws him away from me; and
after that let me decide.'

So the fairy agreed to wait until the husband's next fit of discontent
should come on him; and then, after finding out by what means he sought
a remedy, she would let the wife into the secret and leave her to make her
own choice in the matter.

So unbeknownst to the husband, the fairy stayed at hand and kept
watch; and to be sure, before very long, one day the old man got up
without saying anything to his wife and went away on some secret
errand of his own. But this time he was not quite so solitary as he thought
himself.

The fairy came back smiling, and kissed her godchild, saying, 'Now
you need have no further fear of your husband's love for you. When he
goes away and leaves you alone, it is that he may look at a portrait of
you which he keeps in secret, and which was done when you were still
a young bride. Surely such a husband is the most perfect and faithful
lover in all the world.'

But the old wife, after thinking of it for a while, did not like it; she
became as jealous of that former self as though it had been another
woman.

'Ah, yes,' she cried, 'I know my face is no longer as fair as it was once;
so it is only what is past that he cares about. But what am I to him now
if he has always in his mind's eye the woman that I am not? I said that
when I knew I should be miserable, but I did not think it would be as
bad as this!'

'Well,' said the fairy, 'now I will try to do you some good. So have
your wish, and whatever you think best, that shall be.'

Then the old wife said, 'Let me have back the face of my first youth that I have lost and that he remembers and loves; so will my husband's heart belong to me entirely, and I shall be happy again.'

Immediately upon the word her fairy Godmother, as though she had known already what her choice would be, produced a magic mirror, and placing it before her said, 'Now draw a deep breath, and hold it, and look at your face as it changes in this glass. And when your face is as young as you would have it be, let your breath go, and so it will remain.'

So the old wife drew a deep breath and looked in the mirror, and saw in its magic surface her face change back through all the years from age to youth; and as soon as she saw it as it had been on the day she became a bride, she let her breath go again, and so was as she had wished.

Her gratitude to her fairy Godmother was great; but the fairy smiled a little sadly and said, 'If you want me again, call me, and I will come'. And with that she departed.

When the old husband came home again it was quite dark, and his wife was gone to bed; but he lighted a candle in order that he might see her as he kissed her good night, for his heart was full of contentment once more. And there, when the flame shone, lay the face of his girl wife smiling up at him.

She told him but half of her story — how her fairy Godmother had come and offered her any gift that she cared to choose, and how she had chosen the one which she thought would please him best. And there it was, and the fairy Godmother had departed. As he listened the old man's eyes filled with tears, and he blew out the candle, and in the dark kissed many times the beautiful face that had come back to give him the happiness of the past.

This went on, and nearly a year had run its course when one day the fairy received an urgent message from her goddaughter, begging her to come at once. When she arrived she found the poor dame waiting in a state of profound grief and despondency; her beautiful face was red with weeping, and the house looked as though it had not been swept for days; all was discomfort where once peace and order had reigned. The fairy, however, pretended to notice none of these things. 'Well, daughter, and how goes it with you?' she inquired.

'Alas! Godmother,' replied the other, 'for the last year I have been most miserable. My trouble, instead of being mended, is far worse now than it was before; for where my husband used formerly to go away from me but once or so in a fortnight, it is now nine times that he leaves me: and I know not what it is that takes him, unless it be that my re-covered beauty has reminded him too much of his youth and the times when he had not yet chosen me for his one-and-only.' And, saying this, she covered her face with her hands and wept as though her heart were broken forever.

'Well,' said the fairy, 'we have but to wait, as before, till your husband's next fit of discontent comes over him, and then we shall see what we shall see.'

'That will not need any waiting for,' answered the wife, 'for hardly a day passes now but he leaves me. Indeed, it is only on Sundays that he stays at home, and I think he does that for a penance.' And with that she fell to fresh weeping.

'Is he away now?' inquired the fairy.

'Since break of dawn,' answered the unhappy wife. 'It is seldom I see him now in the day-time.'

'Well,' said the other, 'there's no time like the present. Let us see what has become of him.' And so saying, she drew out her divining-glass.

'Ah! ah!' she cried as she looked in it, 'he is not far away. Let us not waste moments. This time I am going to take you with me, but you must come under my cloak so that he shall not see you, and you must promise not to say a word till I give you leave.'

So the sad wife crept under the fairy's cloak and hid her face for a moment; and when she looked out again the scene had changed, and there was her husband before her very eyes. And first she only saw how happy and contented he looked, and then that he had before him a portrait of herself done little more than a year ago. And into that face of wrinkled age he was gazing with eyes of love, and murmuring to it sweet words of companionship and affection.

Presently he sighed and rose, for it was growing dark, and looking at the picture for the last time, he kissed it tenderly. 'Alas! sweet wife,' he said, 'to think that I may never see you with that dear face again! Though the face you have chosen is fairer, it is only the face of one part of you, and that the least; for I find not in it the years of the life we lived together when our children were about us; or when later they left us, and went out into the world to find homes and children of their own. When I look into this face, then I remember them and all their beauty and youth, and the love they had for us; but the other face tells me nothing of these things.' And with that the old man turned the picture back with its face to the wall and went softly away.

In the darkness of the chamber the old wife and the fairy Godmother were left alone, and for a time no word was said. 'Little one,' said the fairy at last, 'why are you weeping?'

'Because I am happy!' answered the wife. 'Oh, Godmother, let me look in your glass again!'

The fairy seemed to have known what to expect, for she had the glass there ready. And the wife took a deep breath and held it hard, and looking into the mirror once more, she saw all the beauty pass quickly from her face and turn again into age. She watched and watched until there was not a remnant of beauty left, but only the peace and contentment that the years had brought. And then, when she saw herself quite old once more, she let her breath go again and was as she wished.

She kissed the fairy's hand. 'Good-bye, Godmother,' she said. 'This time it is good-bye indeed. For I know that I shall never send for you again; and if I were happier than I am now I should die.'

So there they parted; and as fast as her legs would carry her the old wife went home. It was quite dark when she got to the house, and her husband was already in bed; but she lighted the candle when she went up to bid him good night.

Little Plays of St. Francis (Second Series)   (1931)

THE PEACE-MAKERS

FRANCIS *has come to make peace between the* LORDS *and the* CITIZENS.

FRANCIS These now are all dead, Brothers; and if, as we pray, they be in God's keeping, then they have forgiven those on whom ye still seek vengeance. Pray for thy son, Brother, that thou and he may be of like mind! Pray for thy men, Brother, that as, in this life, they were thy faithful servants, thou mayest now do like service to their souls in Purgatory!

FIRST LORD These things are not done — on earth, Father.

FRANCIS Not often, Brother; men not having the right will.

FIRST CITIZEN Is there to be no such thing as justice?

FRANCIS With God, Brother: but with men the only justice is — mercy.

FIRST LORD We ask not mercy of *any*!

FRANCIS Some day you will have to. And God will then hear you better, if you have shown mercy to others.

FIRST LORD As *they* showed mercy?

FRANCIS Why make choice of so poor a pattern, Brother?

.   .   .   .   .

FRANCIS O Brothers, is not Assisi one city? Do not her walls embrace all, and her gates open and shut as with consent, so that men going forth free, here come back to find shelter? How then can it be for good that, in her midst, ye her own children are divided? Only come together, Brothers, and ye shall miss nothing! For this contention, costing so much, does but breed weakness; and though ye swear ye love her, it is only yourselves; and while your lips say, 'It is for Assisi!' your deeds say, 'Down, down with Assisi!'

CROWD Assisi! Assisi! Life and peace for Assisi!

FRANCIS O Brothers, heal her of her wounds, strengthen her gates, build up her walls, and let her towers have eyes, that — thence looking — ye may see the day-spring from on high visiting her, and the bright and the morning star, which is God's love for all of us!

O little Children, if He denied you His love, as ye deny it to each other, what hope in the world would be left? Brother sinners, be a little like God — only a little! Is it so hard for you to find, each in his own heart, that ye are His children? Must the other first be penitent, ere ye will do each to other the work of Christ? For had Christ waited till our repentance, He had never come!

The Queen's Progress (1932)

THE SIX O'CLOCK CALL
(1837)

The QUEEN *has just received the news of her accession, and realizes that she can now decide for herself matters which have hitherto been decided for her.*

VICTORIA Then my reign has already begun? I can do — as I like?

DUCHESS Yes; as you like! Do not mind what anyone says. If you want to do it — do it!

VICTORIA Oh! . . . Then . . . Mama. There is something I would like.

DUCHESS Ah, yes! Say it! It shall be done . . . But now, my love — do not stay here to catch cold. Come back to your own Mother's bed!

VICTORIA No, Mama dear. As I may now do as I like, I wish in future to have a bed, and a room of my own!

DUCHESS *Of your own?*

VICTORIA Yes — please, Mama.

DUCHESS Oh! so you have been waiting — for *that*!

VICTORIA I should be glad, if you don't mind — now that I am my own mistress. Yes, I would rather be alone.

　　(*She does not wait to hear more*)

DUCHESS Mind! . . . Glad! . . . Alone! . . . O God! What is going to become of me?

　　(*She stands and watches, while* VICTORIA, *mistress, henceforth of her own destiny, turns and goes quietly upstairs.*)

UNDER FIRE
(May 30th, 1842)

An attempt upon the QUEEN's *life has just failed; but, as the* QUEEN *sensibly remarks, there may come another time.*

ALBERT Oh, my Dear, my Dear! And you can say that now — as if you did not mind if it should come again! Is that really true?

THE QUEEN Yes, Albert; for with you I felt so safe . . . Didn't you?

ALBERT No, Weibchen, I was afraid.

THE QUEEN Afraid?

ALBERT I was afraid that if he missed one of us, it might be *me* that he missed. Ah, no, no! Do not talk of another time. I could not bear it — another time!

THE QUEEN Oh, Albert, had I thought for a moment that it might be *you* — I couldn't have gone!

ALBERT What a good thing it was, then, my Dear, that you did *not* think. Queens must not think too much about others: only about themselves.

> (*And having made that little joke, very much to his own satisfaction, he kisses her*)

THE QUEEN Dearest, have I pleased you?

ALBERT Very much. You have more than pleased me. You have behaved like a Queen.

THE QUEEN Then now I must go and take off my things. Oh, dear! what a lot of letters I shall have to write now! To Uncle Leopold, and to everybody. How it will interest them! 'Just think!' I can hear them say, 'Poor Vicky's been shot at!'

> (*And out she goes, very conscious that, having been shot at, she has something worth writing about.*)

INTERVENTION
(November 30th, 1861)

The PRINCE CONSORT *intervenes, and saves England from war with America.*

THE QUEEN Oh, Albert, why did you wait to change? I have been so wanting you.

ALBERT My uniform was wet through, my Dear; and I was feeling very cold *. . .* What is the matter?

THE QUEEN It's about that trouble with America, for having taken the Confederate Envoys off one of our ships. And most wrong of them it was! This is the dispatch Lord Russell is sending to our Ambassador in

Washington about it. He wants it to go to-night . . . Read it quickly, Albert. I want to know what you think about it.

(*The* QUEEN *sits watching the Prince as he reads. Not till he has finished it does he speak*)

ALBERT This means War.

THE QUEEN Yes, I was afraid so. How foolish of them not to give in! For they must know they are in the wrong. And everything that Lord Russell says is true, is it not?

ALBERT Quite . . . Quite . . . But it won't do.

THE QUEEN But, Albert, as we are in the right, what else can we do?

ALBERT Alter a few words . . . Say it; but say it differently. Often it is just the way a thing is said that decides whether it shall be peace or war. It is the same when two people quarrel. You and I, Weibchen, might often have quarrelled, had we said the same thing that we did say — differently . . . Russell? Oh, no: this is Palmerston, I think. He is the man that would *like* to have war with America. He has worked for it; and this is his opportunity — that we are in the right . . . He shall not have it! War? Oh, yes; and this time we should win. But another would come and we should *not* win.

THE QUEEN But we could always beat America now, Albert.

ALBERT Ah, so? What if we were fighting someone else, Vicky; and America chose her time then? No; that is what these 'patriots' never think about . . . It is always — '*This* time, *this* time! We are *right*, and we shall do what we like!' What fools their patriotism makes clever men to be! And Palmerston the cleverest fool of them all! . . . And when he dies, they will say of this man — 'Oh, yes; he had his faults; but he always upheld the Honour of his Country.' And when they say 'Honour', they mean Pride. Again and again, he has been ready to sacrifice the Honour of his County to its Pride. For Honour means that you are too proud to do wrong; but Pride means that you will not *own* that you have done wrong — at all. *That* is the difference.

THE QUEEN Then that applies to America, now.

ALBERT Yes. Here is America; she has done wrong, and she knows it . . . Invite her to reconsider — a mistake: something done by her agents without her instructions. She will think, and will behave reasonably . . . But say 'I order you!' and she will *not*.

THE QUEEN But, Albert, ought we to make it so easy for them as all that?

ALBERT Yes; because we should do just the same ourselves, if we were ordered. And we should call it 'Honour'. And for that honour we should send thousands and thousands to die. What a wicked black thing honour can become — when men make use of it — *so*!

HAPPY AND GLORIOUS
(June 20th, 1897)

The triumphal Procession is over. The QUEEN *is back at Buckingham Palace, and seated in her wheeled chair, with all the members of her Family round her, she speaks to reverently-attending ears.*

THE QUEEN It's very gratifying, very, to find — after all these years — that they do appreciate all that I have tried to do for them — for their good, and for this great Country of ours. We have been so near together to-day — they and I: all my dear people of England, and Scotland, and Wales — *and* Ireland, and the dear colonies, and India. From all round the world I have had messages. Such loyalty — such devotion! Most extraordinary! Tell Mr. Chamberlain how very much I approve of all the arrangements he made for the proper representation of all parts of my Empire in the Procession. Everything so perfectly in order. Most gratifying! . . . Well, I must go now and rest, or I shall not be able to take my place at dinner to-night, and that would never do! . . . So happy! . . . As we were coming back — you were in front, Bertie, so perhaps you didn't see — it was just by Hyde Park Corner, there was a great crowd there; and a lot of rough men — of course it ought not to have happened, but it didn't matter — broke right through the lines of the police and troops guarding the route; and they ran alongside the carriage, shouting and cheering me. And I heard them say: 'Go it, Old Girl! You've done it well! You've done it well!' Of course, very unsuitable — the words; but so gratifying! And oh, I hope it's true! I hope it's true! . . . Hark! They are still cheering . . . Albert! Ah! if only you could have been here!

Ye Fearful Saints! (1932)

THE GODS WHOM MEN LOVE DIE OLD

In the inner chamber of his own Being sits an old QUIET GOD, *warming himself at the fires of life. Here, in symbol or in fact, is the world of his making; and since we find them thus together, they still have, we may assume, some use for each other.*

On the outer door of that misty chamber, whose walls melt into a cloud-like obscurity, comes a knock, which, after a while, is repeated.

QUIET GOD Come in!

> (*The figure which enters is of a different character. Half priest, half warrior, he carries about his Person symbols of godhead which no one can mistake; and they still excite awe and reverence among minds trained to accept them. And, as we look at these two, we wonder by what names we shall distinguish them. '*QUIETUS*' may stand fairly obviously for one; and '*DECUS*' (at his own valuation) will do sufficiently well for the other*)

DECUS Well, Brother, how are you getting on?

QUIETUS (*cheerfully*) Oh, nicely. I'm getting old.

DECUS Getting old? But a God shouldn't grow old. Gods are immortal.

QUIETUS Yes: I used to think so. But it's not true. You know, yourself, many of the Gods have grown old: men no longer know of them — they have gone utterly.

DECUS *False* gods, yes.

QUIETUS Oh no. They were true enough in their day. Men believed in them. Now that they don't, they're gone.

DECUS The life of a God — if he be a true God — does not depend on man's belief in him.

QUIETUS Doesn't it? I'm not sure. I can't myself remember the time when I had not believers — worshippers.

DECUS But you made *your* world (as I made mine) before men came into it.

QUIETUS Well, they say so. Perhaps, in my subconscious mind, I did; but not consciously. Can you remember anything — before?

DECUS Yes; I can remember — storm, tempest, the raging of seas, the howling of wolves, the scream of the eagle, the roar of the lion: pain, darkness — death.

QUIETUS Yes; but nothing else — till man came. The idea that you *were* a God did not occur to you till then. That was your own voice you heard: but it was only a voice, and a divided one. You weren't a God then. You were only hungering to become one — without knowing what you were hungering for.

DECUS Can one be hungry for that which does not exist?

QUIETUS Why, yes. I am hungry to-day for something man has not yet given me: something which I may never live to receive. But I *may*! I'm waiting.

DECUS And while waiting, you are growing old? I'm not!

QUIETUS Then what *are* you doing?

DECUS Ruling, directing, ordering all things to my will.

QUIETUS And do they always obey?

DECUS When they don't, I punish them!

QUIETUS Do they obey then?

DECUS Sometimes.

QUIETUS And when they don't?

DECUS I punish them again.

QUIETUS Do you never cease punishing when they disobey?

DECUS No! If I did, my Kingdom on earth would be over.

QUIETUS Ah! I *have* ceased punishing.

DECUS Then no wonder you've grown old!

QUIETUS You are right, Brother. It is the way of age and wisdom, that I have found at last. I leave men to punish themselves.

DECUS (*incredulously*) And do they?

QUIETUS Oh, yes! Yes, indeed! Terribly! Far worse than I should have the heart to punish them myself.

DECUS Then why don't you go on punishing them?

QUIETUS Because, punishing themselves, they learn more than if *I* did it.

DECUS What do they learn?

QUIETUS Their mistakes. Punish a man, he may still stick to his opinion — think you are unjust. Leave him to punish himself, he learns better.

DECUS You are a strange God!

QUIETUS Yes: strange even to myself; for I, too, am learning.

DECUS Are you punishing — yourself?

QUIETUS In a way, yes. I am finding out where I have made mistakes.

DECUS A God *never* makes mistakes!

QUIETUS That is what your worshippers always say as a preliminary when they pray to you — *not to make them*! But you still do; and keep yourself young by punishing them! I — am growing old.

DECUS And you mean to go on — growing old?

QUIETUS Yes.

DECUS And when you have grown so old that you cannot grow older — what then?

QUIETUS Then I shall die.

DECUS A God can't die.

QUIETUS Oh, yes, he can! Did not Saturn eat up his own children, who would have become Gods had he *not* eaten them? And where is Baal? Where is Ashtaroth? You call them 'false gods'. But they were true once; and, in their worshippers, were very much alive.

DECUS And do you propose to die, too — like them?

QUIETUS Not *quite* like them. *They* didn't want to die.

DECUS You mean to die willingly?

QUIETUS Willingly? Oh, yes.

DECUS Now you do interest me. How do you propose to die — willingly? If a God dies, it must mean that His worshippers have learned to do without Him — don't want Him any more.

QUIETUS Yes: I agree.

DECUS Therefore has already ceased to be a God.

QUIETUS Quite so.

DECUS What do you think a God is for, then?

QUIETUS Mainly the means to an end. He helps men to find themselves. When they *have* found themselves, they don't need him any more. The Two have become One . . . I'm waiting — for that.

DECUS Is that why you are feeling old?

QUIETUS Yes, I think so.

DECUS Because men don't need you?

QUIETUS Oh, they need me still — I don't feel dead yet; but they won't always. When I've taught them to love — really to love — I shall have done my work.

DECUS But — be honest! — don't you need something yourself to make you satisfied — from them? Don't you want to receive their worship?

QUIETUS Yes: if they want to give it, I want to receive it. But not otherwise.

DECUS Which decides?

QUIETUS I don't know. We do it between us.

DECUS *I* don't! You make yourself too cheap, Brother! Little should I get if I took nothing but what was given me willingly. I make *my* worshippers give me what they don't want to give me!

QUIETUS For instance?

DECUS Whatever they hold most precious on earth — I demand in sacrifice: their own children sometimes.

QUIETUS Yes: but if they sacrifice these, it is because they want to. If they did not, they would not do it.

DECUS *Wouldn't they?*

QUIETUS No. What we get in sacrifice depends entirely on what men *want* to sacrifice. We are in their hands, though they think they are in ours.

DECUS They don't *think* — they believe it, they know it!

QUIETUS Yes; but *I* don't. As I've grown old I've grown wise. My sacrifices have changed; and it isn't *I* that have changed them. Men give me the sacrifices that suit their own needs best.

DECUS What sort of sacrifice do you get now?

QUIETUS Love.

DECUS Love, eh? Didn't they always love you?

QUIETUS No. They feared me; just as yours fear you. When they sacrificed to me with blood and burnt flesh, they didn't love me; nor did I love them.

DECUS What did you do, then?

QUIETUS Do?

DECUS Yes. What did you feel toward them? Fear?

QUIETUS No, no. I was never afraid of them. They puzzled me. I liked the smell of their sacrifices — their blood, and their burnt-offerings, though I didn't quite know why. But it took me a long time to find out that they feared me. Had I feared *them*, I might have found out much sooner.

DECUS Oh? Why?

QUIETUS Because it would have made us nearer to each other.

DECUS Nearer, eh?

QUIETUS Yes: we should have been more alike. True worship only comes when the worshipper gives back as he receives. Only then do the worshippers and the worshipped really know each other . . . Fear separates. When I found they were afraid of me, I was sorry for them — that they did not understand.

DECUS Did not understand what?

QUIETUS Me . . . That I had no wish to hurt them. But though I pitied them, I could not tell them. They had to find it out for themselves. It took a long time.

DECUS Yes? Well?

QUIETUS And all that time they went on sacrificing to me. But, as I watched, I saw that it meant less and less to them. And as it meant less and less to *them*, so it meant less and less to *me* . . . I left off caring for the smell of blood and burnt flesh. All my taste for it was gone. So when they left off, I didn't miss it. Other things had come in its place. They still worshipped me, but in a different way.

DECUS In what way different?

QUIETUS Not in doing, but in being. It was very curious to watch them — very puzzling: for I saw they were trying to be something different from what they had been before. And one day I made a great discovery: they were trying to be like — me!

DECUS How blasphemous! Did they succeed?

QUIETUS Indeed, no! Far from it: for, still having their old fear of me, they were trying to make others fear *them*, in order to please *me*! Fear was to make men what they wanted them to be — what they thought *I* wanted them to be. Yet what I wanted them to be, I did not know myself. I only wanted myself to be known and understood. And there they were — in worship of *me* — filling the world with fear! Fear! What a mistake.

DECUS Well, I don't find fear a bad thing myself. I rule my followers by fear; and *I* don't feel old — yet. Try it again for a bit!

QUIETUS No, no. I couldn't go back to it. Only if I feared *them* would it be possible.

DECUS But how *can* a God fear man — his own making?

QUIETUS Only if he is afraid to die.

DECUS Die!

QUIETUS Yes. A God mustn't be afraid to die. I've found that out. When he is no longer afraid to die, men no longer fear him. They love him. He enters the lives of those that worship him, and lives — in *them*.

DECUS I don't understand —

QUIETUS I didn't till I began to feel old. Then I began to understand: I was learning to die.

DECUS But you said just now that you didn't feel like dying.

QUIETUS No, not yet — because, still in want, men worship me. But when they no longer worship me, then I shall know my time has come to die.

DECUS Why should you let them cease worshipping you?

QUIETUS I can't help it.

DECUS That seems a poor end to me!

QUIETUS Yes. I used to think so. But one day I heard one of my worshippers say: 'God is love'. At first it surprised me. And then found it was true. I love my worshippers. I love those that don't worship me. I love every one. When it is equally true that men love — as much as I do: when it can be said 'Man is love', he won't need *me* any more. Love will have become man. It's coming; but it's taking a long time.

DECUS And so — you are feeling old?

QUIETUS Yes: feeling old. I don't mind feeling old. It means that the time is coming when man won't need me. But he needs me still . . . I'm waiting. And while I've been waiting, I've found out something that I did not know before.

DECUS What?

QUIETUS Something beautiful: something that makes me quite contented to feel old.

DECUS Well, what?

QUIETUS The Gods whom men love die old . . . They love me. I've had a long life . . . I shall die — old.

THE NEW HANGMAN

It is the morning of an execution. The HANGMAN *refuses to do his job, and states his reasons.*

GOVERNOR Why, if you had such an objection to hanging, did you apply for the post?

HANGMAN I applied for it, sir, because I thought that, by doing this, I might save just one man's life, and shame a few others from ever taking part again in such a dirty business as this.

CHAPLAIN But do you not realize that you are putting us all in a very awkward position?

HANGMAN Yes, sir. But not such an awkward position as you are asking me to put someone else in.

GOVERNOR That is not *our* doing. That is the law.

HANGMAN Yes; the law: made by human beings, expecting others to do for 'em what they won't do themselves. And it's human beings, sir, are going to *unmake* that law . . . I'm making a start — on my own.

GOVERNOR By getting yourself dismissed?

HANGMAN Oh, yes, sir. That follows, of course. But there's not a music-hall in London, sir, wouldn't give me three hundred pounds to-night, just to stand up and be looked at for a week — the hangman that wouldn't hang people! And a Sunday paper would give me another hundred for an interview — all to itself. Well, sir — that being so — I'm hoping there's somebody'll give me a cleaner job — for a bit less pay. What else is a hangman but a man who murders to order — for money — in cold blood? D'you think a hangman does his job for 'love of society'? *He doesn't get any!* He has to hide himself under a changed name. Decent men won't know him; a decent woman won't marry him. Nobody in my street knows who I am. I got this job because for five years I'd been assistant to the last — 'knew the ropes', I suppose! When one of 'em broke, we had to do it over again. *That* didn't get into the papers, though. No fear! . . . The last time I assisted, we hanged a man who, I believe, was innocent. Others didn't. But if the jury had been made to come and see their verdict carried out — maybe they'd have thought so, too. The truth shows clearer on the drop sometimes than in the witness-box. If 'twas part of the law that judges and juries must be in at the death, there'd be more acquittals, sir. They leave that to us: we finish the job for 'em; and they despise us for it! But they say, 'It's got to be done'.

What-O'Clock Tales (1932)

WHAT-O'CLOCKS

IN meadows, when the months are green,
What gangs of golden flowers are seen;
While cowslip, crowsfoot, buttercup,
And dandelion keep coming up,
And, peering from a million eyes,
Fill all the fields with sweet surprise.

Aye! sweet they are! But not for 'keeps';
Over their heads Time lightly leaps;
Into the daily winds that blow
They break and part, and off they go;
And out along the wandering air
Divide and vanish — who knows where?

The grown-up grass has turned to hay,
And buttercups are all away;
The dandelions among the docks
Have seeded into 'what-o'clocks';
And when their little hour has struck,
There's nothing left for hand to pluck.

For fleeting Time leaves nothing long,
And brief are flowers like notes of song;
Rising in tender tremolo,
They shake a little while, then go.
'When the wind blows the cradle rocks,'
And off they go like 'what-o'clocks'.

So with my tales. They cannot last,
With readers growing up so fast;
Bleak Time will take and blow to bits
Things written for such little wits:
Up till eleven they stand his knocks;
But twelve ends off my 'what-o'clocks'.

But, Readers, you, who up to twelve,
In fairy-tales delight to delve,
May you in mine, for that short while,
Find fancies which can make you smile,
Until, in the more grown-up way,
Your grassy minds have turned to hay!

THE RAIN-CHILD
An Indian Fairy Story

LALOO, the only son of the deposed Rajah now dead, dwelt without state in a small hut under the walls of an old ruined temple, a few miles away from the head city of his ancestors. With him, sharing his solitude and poverty, lived old Junga, too faithful to lend himself to that desertion of fortune which had made the child of his old master both an orphan and an outcast.

The poverty, indeed, was Junga's own; for Laloo had nothing but the blood of his ancestors with which to bless himself; and that indeed would have been a danger and a sufficient cause for his riddance, had he not also been a Rain-child . . . a very great Rain-child. That saved him. All the world knew that, were he to die by any other hand than that of God, the drought that had ended at the moment of his birth would come and wither up crops, and herds, and people. So the popular saying went:

Laloo born, brought corn;
Laloo slain, kills rain.

Thus he lived, the last of his father's house, in the very midst of his enemies, luckless, almost friendless, but unharmed. 'Let God take him!'

said they, and reluctantly resigned to the ways of Heaven, left to the child such small chances as he had. Junga was old, and after Junga's death no one need go out of his way to feed Laloo: God would take him. It would still rain; grass would grow over the child's grave; perhaps, then he, the Rain-child, would become a blessing to the land, making it fruitful.

But if he received small honours now from those who had welcomed his birth with bonfires and rejoicings, in the hutch under the old temple-walls things still went on.

When it was Laloo's bed-time, he had not to go to sleep like a poor man's child, panting in the hot close air of the small hut. Over his head Junga had rigged up a little punkah, and, at his feet, Junga sat and pulled it, singing the while. His song had only one word in it, many times repeated. 'Salaam, Salaam, Salaam,' went the old man's patient lullaby, growing softer and softer, till the little son of the late great Rajah had fallen fast asleep. Whether the time were short or long, the loving heart of old Junga never found it too much of a tax, though he himself was often ready for bed before Laloo's little snores ordered him to rest.

In the morning it was the same thing. 'Salaam, Salaam, Salaam,' murmured the old man to the sleeping child: 'Salaam, Salaam' . . . the words grew louder, till the sleeper stirred: 'Salaam' . . . light flew under the long sunk lashes, up flew the lids to let the eyes have their stare; and there, stationary as a statue, sat old Junga waiting for his master's look. Laloo was always pleased at that.

'High One,' Junga would say, when the early meal had been taken, 'now I must go forth and work. It is permitted, is it not? Thy meal shall be ready for thee in right time. Go, then, O thou priceless one, and, meanwhile, get an appetite. Let thy high-born legs run about with thee. Till the day grows hot, be like an antelope; but thereafter 'tis like a brood-dove thou shalt stay till I return. Little lamb, thou shalt have a golden fleece if thou wilt do so.'

Left alone, Laloo would play in solitude; he did not mix with other children, yet he was not lonely. One remnant of old days of splendour was still his; it was one of the hundred toys with which, in former times, his servitors had coaxed and cajoled him to get out of bed or to lie down again. By some strange chance, Junga had been able to save it for him from the wreck of his fortune; so it remained Laloo's one bit of wealth.

True, one of the wheels was gone; but the three others, all solid and wooden, still bore up the square cart with its gilded canopy, so as not to tip out the magnificently dressed Rajah who sat within. There were oxen to draw it also; by leaning against each other they still had a sufficiency of legs to stand on, and their trappings of gold and blue and red, were still a joy to look upon. No other child in the village had such a thing to show.

Laloo did not conceal the pride he felt in that possession, but he would not take it with him when he went by other folk's houses. That would not be fitting; for whatever he was in the eyes of the common people, he remembered what he was by right, and became a man.

Junga, on his return, was always anxious to know where Laloo had been, and whether peradventure anyone had spoken to him. Or had they looked at him, and talked afterwards among themselves? Junga wanted to know that.

Laloo said one day, 'As I came through the village at noon, it was empty save for one, a woman. She stood waiting by the corner, and as I passed threw this wreath of flowers over my head'.

'Did she speak?' asked Junga.

'She spoke words which you also use. "High One," she said, "I am thy servant".'

'And then?'

'With my hand I gave salutation, pardoning her; for she was a poor woman and meant well.'

Another day he said, 'By one house where I go, there is grain thrown down, so that I walk on it. Afterwards it is gathered up, and I see the man sowing it. He says nothing to me'.

And yet another day he said, 'A boy threw mud at me as I passed; it did not hit me, but I saw the boy's father punish him'.

'Why dost thou go so often through the village?' asked Junga. 'Since thy will is to be lonely, be lonely!'

'It is because by that way I come where the wells are,' answered Laloo.

'Why should the High One go there at all?' inquired Junga. 'His servant brings him all the water he needs.'

'Thou canst not,' said Laloo, 'bring the sound of water to my ears.'

'What is the sound of water to thee?'

'My ears drink it.'

It seemed often that Laloo had thirsty ears, if that was what took him. Towards evening, when the villagers went out to draw water for their households, Laloo would go and sit on a slope overlooking the wells. From within their hollow sides came the cooing of doves; and the birds came and went to their nests in the crannies, not heeding the drawers at all. Through the quiet air, as it reddened into dusk, sounded the slow creaking of ropes as the oxen drew, lifting the leather bucket to the well's brim. Then followed the long 'swish' of the water as it poured itself out into the stone conduit at which the vessels of the water-carriers had to be dipped.

So it was till darkness set in, and the earth began to give out its heat to the cooling air; and of all sounds, only the cooing of doves was heard till that also died away. Then Laloo, having drunk with his ears and been satisfied, would rise up, and returning to the hut, find Junga already preparing the evening meal.

One night, watching him do this, Laloo said, 'Junga, why art thou so thin?'

'I am old,' said Junga. 'Little by little God takes the flesh off a man's body, to make him fit for his end. Far be that from thee, Lamp of my heart! What is the use of fat, when a body has soon to be ashes?'

'But thou,' said Laloo, 'art thinner than most live men. Art thou then so near death?'

'That is God's will: let Him say!' answered the old man, moving to and fro with stiff joints.

'Canst thou not ask Him to spare thee awhile? Do not prayers and gifts bring a man more life?'

'I may pray,' said Junga, 'but I have no gifts.'

'Have I not heard thee say that there is a well, which, if one drinks thereof, renews youth?'

'Many have told of that well,' answered Junga, 'but they have not found it.'

'A gift might bring it to thee.'

'I have no gift but thee,' said the old man. 'Should I want youth if I had not thee?'

'Youth is good,' said Laloo.

'Many years of it may God give thee!' replied Junga.

'But first I want to grow up,' objected Laloo. 'I need strength and wisdom.'

'Thou art a Rajah's son,' answered the old man. 'It will come.'

'Do Rajah's sons grow up sooner than others?'

'If they have cares. Have thou none, Beloved of my heart. But now see, it is time for the High One to lie down and take rest.'

Laloo lay down, and the old man sang his lullaby over him till he slept.

The next morning Laloo awoke to no call from Junga. The old man lay on his bed, unable to rise.

'High One,' said he in feeble tones, 'let thy servant be forgiven, and let what remains of last night's meal be enough for thy present need. In a while I shall be better, and will rise. Then I will get water.'

Laloo looked at the old man, and saw how thin and worn he had become. 'Peace be with you, my father,' he said; and taking up one of the water-pots, he went out softly, and down to the well.

It was yet early, but on his return he met a few villagers, who stared at him bearing a water-pot, and no Junga there. When he was alone a woman came behind and said, 'High One, shall I carry the water?'

'Thou shalt not carry it,' said Laloo. So he brought the water home, and set it down by the door; and behold, there within was Junga, scarcely able to move, but up and making ready to go out for his day's work.

'Lie down, my father,' said Laloo softly as he entered. 'Here I have brought water for thee.'

'Fountain of my heart!' cried the old man, 'why wouldst thou not have patience? In a while I would have fetched it.'

'I have fetched it,' said Laloo. 'Lie down.'

'Pardon me, Jewel of my delight, yet must I go forth; for we have but one day's food in hand, and I must get more. After that I think I will lie down.'

'There is no need,' said Laloo. 'Bread shall come. Lie down, my father, and let me be as a tree whose shadow is over thee.' So Junga lay down again, and for many hours spoke not.

Twice during the day Laloo brought him food; towards evening he slept. It was already dark when Laloo rose up from the old man's side and made ready to go abroad.

He took the largest water-pot he could carry, and set it on his head, then he took his ox-cart, and with that started upon his way. By help of the leading-string he lifted the feet of his oxen from the ground, and made the cart run well on its three wheels.

At the cross-ways before the entrance to the village, Laloo stopped and let go the string.

'Ow, wow!' cried he. 'To-morrow they will find it; and all the village will know that it was mine. Perhaps he that threw mud at me that day will take it, and I shall see him prouder than all his fellows with my two oxen, and my cart with its three wheels following him. He will not fail to let that be seen when I go by. Wah! Let me break it then. Will that not be sacrifice enough? So they shall have the pieces, but only I, Laloo, shall have the whole!'

Then he thought of Junga, himself almost in pieces, with his bones just held together by the skin over them; and sighing he turned quickly away, and went along till he came to the well.

Black as death gloomed the stone pit, within which the water lay: the very root of darkness seemed to be in it.

Overhead the stars flashed and sparkled, but down there no light showed, and not a dove made a sound. Laloo set down his pot, and lowered the great leather bucket to the depths. Then only did he remember how weak he was; how was he to draw the weight of the filled thing up again? He had forgotten to bring a rope of his own. But there was no water left in the conduit by the well's side: either he must draw up more, or Junga must thirst.

All at once he heard a soft tinkling of bells, and saw, not from the village, but from the open country, a woman stepping with many water-pots upon her head, and more under each arm. Laloo was very much afraid; he crept into hiding behind one of the well-parapets, and watched the woman set down the water-pots in a row.

The big bucket was down where Laloo had left it. Lightly with one hand, she touched the pole, making it rise. All the way up could be heard the sound of water-droppings within; and one by one the doves, awakened, began softly to coo. The woman threw in grain, there was a flutter of wings, then silence again, as if the magic of sleep had fallen on all. Three times she drew up the bucket and let down, till her water-pots were full.

Was ever such a water-carrier seen? One by one, she hoisted the full pots, and piled them above her head; with no rest by the way, straight from the ground to head, she lifted them; they went up like bubbles between her hands.

Laloo watching, lost count; the water-pots seemed to reach Heaven, when at last the woman stood upright under them all and started to go back by the way that she had come. The sound of her anklets died away. Laloo was left alone.

Trembling very much, he crept from his hiding-place, and there, where he had left it, was his own water-pot, filled so full that he could hardly lift it to his head. Bearing it home, he passed at the end of the village his ox-cart standing by the road, and knew that it would be no longer there when he passed the next day.

'Let Junga get well!' he said, making haste to get by.

He was very tired when at last he reached the hut; Junga was still asleep. He set down the water-pot by the old man's side, and fell upon his own bed.

Whether he had slept at all, Laloo did not know; it was still night when he heard a voice saying softly, 'Salaam, Salaam, Salaam'. Was it Junga celebrating his recovery from sickness, or was Junga feverish and dreaming?

He turned to see; by the water-pot at Junga's feet sat a beautiful woman, whose lips moved as she sung in a slow murmur the word that he had heard. Soft raiment fell about her limbs, on her wrists were bossed circlets of gold.

It was to Junga she sang.

Sorrowfully at last the old man opened his weary eyes, and looked at her. 'Wilt thou drink, my father?' said she; and dipping into the water a small cup chained to her girdle, she held it out to him.

Junga stirred feebly on his pallet, and tried to rise.

'Lie down, my father, lie down!' said she. 'The High One has ordered it. Do not move, or thou wilt wake him. When thou wakest to-morrow, thou shalt be well; but if thou know thyself then, it will be a wonder.'

So she soothed him with sweet words, making him rest.

'Salaam, Salaam, Salaam,' she sang, and the singing touched Laloo's eyelids also with such magic that, in spite of his wonder, he too fell asleep.

When he opened his eyes again, daylight was abroad; he heard the voice of Junga calling to summon him from sleep; but Junga he saw not. In his place was a strong man whose face Laloo did not remember. Yet the voice was Junga's.

'Where is Junga?' he cried.

'Oh, Apple of my eye,' replied the other, 'dost thou not know thy servant? Am I, then, fallen from thy favour, that thou art slow to know me? Look! To-day I am well again. I have already fetched water and made ready for thee to eat. Pardon me, that I was profitless to thee for one day.'

Then Laloo remembered the woman at the well, and his own water-pot, how she had filled it; and the woman also, that had sung by Junga's bed, and given him drink from a small cup chained to her girdle; and he knew that the same woman had done all. Nevertheless, he told none of these things, saying only, 'Because I love thee, Junga, I know thee; but there is none that will know thee when to-day, thou goest abroad. God has been good to us, and has sent thee back strength.'

When, presently, Junga went out to his work, Laloo went after him, for it was good to see how strong and vigorous the old man had become. Though nobody else might know him, Laloo was proud.

As Junga walked down the village, the people looking out thought they beheld a stranger. They came out and questioned him so much, that presently Junga grew angry. For when he said, 'I am Junga', they laughed; and the more he said so, the more they mocked at him.

Thus standing, the centre of a jeering crowd, all at once Junga caught sight of a child of the village, dragging behind him a toy ox-cart. And the cart went badly, for the new owner knew not how to humour its infirmities.

There could be no mistake about it: Junga, all fury, sprang forward and seizing the boy hard by the ear, cried, 'Ah, rascal!' 'Ah, thief!' and spun him this way and that.

'Ahrri-ahrri-ahrri! Wee-wee-wee!' cried the child, finding himself thus mishandled.

'Little thief, whence hast thou stolen this?' cried Junga, never loosing him.

'It is mine; yea, for I found it,' whimpered the boy.

Junga began shaking him violently.

'It is his, Junga, let him go!' cried a voice. There behind them stood Laloo.

'High One, how can this be his? It is thine,' replied Junga.

Nevertheless he let the boy go.

'Was it not broken?' said Laloo proudly, yet not letting his eyes fall on the cart. 'Why should I not let it go when it becomes of no use to me? Let it be his, Junga, since he found what I threw away.'

'The High One's will is mine,' answered Junga, a little hurt.

The crowd fell back astonished. This was Junga after all, then. What — a strong man? Yesterday he was old and about to die! The people ran into their houses, and from that shelter once again looked at him; no one would come near or speak to him now.

'This must be told!' said one, when Laloo and Junga had gone by. 'It is not what the Rajah will like to hear.'

All that day, Junga was left lonely at work on the fields; men looked at him from far off, saying nothing.

The next day, when he came back, he found that half his crop had been destroyed, and the cactus-fence broken. It was as though cattle had been driven through it, this way and that. Junga had to spend the whole day mending the gaps that had been made.

The following night, he stole out to keep watch. Towards morning he crept back to his hut, bleeding and bruised from head to foot . . . some of his ribs even were broken.

The Rajah had heard of Junga's new lease of life, and it had not pleased him.

Junga knew that no villagers had done this; though it was they who had damaged his crops; they had not the courage to touch Junga, the man who had become strong.

So Junga fell to bed, and there lay groaning out the hours; and throughout the night Laloo tended him, bandaging his wounds. Towards evening, the sick man spoke. 'It is the Rajah's message,' said he. 'He is weary of waiting for Junga to die. Little one, if I obey the Rajah, what wilt thou do?'

'I will put my hook in the Rajah's nose,' replied Laloo, with bitterness; and soon after he rose up and took his water-pot, and went out.

It was still day, and folk were abroad; but Laloo was not ashamed to be seen now. His heart was full of anger as he went down to the well. Let the High One hear him! Though he himself was weak, God should punish!

With the rope which he had this time brought with him, he let down his pot and drew up water. Back he went through the village, bearing it upon his head.

Laloo did not know why all the villagers were staring, wide-eyed and speechless as he went by; for, not looking behind him, he did not see now how after him came a tall woman, round whom the darkness of dusk gathered fast, bearing on her head a tower of water-pots. Behind her rose night; before her as she moved the last of twilight fell.

Night was over all as Laloo came to Junga's bedside.

'Here is fresh water for thee, my father,' said he, and gave the sick man to drink. Outside he heard the sound of bangles striking on metal rims, and looking, without, he saw the water-carrying woman set to ground a shining row of water vessels all full.

She came to the door of the hut, and salaamed low.

'Henceforth,' said she, 'I bring water each day to my lord; since it is ordained that the wells shall be dry.'

So the villagers found it next morning; and also the Rajah in his palace. There was barely enough water left in the land to keep body and soul together.

Word went to the Rajah: 'The day that his man was struck, Laloo the rain-child went down with his water-pot and carried away the wells. He keeps them at his door, there they brim and fail not; but not a soul dare go near, lest his curse should be upon us. Mud only is left for us to drink.'

It was even as they had said. For many days, while the whole country withered in the drought that had fallen on it, Laloo stayed within and nursed Junga, caring nothing for what went on outside.

After a while, however, came messengers from the Rajah, begging for the curse to be removed. All the gifts that they brought Laloo threw back at them.

'Let the Rajah come himself,' he said, and returned to his nursing.

At last there was no help for it, the Rajah came. All the people came with him. Laloo looked out and saw the plain covered with people waiting for him to appear. 'My father,' said he to Junga, 'hast thou enough strength to rise and sit up, and be in state? My hook is in the Rajah's nose, and he is waiting to come to thee, but it were better for all the people to see.'

'High One,' answered Junga, 'command my limbs, and they obey.'

So Junga came and sat in the doorway of the hut; and Laloo stood by his side, and spoke.

'Your Rajah,' he said, 'has beaten my servant, who has also been father to me. We were peaceful, but he made war. I am the son of many Rajahs, was I to suffer it?'

'The men that did it shall die!' said the Rajah, very meekly; for he spoke in the ears of very thirsty people.

'The jackal said, you may kill my fleas!' answered Laloo scornfully. 'Brother-in-law, would you be less thirsty, it were well for you to take off your turban!'

'I, a Rajah!' cried that potentate, greatly scandalized, 'unloose my turban to the son of him that I dethroned?'

'Nay, not to me!' said Laloo smiling. 'Not against me hast thou sinned.'

'To whom, then?' inquired the Rajah. 'Dost thou speak for the Gods?'

'As may be,' answered Laloo. 'For the matter in hand my father Junga shall be thy go-between. Take off from thy head the top-storey of thine arrogance, and go to him. It is an easy matter!'

The Rajah hesitated, trembling with shame and rage.

Laloo said, 'Rajah, look over thy shoulder! There are people who remember that I am the son of their old Rajah. Maybe I have but to lift a finger!'

It was true. By the sound of them they were a very thirsty people. The Rajah hesitated no longer; he came forward and uncovered at Junga's knees. A strange silence fell upon the crowd.

'It is enough,' said Junga simply. 'Let the Rajah cover himself.'

'Is there nothing else, Junga?' inquired Laloo.

'For the High One,' said Junga, 'a new ox-cart.'

'I will provide,' said the abased Rajah.

But provision was not to be in his hands any longer. 'Does he suppose,' cried the people, 'he, who has uncovered and humbled himself in our eyes, that he shall any more be ruler over us? Thou, son of our old Rajah, judge if such a thing be possible.'

'Possible, maybe,' he answered, 'but not in the least probable. Lo, yonder I see signs of rain. Go to your homes in peace, for you are a very thirsty people.'

So from that hour a new Rajah of the old line of Rajahs began to reign.

'Oh, thou fount of wisdom, delight of my heart!' cried Junga, when presently they were alone together in the palace of Laloo's fathers. 'Thou art grown old before thy time; all thy youth has fled from thee!' Laloo answered, 'To-night, the woman from the well shall bring it back to me, for behold the drought is over. When thou wast sick, thy old age fell upon me; soon it shall return to thee. Art thou content, Junga?'

'As the dove that returneth to the well-shadow, O Light of my life,' answered the faithful servant, and laid gentle hands between Laloo's knees.

What can we Believe?
    [Letters exchanged between Dick Sheppard and L.H. from 1922 to 1937]

August 14th, 1932

I SAW a lovely sight in Glastonbury church the other day. You may or may not know that John Camel, Treasurer of the Abbey, lies here — in stone effigy at any rate. And recently he has been brought back to his proper place in the south transept, with a side-altar lying eastward at his feet, and behind his head a window looking west. I went in, just when the sun was at its best moment of downwardness, striking across the tomb from head to foot. It must have been the angle of light for which the sculptor designed it. The face is beautiful anyway and always, a very real piece of sculpture. But seen at that moment, with the light so falling, it was perfectly lovely; the modelling of it became exquisite, and so wonderfully and sleepingly alive, that I kissed him; and, because he was so beautiful, I said 'Pray for me!' which I should *not* have done had he *not* been beautiful. For it was not to the soul of John Camel that I sent word (not being at all sure that his soul exists in any separate sense at all), but to the still present — presenting and presentable — soul of the artist, which was still there, *not* brought down to the dust, but just as much alive as on the day when the figure was finished, even though the tip of the nose has been broken off, and the face tattooed here and there with the initials of silly nonentities who had the cemetery-sense of things — individualism gone rampant.

November 2nd, 1932

In man's own conception of himself, personality is top-notch: so, quite naturally, he ascribes it to his God, as a thing from everlasting. But directly you have, in the evolution of life, that human standard of mind which, with the *élan vital* behind it, starts searching into the unknown with a feeling for connecting-up past, present, and future in a logical sequence, and with the great driving force of evolutionary purpose, or tendency, immanent in all its bones, then, I think, man will inevitably interpret his reachings out towards his future destiny in terms of person- ality — that his quest for 'the one far-off divine event', the Unity of Life that is to be, will seem to him *like* a personal God, personally responding, even though it may in fact be that great spiritual *omnium gatherum* which we call the Communion of Saints — a reservoir of spiritual unity which he draws upon from the past and pours himself into for the future. And just as we say that Christ the perfected man was, by His very perfection, of the substance of His Father, the Incarnate Word, so will perfected man be eventually that Body of Christ which (according to St. Paul in one of his best moments of inspiration), is now a-building: we going to make the joints and articulations thereof. Indeed, is not the work of Creation just God (latent) making Himself articulate and *self*-expressive, first through the disparate and discursive selves of men, until He finds Himself in the ultimate all-uniting Self of Christ — the all-in-all of all selves joined to- gether? For another simile of which, read *Old Bottles*[1], with the *Rose of Dante* as its final vision of the all-embracing fact of immortality.

March 14th, 1933

The 'personality' problem continues to intrigue me. Man, feeling it to be his own top-notch of attainment, gives it an anthropomorphic inter- pretation, and imposes it on the pre-existing Cause of all things. But I'm feeling more and more that what we call 'personality' is just *that* element of the *élan vital* which gives to *every* form of life into which it enters its fullest power of pushing itself, of reaching out to others, and giving into others — impressing, merging, absorbing, and so *forming itself to completion*. And though this is creative in result, we must get rid of the idea that it is 'design' coming from *outside*: it is design from within. No God sat down, or stood up, to design a rose; but into the prehistoric evolution of the rose went the stream of life with a sort of *Will* in it; and on given, or gradually acquired materials, did its best, drawing equally from root and environ- ment, with all the 'Will' of which it was capable; and so, from within and without (and had there *not* been a *within* and a *without*, nothing would have been possible) came the rose into being. And equally, from other roots

[1] *Ye Fearful Saints.*

175

and in other environments came the crocodile into being; quite beautiful and fitting and efficient in its way; but (without any compunction, or reason why not), quite willing and eager to eat up dear little Egyptian babies (including Moses) when they came within the scope of its activities and the scoop of its jaws. Wherever life takes on character (and where does it not?) there, in germ, we have what, in man, becomes personality. The Life-Will gradually rises to a complexity of give-and-take which produces consciousness; then consciousness evolves memory; then memory evolves criticism of life, judgment, power of comparison, an estimate of results produced by past actions, which leads inevitably at last to an acquirement which we call the 'moral sense', or the knowledge of right and wrong. But that moral sense is very largely — if not entirely — a product of the social relation: so that a man, in one type of social relations, would regard as wrong what, in another type of social relations, he would regard as right; and would have quite a clear conscience in doing in one environment what he would be ashamed of doing in another; but always with the possibility of originality of thought leading him in a revolution- ary direction away from one code of morality to another, and a better (or a worse) one. Take as an instance Huckleberry Finn's bad conscience over helping the runaway slave, against 'the law of the land'.

March 5th, 1934

Yesterday such a pitiful tragedy befell us. Our pet robin which came and ate its breakfast with us daily, went and got caught in a trap set for mice in one of our seed-frames. My sister came and found him dead, and sat for an hour or more holding him in her hand hoping to bring him back to life, and weeping over him, because, in a way, *we* had killed him. Of course it was a case of Rousseau's 'social contract'; for had it been the intended mouse that we had caught and killed, we should have been quite callous about it, or even satisfied — though the pain caused would have been just the same. What makes life 'sacred'? Is it merely the value we put on it, according to our likes and dislikes? I was, truly, far more upset and grieved over that small robin, with whom we had contracted friend- ship, than over a young man killed in a motor-smash whom I knew and liked, but who wasn't specially my friend, or my concern. Isn't senti- mentality rather a heartless and self-indulgent thing, when its proportions get so wrong? . . .

June 7th, 1935

Silk is a lovely material; but its use was *not* designed by God, but discovered by man. And I do wish people who talk about God's 'designing' of this, that, and the other, would think a little more directly and less romantically, and realize that, if God did in any sense 'design' the orders and functionings of things created, He did it *entirely* immanently and not transcendentally, and that the mind of the spider was as necessary for the construction of the spider's web as the mind of man for the extraction of a silk-dress from a worm's cocoon. The Word did not pick up the spider, and put him on to the web, and say, 'There, my dear, that's your home!' On the contrary *He* accepted the *spider's* word for it, and only by the eternal process of incarnation, by filtering Himself into and through the life and brain and blood of a spider did His making of a spider's web become possible. He didn't know anything about *singing* till — by the loudspeakers of bird's beaks and men's mouths — larynxes provided it; and if your platonists think it blasphemous not to ascribe the origins of beauty to a pattern hung up in the Heavens before worlds were, let them find compensatory comfort in the fact that God knew nothing about *blood-sucking* till the mosquito taught Him the art, and nothing about the nice trick of eating a titbit out of a live rabbit and leaving it to die a lingering death, till the ferret became a gormandizer, selective in its tastes. It's all tommy-rot to give God the credit for the song of the thrush, if you don't also give Him the discredit for the other darker things which man is reasonably trying to get rid of.

August 5th, 1934

What *are* you going to say to your believers about this wet Bank Holiday? People are always having to make excuses for God, and apologizing for His behaviour nowadays; and must go on doing so until they alter their ideas of what 'God' means. So here's a suggestion, based on the mentality of a dear old Quaker lady-friend (now in the bosom of the Clerk of the Weather, as she believed Him to be): 'You see, a *dry* Bank Holiday would have been so dangerous for the heaths! People are *so* careless with their matches. And it's much better to have a day's holiday spoiled, than heaths and woods which would take years to recover.' My own heterodox explanation — if you want to have it — is that God occupies His creation much as we occupy our bodies, in which a large part of the operations are subconscious and automatic; heart-beat, growth of nails and hair, digestion, etc. go on by themselves uncontrolled by will. And so, by analogy, the thunder is not — as Tennyson supposed — God's *voice*, but only the sounding of his bowels (which, unlike Isaiah's, do *not* sound like a harp); and the rain is a necessary process of micturition (is that the polite word for it?) having nothing whatever to do with mercy and loving-kindness.

And as I am supposed to be one of your religious (or irreligious) influences, I would like to know whether in past weeks you have been praying for rain; and then, when Bank Holiday approached, praying for it to be fine — as you should have done, in case God had forgotten the date, and how much it meant to millions of the deserving poor — and whether in doing this, as perhaps you were told to do by your Bishop (who believes that when he picks up his watch from the pulpit-ledge he 'suspends the law of gravitation'!) whether, in doing it, you *believed* in it? And if you didn't, why did you? Doesn't superstition about God's control of the weather give Him a bad character, and make Him a 'spoil-sport' on a colossal scale? And is not a drought in its operation (if preventable) far more cruel than Hitler at his worst, and more silly (for a Creator who is 'Disposer Supreme') than — — — at his best?

At which point, spiritually out of breath at the high altitude of my theological argument, I stop.

July 30th, 1935

This that follows is not a hymn, merely a commentary on the rabid orgy of self-righteousness which has got hold of nations and peoples at this present time of distress; but I think it has always been the main cause of the world's suffering and wrong — people doing horrible unChrist-like things because they are sure that they are *right*! It's *then* that the evil is so doubly hard to cure.

Deus Loquitur

Oh, me! for this world of mine! 'Tis an old, old song,
The horrible things man does when he knows it's wrong.
But here's the truth . . . I've far more cause for fright
At the much worse things he does when he '*knows he's right!*'

I suppose 'cause for fright' is a disrespectful statement; but you may remember how another 'Commander in Chief' said the same thing about those who were supposed to be under his orders — Wellington, when he inspected the drafts sent out to his army in Spain; 'I don't know how they'll strike the French, but they frighten *me*!' . . .

January 1927

I begin to think that man's theory of God and man's practice of God are very much of a piece, and that you can't separate them; and that it is because there is something wrong in the theology of the Church that she gives her countenance to wrong practices, such as war.

Conditions of war have so enormously changed and worsened in their effects upon society — the interdependence of our international relations has become so increasingly sensitized and extended, and the political and the economic results of war (and I think also the moral results, because war is now on such a large scale that the mind of the whole world is infected by it) have proved themselves so ludicrously bad in proportion to the expected good — that, intellectually, war has become a bad joke. Once embarked on war you *must* be dishonest, you must override the rights of neutrals, and the rights of conscience; you must tell lies about your opponent's doings, while you whitewash your own; you must make unclean treaties to reconcile divergent interests and win fresh alliances. Committed to the arbitrament of physical force (over a dispute which you loudly proclaim to be a moral one) you must — if you would contend successfully — be ready to do all kinds of moral wrong. It seems to me absolutely hypocritical to say that you can hope to win a war without throwing to the winds the bulk of the moral laws which man has made and ascribed to God.

Therefore I don't see how God can be the God of battles (though the Church and the Bible both say that He is), or how we can hope to improve our position by asking Him to take a hand in it. It is an ugly, dirty, dishonest business. You may embark on war for a just cause; but you cannot wage war justly, or make a just peace. (It requires a Bishop of ——— to say that the peace of Versailles was 'not only just, but generous!')

The position, as I now see it, is that the bulk of people who call themselves Christians do really place Country first and Christianity second, making patriotism their God. And by patriotism I mean, 'My Country, right or wrong'. And the question boils down to this. Can anyone be really Christian, whose main article of faith in practice is — 'My Country, right or wrong'?

I myself am so 'unpatriotic' that if I believe we have dealt selfishly and unjustly with — say — China or Russia, then I want our armies and our diplomacy to be beaten, even though the immediate results of the defeat of England by China or Russia might seem more disastrous to the world and civilization than defeat in the other direction. For I don't believe that the rise and fall of Empires, however good and great, is decisive for the coming of God's Kingdom on earth. The fall of the Roman Empire must have seemed, at the time, the biggest possible disaster for the advance of civilization in the then world. But was it?

There is a Christ I so much believe in, that I have faith that He will rise again however much men pile the dead-weight of ruined systems and destroyed nations upon His tomb. The angel-genius of the human race will, at some dawn of day, come and roll away the stone. I suppose it is not usual to think of Rome, all through its history, as the matrix of one part of the body of Christ, and Greece of another, and England, my England, of another; and of these as all having to die and rise again from the dead before the true spiritual part of them can become manifest to the world. Most nations die, I suppose, because of their sins; but if one nation died because of its righteousness, as the Christ of history died upon the Cross, what a wonderful new Incarnation that would be to prove, and what a wonderful new faith for the troubled nations it might give rise to: it might convert nation-worship back to Christianity again.

The Unexpected Years   (1936)

FAMILY PRAYERS

NOTHING in this world is less meek than a child bent upon getting its own way; and if the Kingdom of Heaven really is composed of such material, it can only be because, while according to Scripture, the meek shall possess the *Earth*, the Kingdom of Heaven suffers violence, and the violent take it by force.

The earliest family quarrel that I can remember was over the things of Heaven, which we were trying to take from each other by force. It was a winter's dawn; a quarter of a mile away the high-raised roof of Bromsgrove School, with its small bell-cot, stood out in silhouette against one of those lovely variegated dawns which, ranging from green to gold, and from gold to pale rose and crimson, belong more especially to the season of late sun-risings. Four of us stood on a seat by the night-nursery window, disputing violently as to which of those clouds of glory should be ours. Probably we all wanted the same colours, and what each decided to be his or hers could not be shared by another. Our mother came and caught us at it, and we were sharply forbidden ever again to take, as our own, things so much belonging to Heaven.

My mother's scoldings must have had a virtue about them — perhaps because of their rareness — which other scoldings lacked; for I did, from that incident, carry away an uncomfortable sense of foolish behaviour — the beginning, maybe, of a feeling that beauty was holy, and for that reason not to be quarrelled about.

.   .   .   .   .

Extempore prayer was not a recognized practice in our family; it sounded strange in our ears, for with us prayer was like ritual, and had a fixed form. In its fixity lay its virtue. The earliest prayer I can remember saying — and I said it for years — ran as follows:

> Cargo bress my dear father and mother, my brothers and sisters, and make me a good boy, for Jesus Christ's sake. Amen.

'Cargo bress' was my infantile pronunciation of 'Pray God bless'. I cannot now remember whether to me it meant, 'Pray God bless', or was only an invocative abracadabra — preliminary flourish to the statement that I was a family child, and that I wished my family well; but I am pretty sure that I continued to say, 'Cargo bress' long after I could have said the words, 'Pray God bless' quite plainly; and that I continued to do so because the meaning of the phrase was quite unimportant to me at that time. The gist — the real substance of my prayer — was composed not of God, but of father, mother, brothers and sisters, with a side reference to the Hero of the only storybook I then knew, which had coloured pictures, and was therefore my favourite one.

But in spite of God being the unimportant element in it, it was not a bad prayer as a child's prayers go. In that 'grace before bed' and after, I rehearsed the names of the people whom I most cared about, or who most mattered to me; and in that vital connection I wished myself 'a good boy' for the sake of my favourite storybook. Can a small child's mind go much further in a spiritual direction, until he has had a real and personal experience of what 'God' stands for, and what 'for Jesus Christ's sake' really means? And what exactly is the value of bringing God into it at all, except to establish an association which will afterwards become valuable, between what a child knows and loves, and what — so far — he does *not* know or love? Most certainly at the time when I made that prayer a daily habit — or when the habit was made for me by others — I did love my father and mother devotedly and continuously, and my brothers and sisters with breaks and reservations — on their good days, that is to say. . . .

In that respect my prayer made a truthful distinction: it called my father and mother 'dear', it did not call my brothers and sisters 'dear'. And they were *not*, or not often enough to have the epithet generically applied to them; they had got to earn it. And so, alas, had God Himself to earn or to win the love which was then lacking in me. I am quite sure that during those early years, while my family love was growing, my love for God was non-existent, and my love for Jesus Christ not much more than my love for Robinson Crusoe. And is not that the natural order of things, and only what one should expect, seeing that in normal natures birth, vaccination, and teething come first, and religious experience only second — and very often a bad second at that? It is true that the Roman Church tells us of certain saints who from their very birth have refused the breast every Friday as an act of pious self-denial; but those religious monstrosities do not occur in the Church of England, since there they are not expected to occur; and though such freaks of infantile ritual may please the professional hagiologists, one wonders if they can possibly be pleasing to God — to any God conceivable by reasonable minds.

As years went on, religion in our Victorian family took two widely differing forms — each having its own proper time and place. The dining-room was the place for the one, the bedroom for the other. In its open expression it was rigidly formal and regular — entirely empty of spirituality, almost of meaning; in its private form it was as secret and surreptitious as our daily fulfilment of the needs of nature. For any of us to have been caught praying by anyone else would have been an indecency — we should have felt exposed and uncomfortable for the rest of the day. But when family prayers were being said there was no such bashfulness — to that sort of 'mixed bathing' we were hardened, and we knelt about the room, each in his selected place, and endured with stony indifference while the infliction lasted.

Prayers preceded breakfast; to be late for prayers was to lose one's bacon, and have only porridge and dry bread. A minute after the ringing of the breakfast bell, the maids were summoned from the kitchen. They came and stood facing us in a row before the sideboard. When my father had invoked the Trinity, they whisked round and knelt towards it while prayers were being said. Prayers lasted three or four minutes; they included the Lord's Prayer, in which we all joined. For that there was no fixed place; and I recall one or two occasions in later life when my father, forgetting whether he had said it or not, began saying it again. It was then my peculiar joy to keep him at it — though after the first sentence, becoming aware that he had said it before, he would want to stop; but as he could not stop *me*, he had to go on, and we ran it as a duet, the rest of the family keeping a disapproving silence. They had said it once; they were not going to say it again — it was a waste of words. At that time I was becoming the religious one of the family — which does not mean that I was becoming good: far from it! But a love for ritualistic observance had got hold of me; and since in the Church service the Lord's Prayer was repeated twice, and even thrice, why not domestically also? So, if my father chose to begin it a second time, I made him go on with it.

A much earlier instance of the exceeding uselessness of family prayer for the cleansing of hearts, and allaying of hatred and malice, must have dated somewhere about when I was seven. I had been having a tussle with my brother Basil for the possession of a favourite chair; and just on the entry of the servants at the call of prayers, he had hit me last. From that unfinished conflict our governess had snatched me away to kneel beside her, as I then always did. We prayed, we confessed our sins, we asked forgiveness, we recited the Lord's Prayer. The moment the 'Grace of our Lord' had been said, I leapt to my feet, and gave Basil the return smack that was his due. For that I was sent out to have breakfast in the schoolroom — with no bacon to it.

I felt that it was not fair. Basil had hit me first, and had also hit me last. Neither prayer nor punishment did me any good. And yet with this demonstration before their eyes that prayer meant nothing to me, my elders made no attempt to give it reality.

One hears often nowadays of the great loss to religious life among the young which has come about from the discontinuance of family prayers. Yet I believe that, in our family, it did us more harm than good, and when, in my first years of adolescence religion became more real to me, family prayers were a most painful ordeal, from which I would gladly have escaped if I could, because of their unreality. It was much the same with grace before meat; it did not inculcate the thankful spirit. What we were about to receive were very often the shortcomings of the cook, and we were *not* thankful for them. Complaint was immediate and loud.

Years later, when I had come to London with my elder sister, a relative visiting us found, to her grave disapproval, that we had ceased to say grace, and asked why. I replied, a little restively perhaps, 'In order to try to cultivate a more thankful spirit than the saying of grace ever produced at home'. It was, of course, an annoying thing to say, and perhaps it was meant to be; but one found it hard sometimes not to exact vengeance, when our time came for freedom and free speech, for the afflictions of our youth.

Collected Poems   (1937)

GREEN ARRAS (1896)

THE CORN-KEEPER

A BLIGHT came into the corn by night;
He seemed an angel in God's sight.

All the corn-tops looked at him;
Dark he stood on the moon's rim.

184

Out of the farm a child's soul
Came, and into the moonlight stole.

Shadowy hands reached over the wheat,
And fell upon the child-soul's feet.

'My body sleeps in a warm bed,'
He looked over the corn, and said;

'I am sent to gather dreams,
In among the white moonbeams,

'White moonbeams, all in a row:
I must be back at the first cock-crow:

'What shall I take, and put in the head
Of my warm body in his warm bed?

'I must fashion a dream for him,
Ready before the moon gets dim.'

Said the Blight, 'Then take my hand,
Come with me through the corn-land!'

'Is it not too far to go?
Shall I be back before cock-crow?'

'Not too far, and not too near;
I shall have hold of your hand, my dear.'

Said the child, 'Before I was born,
God was good to my father's corn,

'Night and day, from His Home's great height.
Are you the angel on guard to-night?'

Quoth the other, 'Wherever I go,
I am a sort of a scare-crow.'

Laughed the child, 'Why that's fun too!
Make my body to dream of you!'

But a thousand whispers of wheat,
Following after the child-soul's feet,

Cried, 'Turn back, lest the cock crow morn
While you are wandering over the corn!'

Then the happy soul of the child
Kissed them under their heads, and smiled,

Holding the Blight by both hands,
As they went up the corn-lands.

   .   .   .   .

All of a sudden the cock crew hard,
And the watch-dog howled in the farm-yard;

But the child's body lay too still
For a dream to be under his brain-sill.

   .   .   .   .

One corn-stem they gave him to hold,
A slender sceptre headed with gold.

Never a one of them all could know
Why the corn kept kissing him so:

No one knew how, before he was born,
God was good to his father's corn.

FAILURE

WHEN you are dead, when all you could not do
  Leaves quiet the worn hands, the weary head,
Asking not any service more of you,
  Requiting you with peace when you are dead;

When, like a robe, you lay your body by,
  Unloosed at last, — how worn, and soiled, and frayed! —
Is it not pleasant just to let it lie
  Unused, and be moth-eaten in the shade?

Folding earth's silence round you like a shroud,
  Do you just know that what you have is best: —
Thus to have slipt unfamous from the crowd;
  Thus, having failed and failed, to be at rest?

Oh, having, not to know! Yet oh, my dear,
  Since to be quit of self is to be blest;
Freed from the world, to leave no imprint here, —
  Is this not best?

Spikenard A book of Devotional Love Poems   (1898)

THE SWADDLING BANDS

O LOVE, when human sense first touched Thine eyes,
Bidding them tell Thee naught, save through disguise
Of specious form, and close embodiment,
Seemed it not sad that life such darkness lent,
While to Thy new-born brain the wonder grew
How earthly sight could so shut out the Heavenly view?

For Thou from the embrace of Mary's heart
Must turn and see her play her earthly part:
    Can that poor robe, and this pain-bearing face,
    Cover the highly favoured, full of Grace?
And can this weary elder Thou dost see
The Heaven-taught Joseph be?
    And in this cabin'd space
      Of stable-rock
      Does not the whole world flock
To worship at Thy knee?

Now, this first time, Thine eyes must look on walls:
  Where Thy hands cannot reach
  Hands stretch and do beseech;
Where Thine ear cannot hear, Thine earth for succour calls!

Oh, little Heart,
  Beat fast, and grow!
The whole world's smart
  Through Thee, one day, must flow.
Oh, childish ears, attend,
Being friend to all men's fears!
  Oh, childish eyes,
  Would ye of man be wise,
Ye must the channel be to all men's tears!

So wait, and learn Thy strict estate,
Until to Thee this earth commits her fate!
  Each day a little knowledge brings:
  The shepherd's crook, the crown of kings,
In time shall prove Thee great,
When Hand and Head bear up their awful weight.
  Now round Thee, Holy Child,
  Life dawns in darkness mild:
Out in the star-eyed night a Herald sings
  Of Nature reconciled.
Thou canst not see that star, nor hear those pastoral wings:
Yet first the shepherds come to gaze, and then the kings!

THE SOUL AND THE BODY

UNDER so many shadows am I laid,
Amid these builded walls that flesh hath made
Fivefold about me — every sense a shade,
  How shall I see Light in a light so dim?
  Windows away from God are walls from Him:
Of walls, then, am I made.

These things I do,
  These other things I see,
  Shape not for me
Aught that I dare name true:
  Rather they seem to be
Hard riddles that, with sloth and pain,
I must again
  Undo.

How shall mine eyes
Things, that they love exceedingly, despise?
How shall my flesh defeat
All things my heart names sweet?
  Nay, how shall I be wise,
  When all my brain, led by light folly, lies —
Nor can escape deceit,
  Save by disguise;
Itself at once the cheated, and the cheat!

O dust, have faith according to the term
Of this life's lease! Ere the corrupting worm
Have power to destroy the dust thou art;
  Ere the dark rust
Of death can clog the engine of thy heart.
Great is thine honour, though thou walk in night;
For fringes of thy darkness feel the Light
  Which was ordained to be
  When God, the Just,
From shadow shaping thee,
  Put trust
  In dust.

RUE (1899)

Of old betwixt the gods and earth,
  High-headed, girt with cloud
Dividing misery and mirth,
  Old Atlas stood and bowed.

Close to the high celestial gate
    He bent a drowsy brain:
While far below his feet set weight
    On furrowed fields of pain.

The earth's far cry sang faint, and dim
    Her face toward him grew:
His head was crowned with light; round him
    The immortal laughters flew.

And yet he tired of that high place,
    And thrust away the prize:
Lifting a dead, indignant face
    Of stone toward the skies.

      ·   ·

Long through the night the new-born lamb
    Utters its first complaint;
By the dead body of its dam
    The cry goes low and faint:

Till faint against the dawn this birth,
    Which bears a twilight's span,
Shall pass, and let alone to earth
    The sorry needs of man.

Now, ere the covering darkness yield,
    Lie down, dear lamb, lie down:
Better to die here in the field
    Than yonder in the town;

Where fast before the butchering knife
    A dumb death thins the herd:
Oh, better now to pass from life
    While life seems worth a word!

Out on the downs the shepherds cry
    The silly sheep-dogs yelp:
Then quickly ease my heart, and die,
    Lest I should bring you help!

    ·   ·   ·   ·

You, the dear trouble of my days,
   When life shall let me cease,
Turn once aside from kinder ways
   And look upon my peace!

Let your feet rest upon my roof,
   And for the love we bore,
Forgive the heart, so far aloof,
   You cannot trouble more.

For, if the dead man had his will,
   I doubt not he would rise,
And waste his soul in longing still,
   With looking on your eyes.

So come, when you have lost your power,
   And pardon my release:
And set your feet to rest an hour,
   A seal upon my peace.

The Little Land   (1899)

THE CITY OF SLEEP

MANIKIN, maker of dreams,
   Came to the city of sleep:
The watch was on guard, and the gates were barred,
   And the moat was deep.

'Who is on my side, who?'
   Moonbeams rose in a row:
He tuned them loud betwixt town and cloud,
   But his voice was low.

He sang a song of the moon
  For loan of her silver beams;
Misty and fair, and afloat in air,
  Lay the ladder of dreams.

He harped by river and hill;
  And the river forgot to flow,
And the wind in the grass forgot to pass,
  And the grass to grow.

He harped to the heart of earth
  Where honey in hive lies sweet;
And that sound leapt through the gates, and crept
  Through the silent street.

Manikin, maker of dreams,
  He pursed his lips to pipe:
And the strange and the new grew near and true,
  For the time was ripe.

He piped to the hearts of men:
  And dreamers rose up straight,
To drift unbarred by the drowsy guard,
  And beyond the gate.

He piped the dream of the maid:
  And her heart was up and away;
And fast it beat, and hurried her feet
  To the gates of day.

He piped the dream of the mother,
  The cry of her babe for food:
She rose from rest to give it the breast;
  And that was good!

He piped the dream of the child:
  And into its hands and feet
Came tunes to play of the livelong day;
  And that was sweet!

He piped to the heart of youth:
   And the heart of youth had sight
Of love to be won, and a race to run;
   And that was right!

He piped the song of age:
   And that was a far-off song, —
When life made haste and the mouth could taste: —
   But that was wrong!

Manikin, maker of dreams,
   Had piped himself to sleep:
The watch was on guard, and the gates were barred,
   And the moat was deep!

Mendicant Rhymes   (1906)

DEUS NOSTER IGNIS CONSUMENS

To Him be praise who made
   Desire more fair than rest:
Better the prayer while prayed,
   Than the attained bequest.
Man goes from strength to strength,
   Fresh with each draught of pain,
Only to fail at length
   Of heights he could not gain.

The soul of live desire,
   How shall it mate with dust?
To whom was given fire —
   For ashes shall he lust?
Man's tenure is but breath,
   His flesh a vesture worn:
Let him that fears not death
   Fear not to rest unborn.

THE HEART OF PEACE

The crown entails the curse;
   Here all the fame that's won,
A harvest for the hearse,
   Falls withered to the sun;
There, weary of reward,
   The victor strips his wreath;
There, sick with deaths, the sword
   Sighs back into the sheath.

THE FELLOW-TRAVELLERS

FELLOW-TRAVELLERS here with me,
   Loose for good each others loads.
Here we come to the cross-roads:
   Here must parting be.

Where will you five be to-night?
   Where shall I? We little know.
Loosed from you, I let you go
   Utterly from sight.

Far away go taste and touch,
   Far go sight, and sound, and smell.
Fellow-travellers, fare you well —
   You I loved so much.

The Heart of Peace   (1919)

THE TRUE LOVER

So much have friends deceived me
And fickle lovers grieved me,
   Of so much wealth,
   And youth, and health
Has travelling Time relieved me,
   That being thereby set free,
   Now back I come to Thee.

By such dark fates befriended,
Deserted, unattended,
  O'er hard and rough
  I've jogged enough,
Down ways that never ended.
  So, footsore though I be,
  Here back I come to Thee.

But wouldst Thou further ask me
Of my deserts, or task me
  To show Thee why,
  Abandoned, I
Seek *Thee*, — and so unmask me
  Of any proof or plea
  That brings me back to Thee:

Lord, in such uncouth places
Have I beheld kind faces,
  Where dross for gold
  Was bought and sold
Have met such kind embraces, —
  Such memories, oh see!
  Have brought me back to Thee!

For man, that was Thy making,
Sleeps long, but at awaking
  Finds in his breast
  Th' unbidden guest;
So, after all forsaking,
  As blind men made me see,
  Here back I come to Thee.

A thousand times man faileth,
Him trouble so assaileth;
  Heart cries in haste,
  'All flesh is waste!'
Yet, here, too, love prevaileth.

So, when thereof I taste
In hearts that are not free,
    To freedom's Home I haste; —
And back I come to Thee.

The Love Concealed (1937)

THE HELP-GIVERS
(E.T. and F.B., ob. February 1923)

Pride held my will:
Too much was to disown,
Too many a need I still could not unsay;
High Help at hand,
I willed to stand alone;
Fearful for self, for self I would not pray.

Then came a day:
Judged and condemned, enduring without hope, —
I learned how near at hand two prisoners lay
In separate cells, each waiting for the rope:
Fearful of that whose touch would put away
All griefs and fears:
And helpless I, to aid
Their hapless state —
Lighten, or lift from them that stroke of fate —
With heartfelt tears,
For those poor souls I prayed,
That them from utter wreck
Some Help might save.

Then to my heart there came a rending wave:
Across *my* neck a sudden rope was flung;
Up went a light,
And I of land had sight, —

Where, dark against the sky, two murderers clung,
And in the baffling storm, hand over hand,
Hauled on the line
Which drew my feet to land!

Lord, in Thy Kingdom's day, remember them —
Whate'er they did — who helped me in my need,
To touch Thy raiment's hem!

VALE!

Once I shall see you again, or twice,
    Ere we part, my friend:
One more coming or two must suffice
    To a whole life's end.

Then, shall I miss you so much?
    Or, fast as I hold you now,
Faster for ever find you in touch? —
    From the past, guess how.

Near or far, knit or apart —
    Think of me well or ill;
Here in my lonely heart
    You will be coming still:

Here, at the thought of your face,
    Your hand will be at my door:
Quick! and my heart in its place
    Upon yours evermore.

What Next? Provocative Tales of Faith and Morals   (1938)

THE MAN WHO DID NOT PRAY

NAHTI-POO, son of Kayrahmam the rope-maker, had been left motherless from his first year, to a bringing-up which was all his own. The hum of his father's wheel, as he lay below watching the spin of the loop which seemed never to end, had been his only cradle-song. Through the green shade of overhanging boughs came tempered light; and the large gentle kine roving the village street stepped over but did not tread on him. As soon as he could crawl, he began to explore the world, and presently (when he got upon his feet) to adventure in it; and so long as Nahti-poo in his goings kept clear of the loop, his father, busy at making ends meet, left him benevolently alone, and caused him no grief.

Twice a day they dipped fingers in the same bowl, and at night shared the same sleeping-mat under a common roof; and with this and that, the sum total of parental care, Nahti-poo's needs were satisfied and his mind content. All about the world he saw the wonderful beauty of things left to themselves, of sunlight and shade, of leaves that grew, and water that ran; of clouds adrift on the blue air; and of winds that slept and woke, yet had no form, and whose cause he could not discover. But things which moved were good to the eye, sounds good to the ear, fruit and grain good to the taste; the days were beautifully long, the nights were beautifully short; clay mixed with water made mud-pies; curled leaves floated like boats upon the stream; thrown pebbles skimmed over it like wild geese; other children shared in his games — what more in the world could he want? For a long time life was so simple he never questioned it. But as time went on, sometimes alone, sometimes in company, applying its ways and means to further uses he formed habits, opinions, acquaintances, and so, presently, a mind of his own. Then with his mind he began to discover the meaning of things, and life became more interesting.

In the centre of the village stood the temple, guarded by an old priest; and every day, singly or in groups, or at times of festival all together in a crowd, the villagers went in to the temple to pray. Sometimes, but not so often as others, Kayrahmam the rope-maker went too; and on high and special occasions he took Nahti-poo with him. Then Nahti-poo would behold his father arrayed in a long white robe, which at other times he never wore, and would hear his voice lifted in a high melancholy wail, the sorrowfulness of which caused his eyes to fill with tears. Inside the temple indeed, Kayrahmam the silent one became quite talkative, always repeating with the rest the same form of words; and meanwhile, from all alike, went such a swaying of heads, and bending of backs, and spreading abroad of palms, as never was seen at any other time.

'Father,' said Nahti-poo as they returned together from the temple one day, 'what were you talking about in there?'

'I was praying,' said his father.

'What were you praying for?'

'The needful, my son; that without which a man would die, or live in misery.'

'But I have all that without praying for it,' said Nahti-poo; 'and other things too.'

'One may not always have them,' replied his father as one who repeats a lesson; 'man must pray, lest want come suddenly and devour him. You also, being in need, will have to pray some day.'

But Nahti-poo was no longer paying attention. Things that he had not yet come to want did not concern him. He threw up his heels and ran; life, good and abundant, surrounded him. Stretching out both hands to sunlight and air, he clasped and unclasped them as he ran; yet were his hands still empty, and the world still full of them. This was a new discovery.

'Why should I pray?' thought Nahti-poo. 'I don't want anything: everything is here.'

Suddenly he stopped. Down the street came the child of a rich man, led by his nurse, drawing upon a string a toy bullock-cart. It had coloured wheels and bells and silk tassels hanging from the yoke; and the bullocks were white with gilded horns; and the little wooden man who sat in the driver's seat had a gold turban on his head, and underneath one could see the whites of his eyes.

Nahti-poo gazed with envy and astonishment; his soul became a thing of hunger. 'If I do not have that bullock-cart,' he said to himself, 'I shall die!' So going up to the rich man's child, he said, 'I want that bullock-cart; give it me! I am bigger than you, so mine is the bigger want'.

The child stared proudly, and the nurse looked down at him with angry contempt, but did not speak. Reaching up her foot she planted it firmly and well, and Nahti-poo was left sitting in the road, very weak and small and sorry for himself, but in no wise cured of his want. There was nothing in the world he so much wanted as that toy bullock-cart. Then he remembered his father's word: want had come suddenly to devour him; he must pray. He went back to the temple; the door was still open, but the congregation had gone. This surely was the right time, for now he could pray, all alone, and the God, having no one else to listen to, could the better attend to his need; at another time chances might be against him.

Softly he approached the shrine; up there in the gloom sat the black stone image, and from the midst of the forehead, set like a jewel, the Eye of Heaven looked at him. Nahti-poo put up his hands and was about to begin his prayer — the first prayer he had ever prayed — when he heard quite near him a low sound of weeping; and there, crouched at the feet of the image he saw one whom he knew, a young woman of the village whose husband had died after they had been married only a few weeks. Though she choked and sobbed, Nahti-poo could hear plainly the words of her prayer, for many times over she repeated it, and always in the same words 'A son! O God, give me a son! That is all I ask, so that I may not have to live alone.' And as he heard, Nahti-poo drew back, for all at once he felt empty of purpose and ashamed. 'Surely,' he said to himself, 'her need is greater than mine; if I cause the Eye of Heaven to turn on me now, He may forget what she has been asking for. I will wait till her prayer has been answered, then I will come again.'

So Nahti-poo went out of the temple, not having prayed at all; and while he waited for the widow's son to be born, his desire for the bullock-cart ceased to trouble him; other things came to fill his mind and brought content.

And so it was afterwards and always. Whenever he went into the temple to pray, he found others praying before him whose need seemed greater than his, and whose prayers though often made had not been granted. It was wonderful how many things people were in need of, and, though a thousand times disappointed, went on praying for. Nahti-poo began to notice how few of all the prayers he listened to found an answer. 'It is because so many are praying,' he thought. 'God has not time to answer them. If fewer prayed, more prayers would be answered. I will wait my turn.'

Years went on, and Nahti-poo's turn never came; nevertheless he throve and grew strong, and was as happy as most people; for when he put off praying for the things he seemed to need so as to leave room for others, he would find presently that he could do almost as well without, or sometimes would even forget that he had ever wanted them. Then another want came, and then another; and Nahti-poo put them all by, because it was not his turn, or because there were others in greater need.

Now and again, however, good things would come to him quite unexpectedly, though he had not prayed for them; then Nahti-poo would laugh and sing and enjoy it as a great joke; for truly it was a thing to laugh about that so much good should come to one who had done nothing to deserve it. And he wondered to himself; 'Does God laugh also? When He does things like that, is it for a joke?' This was something he would like to know.

Nahti-poo went to the temple and inquired of the priest whether God ever made jokes; but the priest, angry at being asked such a question, cried on him as a blasphemer and drove him out. What right, indeed, had Nahti-poo to ask such a question of him — Nahti-poo who came to the temple along with the rest, but did not pray or make offerings as others did? And so, untaught by the priest, Nahti-poo went on making thoughts to suit himself, and therewith remained satisfied.

One day he saw a young calf going by in a cart, with a net over it, and its mother followed after, lowing as she went.

Nahti-poo said to his father: 'When cows pray, do the Gods answer their prayer?'

'Silly one!' said his father, 'cows cannot pray.'

'They live,' said Nahti-poo, 'and have needs just as we do.'

'They live only to die,' said Kayrahmam; 'they have not souls as we have.'

'But men die also.'

'The soul does not die. The body dies, but the soul lives on for ever. Men pray because they have souls.'

But Nahti-poo was no longer attending; he was not thinking about souls, he was thinking about cows. He went into the temple; it was quite empty. He drew near to the great image on the shrine; he and the God were alone there together.

'Eye of Heaven!' he said, but could get no further; he stopped. 'After all,' he said to himself, 'how do I know that the cow needs praying for? The Eye of Heaven sees her better than I can.'

Upon his return home, remembering his father's word, he inquired of him: 'If men's souls live for ever, why do they pray not to die?'

'Life is good,' answered the rope-maker. 'What will happen to us after we do not know.'

'But it happens all the same.'

'If we please the Gods by our prayers, they make things better for us.'

'Does it please them to be prayed to?'

'Of course! Why else should one trouble?'

'My father,' said Nahti-poo, 'I have never prayed to thee, yet thou feedest me. Art thou better than the Gods?'

Kayrahmam sat and considered awhile, theological discussion being strange to him. 'I feed thee,' he said, 'so that when thou art grown thou mayst be a support to me in my old age. Thou, also, wilt beget a son to take care of thee hereafter.'

At these words Nahti-poo's mind was filled with a great sense of worship; he went softly out and stood looking at the light. 'O Eye of Heaven!' he cried, 'I, too, shall beget a son!' It had never occurred to him before that this would happen, though every day in the temple he heard others praying that they might have children. 'Wait, wait!' he said to himself. 'It is not my turn yet. When it is, the Eye of Heaven will show it to me.'

Yet there were some he knew that went on praying in spite of everything. One was a poor woman who had been married for ten years, and in that time had born to her husband nine daughters, but no son. Every time she prayed for a son and each time a daughter came to her; on the last occasion, two. 'I should stop praying at once,' thought Nahti-poo, 'if God did that to *me*! And now, there she is going home to have more daughters! Truly the ways of men with Heaven are marvellous. Is it God, or is it themselves that they are praying to?' But though he listened hard, and considered the matter well, he could never be quite sure.

Nahti-poo was very sorry for the people whose prayers remained unanswered. 'We are too many,' he said to himself, 'and we ask too much; God cannot attend to us. Perhaps, if one were to help him, more prayers would be answered.'

The thought smiled at him. From that day forward Nahti-poo began playing a curious game; but he told nobody. If he told it, if people got to know, the fun of it would be spoiled. Standing silently in the temple, he would listen while people prayed; then secretly he would set to work and answer their prayers for them — those at least which he could.

Often they would ask for things beyond his reach or theirs; but sometimes they would ask for quite simple things, things which with a little trouble could be made, or found, or bought out of savings, but which they had not the energy or the patience to acquire; so, as the easiest way, they prayed for them. And Nahti-poo, all by himself, would set to work secretly to meet the demand; and one day as they got up from their beds and opened their doors, or were going solitary along a road, there the supplicants would find the answer to prayer awaiting them. That their prayer should be so answered always filled them with great astonishment — evidently they had not expected it; and Nahti-poo, watching secretly, would clap his heels with delight, as they ran hither and thither, crying to their neighbours to see the wonder that had happened to them, or sometimes (which was funnier still) they would look furtively up and down the road, and then take up and hide the answer to prayer under their cloaks, as though it did not really belong to them.

But Nahti-poo, though he answered many prayers, was not sure that by so doing he made people any happier. Sometimes they quarrelled fiercely as to whom the answer really belonged to; and Nahti-poo had simply to leave them to fight it out in their own way. He could not go forward and say: 'It was I who answered the prayer, and I intended it for so and so.' No; that would have spoiled everything. But he wondered sometimes if the Eye of Heaven had not just the same difficulty and the same sadness over the prayers that he answered. Did not people sometimes quarrel about them also? And if they did, what did the Eye of Heaven think about it? He began to wonder less why so many prayers were not answered; he could not doubt that the Eye of Heaven made a better choice than he did. And so, as Nahti-poo grew older, he left off playing his game, though it had so much amused him; at least he did not play it in the same way. It is not good, he thought, to deceive people.

Time passed, and Nahti-poo came to man's estate, and plied his trade of a rope-maker as his father had done before him. Kayrahmam, who had only married late in life, was beginning to be old and feeble; and Nahti-poo, fulfilling his expected use, worked to support him.

It was known now by all the people in the village that Nahti-poo was one that did not pray. This gave him a bad name, and many avoided him because of it; others shook their heads at him. 'Some day he will know better,' they said, 'but then it will be too late.'

But what puzzled them most was that although he never prayed himself, he would go into the temple regularly and listen to the prayers of others. When questioned about it he said: 'It is by what they pray that one gets to know people. What they want, tells you what they are.' If that was true, then Nahti-poo, who wanted nothing, was a difficult person to know; and of a truth none knew what to make of him — he was so different from all the rest.

The one who thought and spoke most of him was the temple priest; for neither by threats nor coaxings had he ever been able to get from Nahti-poo the offerings of meat and money which he got from others; and sometimes he would stop as he passed, and watch Nahti-poo at his rope-making with an angry eye.

'You are making a rope to hang yourself!' the priest said to him one day.

'Well,' replied Nahti-poo quite contentedly, 'that is one way of coming by one's death; and it is a shorter way than praying for it. I had an uncle who prayed five years to die of the disease that was killing him; and then ended by cutting his throat, so that the prayer could not be granted. If I ever come to hang myself I shall not ask God to tie the knot in the rope; I shall do that foolishness for myself.'

'Nahti-poo,' said the priest, 'you are a wicked man, and your mind is full of evil; God will punish you.' And more than ever he warned those who came to worship at the temple to avoid him, lest they, too, should fall into like ways of unfaithfulness.

Now all this time, while Kayrahmam his father was growing old, Nahti-poo had remained unmarried, for with the feebleness of age Kayrahmam had been taken with a curious jealousy. 'I do not want a strange woman in my house,' he said, 'to remind me that I am old.' So Nahti-poo putting off his own need, had answered his father's prayer and remained single.

But a day came when Kayrahmam was stricken for death, so that he could no longer sit at his rope-making under the shadow of the trees; and going into his hut he lay down on his sleeping-mat, and, placing his hands on the centre of his aches and pains, he began groaning aloud, and praying Heaven to have pity on him. And Nahti-poo, hearing him in such a taking, left his work and came and sat by his side, tending him from morning to night with a woman's care. But in spite of all he could do, Kayrahmam's strength failed and his pains grew worse, and on the third day he turned toward Nahti-poo, saying: 'Oh, see what a sore sickness has come upon me from the anger of Heaven at my begetting such a son! Now, therefore, repent and pray for me, lest I die!'

Then Nahti-poo came near and kneeling at the old man's feet took them between his hands and kissed them saying: 'O, my Father, life is good while it lasts, but when it fails, good is no longer in it; therefore the Gods take it from us that we may have rest. Now as I lay my hands upon thy feet because I love thee, so do thou lay thy hands upon the feet of that Life whose raiment is death. Hold His feet without fear, and it shall be well with thee.'

And when Nahti-poo had finished speaking Kayrahmam looked at him and said: 'Hear me, O Ye in Heaven, that have cursed me with a son who will not pray for me! Some day he also shall be in need. Then if he look for one to succour him, let me be that one!' And so saying Father Kayrahmam turned his face to the wall and spoke not again; and soon after he was dead.

So Nahti-poo buried his father, and went back to his rope-making. And soon after, being now free, he married a beautiful maiden named Mazurah, and for a year lived with her in great happiness and contentment. And when her time came for it, Mazurah bore him a son. But things went ill with her, and being in great pain she cried to Nahti-poo: 'Look, I have given thee a son, but behind life stands death! Now I am in great pain, but my fear is greater. Pray for me, Nahti-poo, lest I die.'

Then Nahti-poo bowed down at her side, and laying his hands in worship upon her breast, he said: 'O my beloved, surely life is good, and because thou hast brought life into the world, God will be good to thee. If it be His will that thou livest, thou wilt live; but if His will is for thee not to live He will take thy pain from thee and give thee rest. Take thy little son to thine arms and behold in him the will of God.' Then without any word Mazurah his wife looked at him; long and earnestly she looked at him, and turning her face to the wall so lay till evening, and died.

So Nahti-poo was left with only the child to care for. In his hands the child grew and throve, and Nahti-poo would sit and watch his footprints in the dust, as they went this way and that, and smile because they were so beautiful. But one day the child, when his father's back was turned, ran out in the heat of the day to play in the sun; and presently he came back saying:

'O, Father, a snake has got inside my head, and it is stinging me! If you cannot get it out I shall die!'

Nahti-poo ran to the well and got water; and making strips of linen he wound wet bandages about the child's head to cool it. But it did not ease the pain. The child lay and moaned; and Nahti-poo's heart was so full of grief that it was near to breaking. But in his grief there was one ray of comfort. 'He does not ask me to pray for him,' thought Nahti-poo. 'That is well, for if he asked me, how could I refuse?'

Before nightfall and without having spoken again, the child died, and Nahti-poo was alone. In the days that followed, Nahti-poo wished that he too might die, yet he did not pray for it. He returned to his making of ropes; but though the priest hoped and expected it, he did not hang himself. He accepted life as it came, went on with his rope-making, and gradually grew old.

As he neared his end, people began looking at him curiously, expectantly. They had been told how surely one day the Gods would punish him for his infidelity; but as they watched his growing infirmity there was nothing they could take hold of for the satisfaction of their beliefs. His body was not more weighed down by the weakness of age, nor was his countenance more sorrowful than theirs; nor did he suffer more pain. From his years of prayerlessness patience seemed to have become a habit; in seeking less from Heaven than other people he had, perhaps in the same proportion, found more. But whether it was much or little he did not talk of it; he took what came to him and was content; and though he often went to the temple and stood amongst other worshippers, never did he pray. If anyone said to him, 'Nahti-poo, why do you not pray?' he would reply, 'I have everything that I need; why should I trouble God by praying to Him? Does He not know better than I what is good for me? I hear so many praying whose prayers are not answered; why more should He attend to mine? When so many are crying out that they cannot — is it not better that one who can should wait?'

'You will wait too long, Nahti-poo!' they told him. 'Some day you will die.'

'And when I am dead,' said Nahti-poo, 'what will there be to pray about?'

'You may find yourself in Hell!' they warned him.

'If I lost myself there,' said Nahti-poo, 'then, indeed, I should have something to start praying about. But why make trouble beforehand?'

When Nahti-poo talked like that people called him a blasphemer. 'He will come to a bad end,' said they; 'of that you may be sure.'

Yet Nahti-poo could remember times, far back in his life, when he had wished and even tried to pray; but the prayer would not come. 'Wait! Wait!' he had said to himself then. 'It is not your turn; when it is, the Eye of Heaven will show it you.'

At last came the day that so many had waited for, curious to see what he would do; Nahti-poo lay dying. The people and the priest came and sat about him, and cried: 'Now pray, Nahti-poo, for now you are about to die!'

'What shall I pray for?' inquired Nahti-poo.

'Pray lest from the sleep of death thou awake in Hell!'

'Surely,' said Nahti-poo, 'if it please God that I should awake in Hell, all my praying shall not make it otherwise. How can I will other than the will of God?'

So presently Nahti-poo died, and passed to the confines of the other world, which is the world of spirits. And as he stood upon its borders, all about him was grey mist; there was no before and no after, nor any sign of a place toward which he might go. So Nahti-poo, seeing nowhere to go, stood still and waited, having no cause to hurry himself. And presently he saw, standing before him in the dimness, a man with his face averted, who said: 'Art thou a traveller in this land?'

'I am no traveller,' replied Nahti-poo, 'for I see nowhere to go. But show me a way, and I am quite willing to go in it.'

'Follow me, then,' said the other, 'for I was sent to show thee the way thou must go.'

So Nahti-poo set out to follow his guide; and as the other strode on, swift of foot, Nahti-poo trotted after. Presently being short of breath, he called: 'Truly, friend, if thou wast sent to be my guide there is more zeal than discretion in thy feet; for I came from an old body, and the weakness of my earthly pilgrimage still clings to me. Therefore be patient with one who is not so young as thou art.'

The other answered: 'In this land the weakness of age lies not before but behind; and the farther thou goest the more shall thy strength return to thee. When first I came hither I was older than thou art.'

'Truly, then,' said Nahti-poo, 'this place has agreed with thee, for thy speed is like the speed of an ostrich.'

Then said the other: 'Now we be come to crossroads; tell me thy name and what thou art, so I may know whither on I am to lead thee.'

Nahti-poo answered: 'I am the son of Kayrahmam, the rope-maker, and my name is Nahti-poo.'

Thereat the other stopped, and turned, and looked at him saying: 'O Nahti-poo, thou who wouldst not pray to save thy father from death, farewell, go forward, and find thy way alone; and if thou have need of Heaven, ask Heaven to help thee according to thy deserts; but I will not.'

And as Nahti-poo gazed thereon with eyes of recognition, the face of his father Kayrahmam vanished before him in the mist, and he stood alone.

And presently, as he waited, he became aware of one who stood veiled before him, and said: 'Art thou a traveller in this land?' And Nahti-poo answered: 'I am a traveller, but I have no guide.' Then said the other: 'Follow me, for I have come to guide thee in the way thou shouldst go.'

So Nahti-poo set out to follow his new guide; and now the mist was so deep about him that he could scarcely see the form that went before him. So presently he said: 'If I am to follow thee as my guide, let me hear thy voice, else in the darkness my feet may stray, and we shall be parted.'

His guide said: 'Tell me thy name, and I will call to thee.'

And he answered: 'I am Nahti-poo, the son of Kayrahmam, the rope-maker.'

Then his guide stopped and turned, and, lifting her veil, said: 'O, Nahti-poo, who would not pray for thy wife to be delivered from pain and fear, the way is dark before thee, but thou hast no need of *my* voice to guide thee. Farewell, go forward; find thy way alone. If thou art in need, ask help of Heaven, and Heaven will help thee according to thy deserts.'

And at the word Nahti-poo saw his wife Mazurah bowing down before him, and over her face fell the veil of darkness; and again he stood alone.

Patiently he waited; the air grew dense and dark with mist; not a hand's-breadth could he see, this way or that, before him. The more he peered and searched, the deeper seemed the wall of darkness by which he stood enclosed. Presently he felt a hand touch his, and a child's voice said: 'O thou traveller in this dark world, I am to be thy guide. Give me thy hand, and as I lead, do thou follow.'

But Nahti-poo reached out both his hands and laid them upon the child's head saying, 'O little son, whose head I thus held when thou wast dying, surely I know thy voice and the sweetness of thy intent. Now go thy way, for I am Nahti-poo thy father, that loved thee, and would not pray for thee; and into no deeper darkness than I am now canst thou lead me. Go thy way, little son; if I have any further need, I will ask help of Heaven.'

And as Nahti-poo spoke, all the darkness that was about him broke and passed away in a broad radiance of universal light; and he beheld before him the Eye of Heaven encircled by a million presences, of human form, but of a beauty and a reasonableness and a persuasiveness such as neither in mind or imagination had he ever dreamed to be possible.

But as the Eye of Heaven looked at him, all else became as naught; and he stood absorbed into the oneness of that light, which seemed both to pass through and to embrace him. And as the sense of its power and loveliness grew on him, he bowed down his face to the ground, and becoming blind to the outwardness of things saw only their true inwardness.

Then, as the Eye of Heaven gazed on him, came a Voice also, saying, 'Who art thou?'

And he answered, 'I am Nahti-poo, the son of Kayrahmam, the rope-maker.'

And the Voice said 'Nahti-poo, what hast thou done to show forth My praise and honour among men?'

And Nahti-poo answered, 'Lord, I have not prayed to Thee'.

And as he so said, the Eye and all those presences standing about looked at him with larger gaze; and Nahti-poo's soul was like a piece of pale glass held up to the sun, having no before and no after, and no shadow or secrecy of its nature left.

And the Eye of Heaven said, 'Nahti-poo, wherefore didst thou not pray?'

'Lord,' said Nahti-poo, 'I waited till I had need.'

'And hast thou,' said the Eye of Heaven, 'lived all the years of thy life on earth never having felt need?'

'Truly, Lord,' said Nahti-poo. 'I could often have invented one; but if one begins where is one to end?'

The Eye of Heaven gazed on him for a while, and the pure lustre of its rays changed and burned with a strange twinkle of lights. Then said the Voice celestial, 'Nahti-poo, bend down thine eyes and look on Hell!'

The foundations of the ground on which Nahti-poo stood were shaken and divided from side to side; and between him and the Throne of Judgment there opened a gulf dark and deep, into which he stooped and looked down. And as he looked, he caught back his breath, and covered his mouth with his hand; and up from below came a confused babel of voices crying.

And the Eye of Heaven said, 'Dost thou see Hell?'

'Yea, Lord,' said Nahti-poo, 'I see it, and hear it; and it is not the place that I would go to, for they that dwell in it are full of unsatisfied wants, and of desires that cannot be appeased; nor if they were, would it be good for them. Therefore are they in torment without end.'

Then said the Eye of Heaven, 'What is it, Nahti-poo, that they are doing down yonder?'

'Truly,' said Nahti-poo, 'it seems to me they are praying.'

Then out of the light around him to Nahti-poo came word: 'Lift up thine eyes and look on Heaven.'

And Nahti-poo lifted his eyes, and looked; and his mouth opened and became wide with astonishment as he stood gazing speechless.

Then said the Eye, 'What dost thou see in Heaven?'

Nahti-poo breathed a deep breath and said, 'I see the Joy of my Lord.'

'In what does that Joy consist?'

'He is laughing at me!' said Nahti-poo; and still, as he spoke, the widening of his mouth did not cease.

'Why does He laugh at thee?'

'Because I never prayed to Him.'

Then sweetly the voice of the Beloved spoke to him and said: 'O Nahti-poo, all thy life has been a prayer. Enter thou into the Joy of thy Lord!'

The Distorting Mirror

'I CAN'T tell the truth!' wept the distorting mirror. 'Everything is so beautiful; but as it looks at me, and as I look back, all at once it becomes ugly and misshapen — false, out of proportion, horrible. Why was I so made that I cannot tell the truth?

And so, for many years, with its face set to beautiful things, which, as they looked at it, became ugly, the Mirror led a sad, self-commiserating life, and would gladly have turned its face to the wall (so that if unable to tell the truth it might at least not have to tell lies), but could not do so.

Then, one day, things began to happen — the like of which the mirror had never seen before. Men came and began to break and destroy the beautiful things of which the mirror had always wished but had never been able to tell the truth. Shattered and shapeless the beauty went out of them; their distorted image in the mirror no longer mattered; ceasing to have form or meaning they had become useless rubbish.

Presently, not content with destroying the beautiful things of the world, the men began destroying each other, and themselves also.

With flayings, mutilations, tortures, rubber-snouts, and other disfigurements, they changed themselves from the likeness of men into the similitude of something far worse than beasts; and when they came to look in the distorting mirror — again it was no good; though they had no beauty that one should desire them, the mirror was still not able to show them what they were really like. It was the same old trouble the other way round.

'Alas!' wept the mirror, 'I can't tell the truth! I can't show them how ugly they are.'

(1937)

THE BED-CHAMBER PLOT
(1839)

The QUEEN *has told* LORD MELBOURNE *of her determination to refuse Sir Robert Peel's requirement that with a change of Ministry there must also be a change of her Court-Ladies.*

THE QUEEN But though I am very young and inexperienced as yet, I do mean to be Queen.

MELBOURNE H'm; yes, quite so. And if I may be allowed to say so, your Majesty already is — every inch — a Queen.

THE QUEEN Your saying it, Lord Melbourne, makes me hope that it is true.

MELBOURNE And that, Ma'am, suggests to my mind — a riddle.

THE QUEEN A riddle?

MELBOURNE Which I have just made, but to which I don't know the answer.

THE QUEEN But a riddle must have an answer.

MELBOURNE Then perhaps your Majesty can answer it. The riddle is this — if every inch is a Queen, what is a foot?

THE QUEEN I don't understand?

MELBOURNE There are twelve inches in a foot. If every inch is a Queen, how much is the foot, when the Queen puts the foot down? H'm?

THE QUEEN Are you making fun of me, Lord Melbourne?

MELBOURNE No, Ma'am; not at all. I am only wondering. This United Kingdom of Great Britain and Ireland is not an Empire *yet*; but under your Majesty's foot it may become one. But as an old man, speaking to a very young sovereign, whom he loves almost like a daughter — may I just say — Go slow; only one foot at a time. That will be enough.

THE PRIMROSE WAY
(1894)

LORD ROSEBERY, *having through no fault of his own become head of a Government of which Her Majesty highly disapproves, artfully turns the conversation from politics to horse-racing.*

ROSEBERY Has your Majesty ever heard the story of a horse called Pepper's Ghost? He won a race under very remarkable circumstances.

THE QUEEN No, never.

ROSEBERY He was a splendid horse, and a hot favourite for one of the big events. His jockey was offered £1000 on the condition of his not winning the race. Afraid to be caught 'pulling', what was this jockey to do? The horse's name may have suggested it. Just before mounting he went up to the horse's head, fondled it, and put a pinch of pepper up its nose. The race started, the horse sneezed all the way — and won.

THE QUEEN Dear me! Most extraordinary! And was it found out?

ROSEBERY Yes, Ma'am; directly the race was over, the trainer had the horse's nose examined; the pepper was found and traced; the jockey confessed.

THE QUEEN Was he prosecuted?

ROSEBERY No, Ma'am; he was too valuable. He wasn't even dismissed. They put some pepper up *his* nose as a lesson for him, and told nobody. After that he won several more races for its owner on the same horse. Pepper's Ghost, your Majesty may be interested to hear, came to Windsor on one occasion for stud purposes, and sired Peppercorn out of Cornupia. . . .

> (*By telling this quite untrue story of his own invention he has put* HER MAJESTY *into a good temper, and made himself once more as acceptable as under present adverse circumstances is possible. True to his family name, he has found that the Primrose Way is the one that he can always tread with natural grace, and generally with good results when it takes him away from politics.*)

RIVAL GODS

In everything except name the Nation has become a god, but its worshippers still persist in calling themselves 'Christians', and invoke Christ's name when they do the most unChristlike things. Allying itself to Caesar, institutional Christianity appropriated and applied to its anti-Christian activities and instruments of power the symbol of Christ; and on its banners of war, on the coats of its soldiers, and in the very design of its sword-hilts, it used the Cross, to which all these things were a contradiction.

It does so to this day. Our churches and cathedrals are littered with war-trophies on which are inscribed the names of many unjust wars; and these trophies we revere and hold sacred.

May I recall how, on the night of Christ's agony, a great multitude came out 'with swords and staves to take Him', and to the one (their guide and leader), who came forward and kissed Him, Christ said, 'Betrayest thou the son of man with a kiss?' We call the man who did it 'the Betrayer'. That same betrayal has been repeated by Christendom all down the ages. It has come to Him with its swords and its staves, and (striving to identify Him with the very instruments which are the negation of His teaching and the barriers to the coming of His Kingdom), has betrayed Him with a kiss. It thrusts them into His hands, and crowns Him their king, and blindfolding His eyes, bows itself before Him in lying worship, hailing Him as king — not of His Kingdom but of theirs. Unless the Church cleans itself of that double-faced heresy, it is heading for destruction.

· · · · ·

The real crucifixion of Christ has come far more from Christians than from the Romans or the Jews; for *they* knew not what they did; but we — we who claim to have accepted Christ's teaching, who have His Gospel before us, who say that He is the way, the truth, and the life — what excuse have we?

But if (because of our infirmity of purpose and our feebleness of faith) we accept war as a horrible necessity, why do we glorify it, and make it the crowning-point of our history, of our national pride and honour, as we do? Of course we know partly why. The courage, the comradeship, the self-sacrifice which are displayed in wars however unjust, however cruel, however useless in result, blind us to the evil which lies at the root of them; they are the Devil's best bait to the pit which he has digged for us.

But that is not *all* why. We glorify war because we believe in power, however questionable in our past history were the means by which we secured it. All nations believe in power, but try to compass it in contradictory ways. True power arises out of unity of purpose, unity of direction, unity of principle in the methods we employ. But here we have a world so crammed with conflicting interests, so divided by rivalries, jealousy, hatred, suspicion, that it is producing not strength but weakness: yet is producing it in terms of power! See how power is being pursued by governments and peoples, all declaring that they want peace but still believing in war, manoeuvring for position with war as the final instrument in which they trust.

All these governments, by employing means contradictory to the mind of Christ, make war more inevitable, failure to ensure peace more certain; yet when war comes they will turn round and ask God's blessing on their failures, and on their use of the contradictory means in which failure has landed them.

And when they ask that blessing, their prayer should honestly be this: 'Bless us, O God (who refuse to accept the Christian way) in the results of our refusal. Make *our* methods *Thy* methods, *our* weapons *Thy* weapons. Let us teach *Thee* the way of peace, for we know better than Thou knowest how to bring Thy Kingdom upon earth.'

And when, going our own way, we send out our young men in air-raids to inflict torture and death upon whole populations, men, women, and children, both sides alike will be praying, 'Wilt not Thou, O God, go forth with our armies?' And they will not perceive that it is not, and cannot be, to God the common Father revealed by Christ that they are praying — *but to Beelzebub the God of Flies.*

EXTREMISTS

IF it is true that conscience makes us cowards in a moral sense, it seems equally true that habit makes us cowards intellectually: that when our lives are deeply committed to custom (whether on the physical, the intellectual, or the spiritual plane) we cease to be either free doers or free thinkers. We still fear the sharp driving-point of that great pacific instrument the brain, lest it should pierce defences which it would be very inconvenient to our present habits of life and thought to throw aside — lest, in a word, it should force us to become extremists, in the sense of recognizing that only extreme remedies and changes will suffice to make right that which in our present social order or social philosophy is wrong.

The idea that an extremist must stand for violence, and that free thought must stand for lack of faith, colours most people's minds. And if this were a world where middle-parties ('coalitions' and suchlike) did no violence, or in which the average man, conventional in his opinions, did not still believe in force as a remedy and vindictive punishment as a cure for crime — in which religious conformity was not largely a cover for those whose weekday lives are profoundly inconsistent with their Sunday professions — then one might, in such a different world, have more respect than is possible as things are, for that disapproval of violence and of so called 'infidelity', which wakes to register its protest only when the violence is done by a minority, and the infidelity is merely a breaking-away from the out-worn shibboleths of the past. Average minds protest far more readily against new theory than against old practice to which they have become accustomed, though, of the two, old practice may be much more incompatible with social principles which they now accept, and may have sprung from abuses of the past which no one now dares to defend.

Now just as society produces its own criminals largely, if not entirely, by its own shortcomings, injustices, and indifference to grievances and inequality which it could remedy, but has not the will to remedy — so does it produce the extremists who wish to go great lengths in the alteration of our social and economic system, by its persistent refusal to go short lengths, or any lengths at all, for the remedying of its defects. Those resisters to change, in a world where change is as natural as growth and as inevitable, are the biggest and on the whole the most dangerous extremists whom we have to deal with; for their numbers make them powerful, and they more than any others are the people who cause bloody revolutions and wars. Nothing is more stupidly extreme than refusal to *move* in a world-order which lives by movement, or than insistence that things temporary — the product of a set of circumstances which no longer hold good — shall be regarded as permanent.

We have only to look back into history to see how consistently disastrous has been the effect of that particular type of extremism in all the great crises of human development — the extremism of implacable conservatism and resistance to change; and how in the end judgment has always gone against it. That form of extremism, backed, to begin with, by a large body of public opinion, has always been the biggest obstacle in the way of liberty, freedom, and reform, because its adherents so greatly dislike going to the root of things to which they have been accustomed, and facing up to the inconvenience and temporary discomfort of the scrapping process which is sometimes necessary in a changing world, for ridding us of social leavings which have become refuse.

Acceptance of slavery as a custom produced an extremism which, as civilization progressed, we found harder and harder to justify. But see how natural was the development of slavery. When tribe or nation was the outside limit of any unity which could be understood or looked for among the fighting races, who in battle must prove their fitness to survive, it seemed obvious that to enslave the conquered was the shortest way for the victor to become strong. The addition to material strength was so immediate, the blow to the strength of the enemy so drastic and satisfactory, that any man would have been thought mad, if not a traitor to his country, had he advocated the liberation of all captives taken in war as an accompanying condition of victory.

And so presently the habit becomes universal — an institution of developing civilization, and slavery ceases to be a product of war only, and becomes a product of commerce, even in time of peace. It is no longer, then, the dangerous and conquered enemy who becomes the slave, but the inferior race, or the inferior class, the poverty-stricken and the serf. Habit and vested interest combined produce in the social order a new extremism — the right, under the sanction of law (no longer for military but for commercial reasons) for man to possess and exploit his fellow-man. Habit, custom, blinded men's eyes to the monstrousness of the doctrine; and the low economic status of labour nominally 'free' delayed the discovery — at which we have at last arrived — that slavery is the most expensive and least efficient form of all labour — that it does not pay. We have still to learn that sweated labour and under-cutting do not pay, or make for health in the body politic.

In the years following the Great War one passed from great west-end shops, crowded with luxurious superfluities at extravagant prices — things which people can perfectly well go without — to street-corner musicians, under-nourished and out of work, some of them men who had risked their lives in that 'war to end war', playing for a chance pittance; and elsewhere to 'distressed areas', where men through no fault of their own could not get work; and we accepted and still accept the inequality and iniquity of it, because for these contrasts, under our present consumptive social system, there is no remedy. But the fact that there is no remedy within the system does not make the system right. It cannot be right that while these men and their families live in want, vast quantities of the food-products of human industry are destroyed because there is no market for them — no market, though there are many hungry mouths. What stands first and foremost between us and a remedy is that great army of extremists for things as they exist — who because a thing is a system, a custom, a social institution, sanctioned and defended by law, remain more tolerant of it than they would be of any individual action which produced such evil results.

It is a strange thing that a principle of life from which we are (in practice) further away than we are from principles and practices which we regard as extremist, is yet a principle which haunts us. We cannot away with it. Jesus Christ was the greatest extremist that the world has ever seen, for in a world that believed in violence He abjured violence. 'Resist not evil', 'overcome evil with good' is the teaching of an extremist. 'Love your neighbour, do good to them that hate you, and pray for them which despitefully use you, and persecute you', is the teaching of an extremist. In our so-called free Democracies, we are nearer to Fascism and to Nazism than we are to that. Yet it holds us. We cannot get away from it. Though it may seem unattainable, it is yet truer to human nature than all those other evil things to which we are so much nearer to-day; for surely, if it were not truer to human nature, it would not attract us as an ideal to be striven for. You cannot be attracted by that with which you have no affinity.

People talk of certain things, good or bad, as 'unbelievable of human nature'. But whether good or bad, they have all been done by somebody, at some time in the world's history. If ever you hear or read of something unbelievably base which a man has done, so base as to be out of keeping with your idea of human nature, let it be an encouragement to you to believe also that the things which now seem to you too good for attainment are yet possible; that human nature only stands at a stage of its moral evolution; that man is still not made, but only in the making.

Browning, in one of his poems, tells of a man (it actually happened) who, climbing along a steep and precipitous ledge of rock, so narrow that it would be dangerous even to turn back, comes suddenly upon a stag advancing from the opposite direction, and man and beast stand looking at each other. For the beast it is possible to throw the man over the precipice with its horns; but it cannot turn back. So the man lies down; and the beast with understanding and acceptance advances and steps gently over him. As it does so, the man reaches up with his hunting-knife and tears out its life, and lives to make a boast of it!

Why does that piteous story seem to us so horrible? The stag died with not more pain than is suffered by thousands of animals that die daily so that we may be fed. What does it matter, materially, that the man set his wits against the wits of a beast and by cunning compassed its death? Materially, you cannot give me any reason why that death was so piteous and the man's act so horrible; but spiritually you can. For there, from the man to the beast, went deceitfully the offer of friendship, the Unity of the Spirit; and the beast with its simple, groping mind understood and accepted the higher plea for trust and help and mutual forbearance, and so accepting went to its death.

Surely we find in that story something which, in the animal world, was a Calvary comparable in its degree to the Calvary which the Christian Church celebrates. Wherever that story is told, it is the stag that rises from the dead and dieth no more; but the man who slew means nothing to us. He belongs only to the past, a piece of dead clay. He is not part of human nature any longer; but the stag is.

EXTREMES MEET

It is the afternoon of a certain day in the early seventies; and in the drawingroom of the Deanery at Westminster, CARLYLE has come to meet Royalty by special request — an honour for which, without wishing it, he has had to wait long.

DEAN STANLEY May I present to your Majesty — Mr. Carlyle? ·

THE QUEEN We are so pleased to meet you, Mr. Carlyle.

CARLYLE Your Majesty does me great honour.

THE QUEEN Lady Augusta was so kind as to say that she would arrange so that I might meet you here.

CARLYLE It was from her that I heard of your Majesty's good wish.

THE QUEEN I have long wished it, Mr. Carlyle; more especially since — since your great bereavement.

CARLYLE That's kind of ye, Ma'am.

THE QUEEN It was — (*she seats herself*) — it was nine years ago, was it not, that you lost your dear wife?

CARLYLE Aye: lost my wife, and kept me life. Better had it been the other way.

THE QUEEN Ah, yes: that is how I have always felt since I lost my dear husband, the Prince.

CARLYLE There ye're wrong, Ma'am. Your people still wanted you for great service. But there's few now to be wanting me.

THE QUEEN But your work, Mr. Carlyle.

CARLYLE That's over and done now — such as it was.

THE QUEEN You have finished writing — your histories?

CARLYLE Aye; all but one.

THE QUEEN What is that?

CARLYLE 'A poor thing, but mine own,' Ma'am, as they make Shakespeare say (though he never did). I'm writing it now.

THE QUEEN Your own life, you mean? That must be very interesting.

CARLYLE Very frightening, Ma'am. It's a fearsome thing to look into yourself and see the man you are, and the man you might have been.

THE QUEEN Well, we do all fall short of what we would have wished to do in some things. As I know, only too well.

CARLYLE You've been a good Queen, Ma'am.

THE QUEEN I had a good teacher, Mr. Carlyle.

CARLYLE Aye, aye. But there's wisdom — rare in Kings — of knowing you can be taught. And now, with your Majesty's permission, I'll sit down. I'm an old man.

THE QUEEN (*generously allowing this breach of etiquette*) Oh, yes; do sit down, all of you. (*They sit.*) . . . Have you yet read Mr. Theodore Martin's Life of the Prince Consort, Mr. Carlyle?

CARLYLE I have not, Ma'am.

THE QUEEN I think everyone should read it. Then my people would understand — better — what they have lost.

CARLYLE We all need better understanding, Ma'am, of what we've lost.

THE QUEEN I like to hear you say that, Mr. Carlyle. I've found it so true — myself . . . It was your dear wife you meant, was it not?

CARLYLE I meant everything, Ma'am, that one's let go, that one might have kept had one known better — to be more merciful.

THE QUEEN (*a little surprised*) Merciful, you say?

CARLYLE Yes, Ma'am; it's a thing some of us don't learn till it's too late: more especially with those we love — through not thinking.

THE QUEEN 'The quality of mercy is not strained,' Shakespeare says, does he not?

CARLYLE Aye; so he *says*. But it's a sore strain man puts on it when he least knows what he's doing. When we are thinking only of ourselves, we've small mercy for others.

THE QUEEN You have studied human nature, Mr. Carlyle; and no doubt you understand it better than I do; for I must confess that it often puzzles me.

CARLYLE It's the greatest puzzle that God has set for man in this world; and when we've solved it we shall have solved everything.

THE QUEEN Yes: I suppose it is the most difficult thing of all to understand and treat rightly — especially for those who rule, and hold power. It may sound unsuitable, but Kings do need to be humble.

CARLYLE Ye've said a wise thing, Ma'am, that some would find difficult to follow.

THE QUEEN Yes: to be a good King is very difficult. The Prince, my husband, was really a King by nature. To him I owed everything.

CARLYLE It's a great thing to know, Ma'am; and a great satisfaction the knowing of it must be.

THE QUEEN Yes, I am thankful that I do know it — that I have always known it, so well ... But now about your writing, your histories, Mr. Carlyle: tell me, what is the last history that you have written?

CARLYLE The life of Frederick the Great, Ma'am — 'the Great' as they call him.

THE QUEEN But he was great, was he not?

CARLYLE Aye; with a lot of littleness added to it. And 'twas the littleness, maybe, that made half of his success for him. There's greater men that have died failures.

THE QUEEN Yes: Napoleon was a great man, was he not?

CARLYLE Aye, Napoleon: the man that didn't know where to stop. Had he known that, he might have conquered the world.

THE QUEEN (*with patriotic conviction*) Not *England*.

CARLYLE England, and Asia, and Africa, and America.

THE QUEEN Dear me! Most extraordinary that you should think that, Mr. Carlyle ... But he *didn't*.

CARLYLE No, he didn't, Ma'am; but he'd got the idea of the United States of Europe — the same as they had over in America. But he made the mistake of thinking that France had got to be the head of it. Now if he'd only had the sense to give up that notion, he'd have won; and Great Britain would have had to come in.

THE QUEEN Then I'm glad he didn't.

CARLYLE Well, Ma'am, there's no knowing what you might be glad of, fifty years from now.

THE QUEEN That won't be in *my* reign, Mr. Carlyle.

CARLYLE No, Ma'am; but it's well to think of your sons, and your sons' sons, and what may be happening in their day to this England and Scotland of ours.

THE QUEEN What do you think is likely to happen?

CARLYLE He'd be a great prophet, Ma'am — or a great fool, maybe — who'd think he could say what's likely to happen. There's only one thing we can be nigh sure of — whatever it's to be, it's likely to be bad.

THE QUEEN Why do you think that, Mr. Carlyle?

CARLYLE It's to no good end the way the world's going these days, Ma'am. So many working for a pittance so the rest can play; so many kept starving so that others can go stuffed. Money's a god that has no mercy; he lets none of 'em off; them as have not he breaks one way, and them as have he breaks another — and a worse ...

THE QUEEN Well, of course, there are a great many things being done, that one can't approve of — changes not only foolish but wrong. Still the country is prosperous.

CARLYLE Aye; prosperous — like to those Gadarene swine, Ma'am, which thought themselves prosperous, maybe, while they were all running down the hill: but the water was waiting for 'em at the bottom.

THE QUEEN But do you think England *is* going down hill, Mr. Carlyle?

DEAN STANLEY (*tactfully intervening*) If Mr. Carlyle says Yes to that, Ma'am, your Majesty must remember that he has always taken the prophet Jeremiah as his model, believing that the best way of warning people against danger is to frighten them well beforehand. He has been frightening us for forty years, and as a consequence we have managed to survive the dangers he foresaw for us.

THE QUEEN I see. Well, Mr. Carlyle, I'm not going to let you frighten *me*. But even if we don't agree, I have found everything you say most interesting. You say things in such an interesting way that one cannot help being interested. And now, dear Lady Augusta, I'm afraid that I must go, though I should have liked to stay so much longer.

(*She rises. They all rise with her*)

Good-bye, and thank you very much for asking Mr. Carlyle to come and meet me. Mr. Carlyle, meeting you has given me great pleasure.

CARLYLE Very honoured, your Majesty.

THE QUEEN And I hope it may not be the last time.

CARLYLE Eh, but it will be, Ma'am, I'm thinking: my ganging-about days are over. But I thank your Majesty for the wish, and for having given me this day to remember.

Palestine Plays   (1942)

THE STORY OF JACOB

The wrestling at Peniel: JACOB *hears the voice of his conscience.*

JACOB So . . . to this end am I come!

(*And out of the darkness a* VOICE *answers him*)

VOICE Yes, Jacob.

JACOB (*startled*) What is that? Who called? . . . Who are you?

VOICE *You* called. I am yourself, Jacob. The voice you heard at Bethel you hear again.

JACOB The voice of my fear?

VOICE The voice of your fear.

JACOB I told you to begone.

VOICE Yes; but you are still afraid; so here I am. We are still two, Jacob.

JACOB What do you mean?

VOICE In every man there are two, Jacob; one is his weakness, the other his strength. Sometimes they meet, sometimes they part. Sometimes they wrestle together — to the death. How stands it with you and me — *now* Jacob?

JACOB Nay, I know not. For I no longer know, myself, what I am.

VOICE Know to-night, Jacob. To-morrow may be too late.

JACOB How? How *can* I know?

VOICE Not while you are of two minds. Choose one. Which is it to be?

JACOB You torture me!

VOICE You torture yourself, Jacob. (*There is a pause.*)

JACOB Oh, where is the God of my Fathers, and the Promise that He made me?

VOICE Not here, Jacob. You are alone.

JACOB Aye, surely alone! No help comes now.

VOICE None? Is not a friend speaking?

JACOB What does he say?

VOICE He only bids you be wise.

JACOB Speak!

VOICE All these years you have shown wisdom and prudence; and you have prospered, and the Lord has made you rich. In Laban's service you were safe. Now you are in danger. Why have you come?

JACOB For the Promise that God made to me, and the Blessing it was to bring.

VOICE To *you*, Jacob?

JACOB Aye surely! For to Abraham, and to Isaac my father He gave it, and to their seed after them. And my father gave it to me.

VOICE Did your father know to whom he was giving it?

JACOB He knew — afterwards.

VOICE Will a blessing so given, hold good, think you?

JACOB It was mine! Esau sold it to me.

VOICE Did he know what he was selling?

JACOB You asked me that at Bethel.

VOICE Yes; and you said he did not care. Yet you were afraid of him. You are still, Jacob.

JACOB Yes, I fear him still.

VOICE Why?

JACOB (*after a struggle*) Because then I did him wrong.

VOICE That's better, Jacob. You are nearer the truth now.

JACOB What would you have me do?

VOICE Why not give back to him the blessing which you took from him?

JACOB How can I do that?

VOICE Have the will, Jacob.

JACOB How can I undo God's doing? The blessing was given me by God.

VOICE Only in a dream, Jacob.

JACOB That also came from God. When I woke, I knew that the dream was true.

VOICE Were you sure?

JACOB I *was* sure.

VOICE If you were, of what use was the bargain that you made?

JACOB I made no bargain.

VOICE You offered one ... Oh, yes, Jacob. Did you not say that if God would fulfil His promise, and bring you back in safety to your own land, you would put away all other gods, and serve Him only? Why 'if'?

JACOB I *have* put them away.

VOICE Also you said that of all God should have given you in that day, you would give back to Him one tenth — always one tenth, so long as He kept His word to you ... Are you sure that one tenth was enough, Jacob? You thought so then; are you still so sure?

JACOB Had He asked more of me, I would have given more.

VOICE No doubt. But He never answered. So the bargain was not made. To-morrow you are sending to your brother Esau not one tenth but three tenths of all your sheep and cattle. Are you sure that three tenths will be enough — to satisfy him? And if not, why should the God of your Fathers be satisfied with only one tenth?

JACOB He made His promise freely. He required nothing of me — nothing!

VOICE Why, then, did you make a bargain of it? That wasn't wise, Jacob . . . So to-day you were afraid, when you found that you had Laban's gods still with you — afraid that the bargain had been broken.

JACOB When I found them, I sent them away.

VOICE Aye, aye. But it was a late finding, Jacob.

JACOB Is God no better than man? Twenty years have I been faithful to Him. Will He now be less faithful to *me*? Surely in God must be truth — if God be true.

VOICE Aye. So only in truth can you serve Him.

JACOB How have I *not* served Him?

VOICE You are a coward, Jacob.

JACOB Because I fear death?

VOICE No; a man need be no coward who fears death. He only is a coward who fears truth.

JACOB What truth do I fear?

VOICE The truth about the man you are, Jacob.

JACOB Tell it me.

VOICE I cannot, you must find that for yourself . . . You think that I am the voice of your fear. Yes: because conscience has made a coward of you. Cease to fear the truth; and you will cease to fear me also.

JACOB Your voice has changed!

VOICE *Your* voice, Jacob. It is your own heart speaking now. And you hear me — for the first time.

JACOB Why have I not heard you before?

VOICE Because you did not listen for me. You were afraid.

JACOB Of what?

VOICE Of the truth, Jacob. For when you deceived others, you deceived yourself also . . . How could a deceiver by deceit serve faithfully the God of truth? And you were a deceiver, Jacob.

JACOB Yes.

VOICE You were not honest — to Laban.

JACOB No.

VOICE And you gave your dishonesty to God, saying that it was His doing, not yours.

JACOB Yes.

VOICE Therefore, also, has Rachel deceived *you* — as you deserved. But the bargain that you made with God was broken — not by Rachel, but by you, because you did not serve faithfully the God of Truth.

JACOB Then is He free from His promise.

VOICE So you have come to the truth at last! And you also — are free.

JACOB How am I — free?

VOICE To return by the way you came. To-morrow comes Esau, with his four hundred armed men; and your life, and the lives of those with you, will be in danger. It is still night; escape is easy. Would not Laban be willing that you should work for him again as you have worked for him these twenty years? The forgiveness of Laban you can win more surely than the forgiveness of Esau.

JACOB Why are you tempting me?

VOICE Am I tempting you?

JACOB No! I will not go back to serve Laban. I will not go back!

(*And now a* NEW VOICE *is heard speaking to him*)

VOICE Well said, Jacob — though the saying was hard for thee. But God is faithful and just, and has not taken His promise from thee. For though Esau may slay thee, God's blessing shall be upon thy sons, and on their sons after them; and the land which He gave to thy Fathers shall be theirs; and from thy seed shall come a nation . . . This night thou hast heard the voice of thine Accuser, whom thou didst fear; and that of which he accused thee is true. But he has gone from thee, and thou hearest him no more. For now the truth is with thee, and thou knowest what manner of man thou art, and seest thyself even as God sees thee; and hast judged thyself righteously . . . Therefore thy name shall no longer be called Jacob, but Israel, for as a prince thou hast striven with God, and thy strength has prevailed over thy weakness . . . To-morrow thou shalt go forward and meet Esau.

JACOB This is no longer the voice I heard. It is no man's voice that speaks now . . . Tell me thy name.

VOICE Why dost thou seek my name? Is it not enough that thou hast heard my Voice speaking to thee? You walk lame, Jacob, but you get there at last. Lo, now the day breaks, and the shadows flee away; the day of God's promise has come; and on Israel His light shines.

(*Very slowly the darkness begins to break; and there is a sound of birds*)

JACOB Now have I seen God face to face; and my life has been spared to me. Yea, though I fear death, I will go forward and meet Esau. . . .

THE BURDEN OF NINEVEH

JONAH's *friend* SHEMMEL *gives him good counsel.*

SHEMMEL Jonah, Jonah, let me speak to thee.

JONAH I have heard enough of thy speaking, Shemmel. Where is the mercy of God that you are so loud about? Was there mercy in that which He did, either for the gourd — or for *me*? He keeps His mercy for Nineveh!

SHEMMEL Jonah — I have counsel for thee.

JONAH I have counsel enough of myself. I need no other.

SHEMMEL The more, therefore, it waits for thee. For I think this counsel which I have for thee is of God. Be patient, therefore, and hear me.

JONAH (*after a pause*) Speak, then . . . Aye, speak.

SHEMMEL Jonah, God is good, and full of wisdom; and when we understand Him not, the fault is not His but ours, because we are less good than He, and less wise. Yet does He speak to us according to our understanding. So, in this that He has done to the gourd, has not God spoken to thee in a parable? All things are of God. He sends forth the strong wind, and makes the sun to shine, and the gourd to grow. But these, that are His creatures, know not whether what they do is good or evil; for they know not of themselves what they are. But God knows. So also is man His creature — knowing little. Now because the gourd had given you comfort and shelter, therefore in your eyes it seemed good, and the wind and the sun evil. And you are angry because God has not spared the gourd but has spared Nineveh; and it had pleased you better had He destroyed Nineveh, and saved the gourd . . . Listen, Jonah. When the Lord first called you, you turned away and would not hear; because it was not in your heart to do His Will. And He was angry with you; but He forgave you. And now, Jonah, it is the other way about; you are angry because it is not in the Lord's heart to do *your* will. You wish Nineveh to be destroyed; He wishes to save it.

JONAH Why, then, did He send me to preach against Nineveh?

SHEMMEL Your preaching has done a great thing, Jonah. Nineveh has repented . . . I am no preacher, only a counsellor. But hear now from me the Word of the Lord, which I speak unto thee: 'Thou hast had pity on the gourd, for which thou hast not laboured, neither madest it grow, which came up in a night, and perished in a night. And should not I spare Nineveh, that great city, wherein are more than six-score thousand persons that cannot discern between their right hand and their left; and also much cattle?'

(*There is a long pause*)

JONAH You are a greater prophet than I, Shemmel, for in you is more understanding of God, and of His ways.

SHEMMEL I am no prophet, Jonah; only a reader.

JONAH A reader?

SHEMMEL Of men's hearts, Jonah. And yours has been one of them. Maybe, some day, also a writer. Then will this story of Jonah be written for man's learning. But *my* name will not be known, nor, by any shall I be remembered. What matter?

Samuel, the Kingmaker   (1944)

ACT IV

SAMUEL *lies dying; his sons have fled from the wrath of Saul: he is alone. The* WISE WOMAN *enters, stands looking at him, and speaks.*

WOMAN   The old man is full of sorrow,
           Here to-day, and gone to-morrow.
           Kings come up, and Judges go down;
           All alike when the Gods frown.

SAMUEL Who's there? ... My sons, my sons, where are you? ... They've left me — alone!

WOMAN Aye! Alone — all alone, at last.

(*Hearing the voice he most fears,* SAMUEL *starts to full consciousness*)

SAMUEL Woman, what brings *you* here?

WOMAN *You* brought me. I've a word for you, 'twill be good for you to hear. Will you hear it? ... Or will you have it not said?

SAMUEL Speak.

(*She sits down by him*)

WOMAN You asked me once, Samuel, whether I could put a curse upon a man; and I answered, 'He puts it upon himself'. Aye, it's your own curse that is upon you now, Samuel. For though you still live, all your power has gone from you. Who cares for you now? Oh, yes; you thought to break Saul — to do it, you broke Israel. What good has it done you? Over Saul's head you anointed David to be King. You won't live to see David King — *you* won't, Samuel. Has David come back to you for a last blessing? No. David has fled away from Saul, and gone to give service to the foes of Israel — to Achish, King of Gath. Aye, you've been a sore trouble to Saul — the two of you. And I helped you to do it when Saul became my enemy. *Your* doing, Samuel; you didn't break your oath to me, eh? You set Saul to do it for you. I know it now.

SAMUEL Oh, cease, cease, Woman, from troubling me! Let me die in peace.

WOMAN Peace! What peace have you given to Israel? David was Saul's servant, his friend. Saul loved and trusted him. But behind Saul's back you anointed David to be King. Did David tell Saul? No; Saul was not to know. So at your bidding David became a traitor to his King. For if Saul *was* truly the Lord's anointed — what was David? Was he the Lord's, or was he only Samuel's? Who can tell? A prophet can always speak the 'Word of the Lord' as seems good to him; but we've only *his* word for it. And if there be evil in his heart, the word he speaks will be evil also. And *your* heart was evil.

SAMUEL Go, Woman, go from me! You have cursed my life from the day when first I hearkened to you, and took your counsel for the sign, and did not wait for the Lord. You took the Word of the Lord from me — tempting me; and I heard His voice no more. Though I called upon Him, He heard me not.

WOMAN Call on Him again, Samuel! Make thy peace with Saul, and maybe He will yet hear thee.

SAMUEL I will *not* make peace with Saul.

WOMAN Therefore has this come to pass; that because you also made Ahimelech, and the priests of the tabernacle to conspire with you for David against Saul, therefore has Saul slain them. The priests are dead, Samuel.

SAMUEL The priests are dead!

WOMAN Your doing, Samuel. So now is Israel broken and divided, because Samuel loved himself more than he loved Israel, and was wroth when power was taken from him and given to another.

SAMUEL Ah! God, why hast Thou made me live to see this day?

WOMAN For the better knowing of thyself, Samuel, and of the man thou art.

SAMUEL Oh, God, send down Thy curse upon this Woman, whose life I spared, when I should have slain.

WOMAN You did your best, Samuel, you did your best. 'Twas a fine oath you took that day — took and kept; eh, Samuel? — that I should live to *your* life's end — and further — if it were God's will. Well, it has been — God's will. Now die! and your God — go with you.

(She turns to go)

> Rat-a-tat-tat! 'Twas a rat in the house
> That wanted to kill the old grey mouse.
> But the old grey mouse, for all that,
> Has lived to see the death of the rat!

(She goes out)

SAMUEL (*feebly*) Help, help! Joel, Abiah! My sons, where are you? Oh, God, Thou hast emptied me out, and cast me away; and there is none left to succour me — none to regard me. Abiah! . . . Abiah! . . . Joel!

(He goes on calling. Slowly the curtain falls.)

Nunc Dimittis

NUNC DIMITTIS

AN EPILOGUE, IN TWO SCENES

(*Wherein an Author says good-bye to his favourite character*)

Dramatis Personæ:

ST. FRANCIS   NURSE
BROTHER JUNIPER   DOCTOR
BROTHER DIVES   AUTHOR
ATTENDANT ANGELS

SCENE I

A very beautiful gateway stands in the centre of the stage, and the limelight. Its folding doors are of gold, studded with jewels; and in the arched space above, depending from a chain which passes up out of sight, hangs a large, Golden Key. On either side of the gate stand ATTENDANT ANGELS, *made decoratively beautiful with wings which do not work. As the tails of ermines, which no longer wag, give the finishing touch to Royalty, so these to the livery worn in the Courts of Heaven. Flight is no longer required of them: 'They also serve,' as the poet says, 'who only stand and wait'; and these Angels are, in a celestial sense, Waiters. They are beautiful, but not quite human; they have golden faces, and on their hands gloves set with jewels. They might, indeed, be mistaken for gold statues, but for their sense of humour; for when funny things happen, they look at each other and smile, nod, almost wink. They are smiling now, for at the wicket stands the very human figure of* BROTHER JUNIPER. *Before the rise of the curtain cock-crow is heard . . . then comes to a pause; and we are just in time to see* BROTHER JUNIPER *put his head through the wicket to discover why.*

JUNIPER Go on, Brother! Go on!

    (*The cock-crow continues in crescendo.* JUNIPER *withdraws his head from the wicket, and stands, looking up expectantly. The Golden Key descends, taps the gate with a jar of celestial harmony, reminding one of the spring-call of the curlew. The gate miraculously opens.*

232

'*Ah!*' *cries* JUNIPER, *satisfied; and if his soul delights in marrow and fatness, here it is for him. In walks, not timorously, but in a daze of obtuse bewilderment, a large, fat man wearing a crush hat and a fur coat, and carrying a cigar. He looks round in puzzled apprehension of having come to the wrong door; but* JUNIPER *reassures him*)

JUNIPER We've got you in, Brother Dives! 'Twas a hard push for the like of you, though!

(*Slowly the doors close again on a descending scale of music, locking themselves emphatically on the last chord. The newcomer, who is our old friend,* DIVES (*and like the poor, is always with us*), *feeling that somehow, by accident, he has come to a place where hats must be taken off, takes off his, and looks round for some spot whereon to deposit it. Failing to find one, he offers it to one of the* ATTENDANT ANGELS, *whom he regards as a footman. With the politeness of a Chinaman, the* ANGEL *lifts deprecating hands, and crosses them again. He is not having any.* JUNIPER *comes to the rescue*)

JUNIPER You don't want that! Not here!

(*He takes the hat and throws it out through the wicket; it falls with a reverberation of thunder . . . down . . . down . . . into the outer darkness, to which properly it belongs*)

JUNIPER Nor that!

(*The cigar goes after it . . . More thunder, as the outer darkness continues to digest the things given to it*)

JUNIPER Nor that!

(*He pulls off the fur coat, and throws it out. Thunder again. The evening dress, which now presents itself to* JUNIPER'S *astonished gaze, is something which, apparently, he has never seen before*)

JUNIPER Whatever made you come like that?

DIVES (*with a sulky dignity, but feeling ashamed of it, as being out of place*) I couldn't help it. I was in it. I was run over.

JUNIPER And I don't wonder. Drunk, were you?

DIVES (*not committing himself*) I had been dining.

JUNIPER Had you? Well, you won't get such another dinner here. We can't run to it.

DIVES I begin to hope not.

JUNIPER Ye do? Well, take 'em off, then!

DIVES (*astonished*) Which? . . . What? . . .

233

JUNIPER All of 'em ... You don't want 'em here. (JUNIPER *begins disrobing him*) *And* that! ... *And* that! ... *And* those! ...

(*This indication of the nether garments brings things to a pause.* DIVES *has an earthly sense of decency, which, in Heaven, is no longer required.* JUNIPER *becomes persuasive*)

Believe me, you don't want 'em here, Brother! Your own legs are better. Look at mine!

(DIVES *is still hesitant; but the two* ANGELS *come forward, and, extending over him cloaks of charity, persuade him to be seated. Thus, under cover and countenance of the heavenly bodies, he allows* JUNIPER *to divest him of his last mark of respectability; and, in shirt and pants, of which we catch but a glimpse, he is considerately shepherded into the Courts of Heaven — there to learn better about many things*)

JUNIPER Heaven help you, Brother!

(*With a sigh of relief,* JUNIPER *rolls up the discarded dress suit, and bundles it out to the place whence it came. Down it thunders, and then follows silence. But the quick ear of* JUNIPER *has heard something; out goes his head again, and is still out when* ST. FRANCIS *enters, and stands watching with amusement the ecstatic working of one of* JUNIPER's *legs, as he gathers information from the world below*)

ST. FRANCIS What are you doing there, Juniper?

JUNIPER (*withdrawing his head*) Only listening, Father.

ST. FRANCIS With your head out of Heaven, Brother. Tut! Tut! That won't do.

JUNIPER But, Father dear, if a sound outside Heaven comes into Heaven, isn't one to listen to it?

ST. FRANCIS Yes, Brother. But if it comes into Heaven, why put your head outside?

JUNIPER Because, there outside, Father, I can hear it better, maybe having the longer ears for it; for 'twas the voice of an ass I heard.

ST. FRANCIS An ass, Brother?

JUNIPER Yes, Father; but not one like me. A clever ass this one, by the sound of him. They're the worst sort, aren't they, Father?

ST. FRANCIS Sometimes, Brother. What kind of clever ass is this one?

JUNIPER Sure, Father, he says he isn't a Christian, but he wants to die! And he's ever so fond of you, but thinks you aren't alive. Did you ever know such an ass, Father?

ST. FRANCIS Yes, Brother, often. And what does he say?

JUNIPER He's calling *you*, Father.

ST. FRANCIS Me? Why did you not tell me that at once, Juniper?

JUNIPER Sure, you could have heard him for yourself, Father, had you wanted. It just happened I was the first.

ST. FRANCIS In that case, Juniper, it is surely you that he wants, not me.

JUNIPER Me, Father? Not likely!

ST. FRANCIS Very, Brother, since kind ever seeks kind. And 'ass' you said . . . Yes, I will go; but you will go with me . . . Come!

(FRANCIS *goes to the gate as though to open it.* JUNIPER *looks up, and whistles*)

JUNIPER Hi! . . . Hi! Peter! Peter! Peter! The Little Father wants to go out.

(*Slowly and musically the Key descends, and the curtain follows. The gates open . . . We catch a glimpse of* ST. FRANCIS *and* JUNIPER *passing out.*)

SCENE II

The AUTHOR, *for stage purposes, is lying in bed, preparing to die. And he prepares so well that the* DOCTOR *and* NURSE *are taken in by it, and act accordingly. The* DOCTOR *has just entered the room, and the* NURSE, *lifting a warning finger, tiptoes to meet him.*

NURSE He's asleep, Doctor.

DOCTOR Then don't wake him. It's no good. One can't do anything.

NURSE How long do you think it will be, sir?

DOCTOR I doubt if he can last out the night.

AUTHOR (*feebly, but cheerfully*) Hip . . . hip . . . hurray!

(DOCTOR *and* NURSE *exchange looks of consternation; and the* DOCTOR, *having thus given away a professional secret, which the patient was not supposed to know, makes a helpless gesture, and retreats from the room, leaving* NURSE *to deal with the situation. She approaches the bed cautiously, and, with diplomatic finesse worthy of a better cause, inquires*)

NURSE Did you speak, sir?

AUTHOR (*whimsically*) Did I, Nurse dear?

235

NUNC DIMITTIS

NURSE I thought you were asleep.

AUTHOR Yes, so did I — till I heard you talking.

NURSE I'm very sorry, sir.

AUTHOR Why? ... Why?

NURSE I ought to have been more careful.

AUTHOR Good Lord! *I* don't mind. Dying is not so comfortable that one should wish to prolong the process — more than one can help. Why shouldn't one be told the truth?

NURSE It's what most people don't like to be told.

AUTHOR Because they won't believe it. All my life I have been trying to tell people the truth ... *my* truth. But it isn't *their* truth. If it were, the world would be different.

NURSE Better?

AUTHOR Am I better, Nurse, than most people? No, but I am more amusing. So, if people would only believe what I do, the world would be more amusing too. But not less naughty — oh, no!

NURSE But *you* are not naughty.

AUTHOR When I was still quite small, Nurse dear, and had done something I should not, my old Granny said to me, 'Larry, if you do that, you will go to the Devil!' And I said, 'I 'ikes the Debbil'. It was a good, true answer; and my mother admired it so much that she wrote it down for me.

NURSE You began early, sir.

AUTHOR Being author? Yes.

NURSE You have written quite a lot of books, someone told me.

AUTHOR In my life, more than I ought. My Brother used to say that I wrote faster than he could read. He wrote two books of poems — better than all mine put together.

NURSE But you wrote plays too, sir.

AUTHOR Oh, you know that, do you?

NURSE Why, yes. Last year I saw six of them, done by the students at University College.

AUTHOR Yes, poor dears! It's become a habit with them. They can't break themselves of it. What did you think of them?

NURSE Oh, very nice, sir ... Very beautiful.

AUTHOR The *students*, I meant.

NURSE Oh, well, sir, of course they did their best.

236

AUTHOR They did . . . They always do. They are excellent in parts, like the curate's egg.

NURSE Oh, not as bad as that, sir! .

AUTHOR No? Well, I suppose it takes an author, or a God, to put all the blame on others, and none on himself.

NURSE Or a *what*, sir?

AUTHOR Oh nothing, nothing, Nurse dear! Isn't it time I had my beef tea, or something, to prepare me for the next world?

NURSE A little white of egg and whisky; will that do, sir?

AUTHOR I dare say.

NURSE Then I will go and get it.

(*She goes*)

AUTHOR While I go on with my dying . . . dying! . . . I wonder . . . Is there another side to it? Is there still a St. Francis living . . . anywhere? Or is it only an echo seven hundred years old, that one hears? . . . Little Father! . . . Little Father! . . . Ah! Not for the likes of me. Holy Mother Church would forbid.

(ST. FRANCIS *comes in, and stands by the bed*)

ST. FRANCIS Here I am, my son . . . You called me?

AUTHOR Yes, but I never expected you to hear — *me*.

ST. FRANCIS Why not?

AUTHOR Seven hundred years is a long time, Father.

ST. FRANCIS Have you found that such a difficulty?

AUTHOR To hear *you*? That's different. *Your* sound has gone out into all lands.

ST. FRANCIS And the bleating of my sheep also.

AUTHOR But am I one of them?

ST. FRANCIS Why not?

AUTHOR Perhaps you don't know what I've done?

ST. FRANCIS Don't I? What?

AUTHOR 'Little Plays' — about *you*.

ST. FRANCIS I know. Why shouldn't you?

AUTHOR But are they *true*? Are they in the least like you?

ST. FRANCIS Not a bit!

AUTHOR Then they are no good!

ST. FRANCIS Tut! Tut! Things don't have to be like *me* to be good.

AUTHOR Don't they? Oh! I thought they did.

ST. FRANCIS Then you thought foolishly, my son . . . Like *me*? Why should they be like me? A good piece of fiction is a great work of mercy.

AUTHOR For why, then?

ST. FRANCIS God has savoured it, without making it true. Had I done all the things I am said to have done, I should have needed a hundred legs, or a hundred lives for it. Your tales of me are not all of them true — very few, indeed; but you are in good company, my son. When Father Bonaventura sat down to write my life — the official version of it — he not only put in things that were *not* true, and left out things which were, but he burned everything he could get hold of which had the true things in it. Yet, in spite of all my miracles, I have managed to survive — somehow.

AUTHOR Your miracles, Father? Why should miracles prevent?

ST. FRANCIS They weren't mine, or very few of them. Bonaventura, zealous for the faith, but not for the truth, found that I had not done miracles enough to justify my place in the world as Founder of an Order, and one in whose name Churches were being built. So he got hold of the life of St. Benedict, Founder of another Order, took all the best of his miracles, altered them, and gave them to me.

AUTHOR How did you find out, Father?

ST. FRANCIS St. Benedict told me himself. He was very nice about it, said they couldn't be in better keeping, and that Bonaventura had done wisely. And there is this to be said for it — we don't have property in Heaven, and the good works of one are shared by all. So if, like the loaves and fishes, they multiply miraculously, no one loses and everyone gains . . . So you think you are not one of my sheep, eh? Then what made you write plays about me? Did you do it for mischief?

AUTHOR No, Father — I'll tell you. There are (or were when I wrote them) two monsters going to and fro in the world seeking whom they might devour.

ST. FRANCIS Monsters?

AUTHOR Yes, Father. Not bad monsters, good monsters; but with a terrible appetite for getting hold of people and writing plays about them. One of them was called 'Drinkwater' — but didn't — except sometimes. And the other wasn't called Drinkwater, but did. And Drinkwater was always looking for real people — great and good people — to write plays about; because he thought that if the people were good and great, the play would be good and great also. And the other person, who wasn't *called* Drinkwater, but did —

ST. FRANCIS What was his name, my son?

AUTHOR Shaw, Bernard Shaw, Father. He was afraid that Drinkwater would try to write a play about Joan of Arc. So, to save her from Drinkwater, he wrote it instead.

ST. FRANCIS Yes, well?

AUTHOR: Well, Father, that play about Joan was such a success that he began looking round for some other saint to write about. And so, for fear he would choose *you*, I wrote my *Little Plays of St. Francis*, to save you from Bernard Shaw.

ST. FRANCIS Well?

AUTHOR And I *did*, Father.

ST. FRANCIS And why should not Bernard Shaw have written plays about me?

AUTHOR Because, Father, had *he* written them, he would have made *you* Bernard Shaw.

ST. FRANCIS Even as Bonaventura made me Benedict. Why not?

AUTHOR Ah! Father, you know Benedict; but you don't know Bernard Shaw.

ST. FRANCIS What's the matter with him?

AUTHOR Matter? Nothing. He's a wonderful man. I love him. But he doesn't like fools — hasn't any use for them. So how could he have written plays about you and Brother Juniper?

ST. FRANCIS Ah! There was never a better or wiser fool than Juniper.

AUTHOR No; and it was your doing, Father.

ST. FRANCIS Indeed, how?

AUTHOR Because, by using his foolishness, you made him wise. If we used everybody as you do, Father, all the world would be a-building.

ST. FRANCIS And you, little Brother, a stone in it.

AUTHOR Yes, Father.

ST. FRANCIS When you called me just now, was it because you wanted anything?

AUTHOR Only to see you, Father.

ST. FRANCIS Then is there nothing else you want?

AUTHOR Many things that I ought to want, Father, if I were — sure of them . . . Heaven — if there is Heaven.

ST. FRANCIS Heaven is not in my keeping, Brother.

AUTHOR No, Father; but isn't Brother Juniper?

ST. FRANCIS Well? and if he were, why?

AUTHOR I would like to see Brother Juniper. Somebody said that when I began writing my *Little Plays*, I wrote them for love of *you*, but that I went on writing them for love of Brother Juniper. That's quite true, Father. So — if I may — I would like to see Juniper.

ST. FRANCIS He is here, Brother.

(*Indeed, hardly has the wish been expressed, than* JUNIPER *has begun to make his appearance, coming in gently and slowly, a little interrogative at finding himself 'wanted'. So now* ST. FRANCIS *steps back, and makes way for* JUNIPER *to come forward; and after watching the encounter for a while with amused eyes, he goes quietly out of the picture, leaving the two alone*)

AUTHOR Is it yourself, Juniper?

JUNIPER It is; what's left of me.

AUTHOR Is anything missing?

JUNIPER Sure! What was once the bigger part of me — my sins, Brother. At least, so they tell me. But it's not my doing; it just comes of being where I am now. On earth one was always having to run away from sin, wasn't one? But up there, it's all the other way: sin runs from you, like water off a duck's back, and there's no catching it.

AUTHOR (*meditative*) Sin . . . Anything else, Brother?

JUNIPER All my troubles, sorrows, fears; a heavy load they were. But I don't fear anything now — nor anybody. All the things gone that got in the way of me being any use in the world.

AUTHOR And your foolishness, Juniper? That also?

JUNIPER No, no, God forbid! I couldn't do without that. 'Heaven's Fool' they call me. That's what I am now.

AUTHOR You always were, Brother.

JUNIPER Ah! 'Twas a good world, by God's mercy, needing fools.

AUTHOR And what do you do now, Juniper? Do they need you still?

JUNIPER Sure! More than ever. That's the comfort of it! I stay by the gate, watching for all them that come . . . and seeing that they don't go away from it.

AUTHOR How do you prevent them?

JUNIPER Tell them not to be afraid. 'Where I am,' I say, 'is good enough for anyone.' No! No! I mean — anyone's good enough for where I am, please God. Where Juniper the fool is, there's no fool that's greater. And those that don't love God, or think so — it's only foolishness, through not knowing.

AUTHOR But you haven't the Keys, Juniper.

JUNIPER (*dryly*) No, *I* haven't, Brother.

AUTHOR Then how do you get them all in? Do you?

JUNIPER Aye, all that I see. And if there's others, it's a God's mercy I don't see them, else it 'ud break my heart . . . Aye, if I see 'em, and if old Cock-crow see's 'em, we get 'em all in, by the head or the tail.

AUTHOR Old Cock-crow?

JUNIPER Aye, Peter's Cock, I mean. He's there to remind him. For there is Peter: very good and holy he is now, and careful in his keeping of the Keys; but he wasn't always what he ought to be. So when I see him turning anyone away, I give a wink to old Cock-crow, and he gives me a wink, and starts crowing (with me to keep him company); and he doesn't leave off until Peter's remembered himself, and changed his mind. Oh! he's a wise bird, and a judge of character, and knows well when to crow, and when not to — me helping him.

AUTHOR And what does Peter say about it?

JUNIPER 'The fool's right!' he says. It's what I'm there for. And for that same reason I must be going back now, Brother; they will be missing me.

(*Just then, from outside comes the singing of birds, as has been faithfully given on a certain gramophone record, which, for stage purposes, had better now be used. They both hear it. There is a short pause before the* AUTHOR *speaks*)

AUTHOR What's that noise, Juniper?

JUNIPER It's the birds, Brother, singing. Dawn has come.

AUTHOR Draw — draw the curtains, Brother

(JUNIPER *does so, twilight enters the room. The* AUTHOR *reaches out a hand, and switches off the light*)

AUTHOR Welcome light! Oh, welcome light!

JUNIPER Aye, there it is, waiting for you!

AUTHOR What birds are those, Juniper?

JUNIPER So many kinds, one can't name them, Brother.

AUTHOR I don't hear any cock-crow!

JUNIPER But you shall! You wait! I'm going back now to tell him you are coming. He'll crow you in, Brother.

AUTHOR Then I, too, like one that was my better, shall owe a cock to Aesculapius.

JUNIPER To who, then?

AUTHOR To Luke, the beloved physician — and you, Juniper.

JUNIPER (*listening*) Ah! they are calling me!

AUTHOR Then go, Juniper.

JUNIPER Aye, for a minute, to show you the way, just. And keep your ears sharp for the signal. 'Twon't be long. When you hear us cry 'cock-a-doo', you will know we've fixed it. (*Then, hearing himself called again*) Yes, Brother, I'm coming!

(*And back to Heaven goes* JUNIPER. *The* AUTHOR *lies listening to the birds. He is not at all sure that* JUNIPER'S *signal is going to reach him; and, being in doubt, he questions his own identity and fitness for taking on so large a matter*)

AUTHOR Me? . . . Me?

(*The double 'Me' reminds him of something he wrote in a play a good many years ago, and being rather proud of the passage, he now recites it: a farewell to authorship, in this world at any rate*)

AUTHOR Dawn, Mee-mee, Dawn! Look how the hands of light
Reach up, and lift the covering cowl of night
From the blush-blinded eyes of Heaven. And she,
Heart-woken, and warm-footed o'er the sea,
Her face a fountain of desires long stored,
Goes kindling to the arms of her great lord!
And lo, he comes rejoicing, and flings gold
Till all the earth is with his joy enrolled,
And every life — a mote in his glad beams —
Melts forth to meet him, and, where'er light streams,
Dance till it drowns! Ah! Look! The sun! The sun!

(*The babbling of the birds thins out, pauses, then ends. From far away comes a cock-crow, twice, thrice it repeats itself. Half incredulous, but putting his trust in Juniper's word, the* AUTHOR *sends out a feeble response*)

AUTHOR Cock-a-doodle-doo!

(*The door opens. Too late to administer it to her departed patient, the* NURSE *enters with the white of egg and whisky.*)

CURTAIN

APPENDIX

Pains and Penalties The defence of Queen Caroline. A Play in   (1911)
four acts

PREFACE

THOSE who defend a bad cause have to defend it blindly: otherwise its
life would be short. Driven from one false argument to another, they
still find sufficiency in the last that is left to them. It is the thing, not the
reasonableness of the thing that they are defending.

Last year (1910) this play of *Pains and Penalties* was privately and con-
fidentially condemned by the Lord Chamberlain[1]: for some months the
author was given no reason for the condemnation which he could make
public. Yet before a word of the play was printed, defenders of the censor-
ship supported the Lord Chamberlain's decision with blind and headlong
enthusiasm, and industriously set themselves to assert that their beloved
official must be in the right. The author had dared to pass unfavourable
comments on the character of King George IV; and hostile reference upon
the stage to the great-grand-uncle of our present Sovereign was declared
to be incompatible with respect for the institution of monarchy.

But at last the Lord Chamberlain was persuaded to give his reason publicly; and then, hey, presto! the defence of our monarchy in the person of
so bad a representative as this happily distant relative of our present King
was sent to the limbo of untenable foolishness, and a brand-new reason
was fitted out for public consumption.

The Lord Chamberlain, it then appeared, had refused to license my
play, not for the supposed reasons at all — on those I had been 'mis-
informed' — but because it dealt with 'a sad historical episode of comparatively recent date in the life of an unhappy lady'. The 'unhappy lady', as
I at once pointed out, had been dead for ninety years, and during the
whole of that period her memory had rested under a cloud which the
main trend of my play was calculated to remove. Driven to give a public
reason for his action, the Lord Chamberlain decided that such an attempt
to rehabilitate her character was not to be allowed.

And so the pro-censorists must adapt their attitude of adulation and
agreement with the Lord Chamberlain's thoughts, words, and actions to
the new substitute for a reason which he has given them . . . And the

[1] Lord Spencer.

only thing I wish to add here is my hope that the Lord Chamberlain keeps an uncooked record, not only of the published, but also of the private and confidential communications which pass between his officials and others in connection with the suppression of modern drama, and that a time may come soon when those documents will be collated in the light of day.

Echo de Paris   (1923)

FOOTNOTE

TWENTY years after a man's death is usually a sufficient time to compose, in their proper unimportance, the prejudices and enmities which have surrounded his career. But in this particular case, I suppose, it has hardly done so; and the man who was so greatly overrated by his own following, during those ten years of literary and social triumph which made him the vogue, was, in the ten years after, as carefully underrated, not because the quality of his work had proved itself poor and ephemeral, but because of something that he had done.

The blight which fell on his literary reputation was about as sensible as it would have been for historians to deny that Marlborough was a great general because he peculated and took bribes, or that Mohammed was a great religious leader because he had a number of wives, or that David was a great poet because he preferred the love of Jonathan to the love of women. In which last-named absurdity of critical inconsequence we have something very much to the point; and it is upon that point, and because the world has been so unintelligently slow in seizing it, that I am moved to write this footnote to my dialogue, with which, in subject, it has so little to do.

Always, so long as it stays remembered, the name of Oscar Wilde is likely to carry with it a shadowy implication of that strange pathological trouble which caused his downfall. And whatever else may be said for or against the life of promiscuous indulgence he appears to have led, his downfall did at least this great service to humanity, that — by the sheer force of notoriety — it made the 'unmentionable' mentionable, and marks the dividing of the ways between the cowardice and superstitious ignorance with which the problem had been treated even by sociologists and men of science, and the fearless analysis of origins and causes which has now become their more reputable substitute.

Obscurantists may still insist on treating as an acquired depravity what medical research has now proved to be an involuntary or congenital deflection from a 'normality' which exact science finds it harder and harder to define. But in spite of these surviving resistances to the formation of a new social conscience, intelligence is at work, and to-day it is no longer eccentric or disreputable to insist that the whole problem shall henceforth be studied and treated from the medical rather than from the criminal standpoint; so that in future, whatever limitation of reticence or segregation society decides to impose on men whose tendencies are ineradicably homosexual, the treatment shall be health-giving in character and purpose, carrying with it no social or moral damnation of those who, in the vast majority of cases, have been made what they are by forces outside their own volition, either at their birth or in early infancy.

The comical ignorance and ineptitude of which quite brilliant minds are capable in regard to a matter that they wish to relegate to mental obscurity, was well exemplified in the remarks made to me on this subject, only ten years ago, by one who ranked then as now among the most eminent of British bacteriologists. He had been told, he said, that homosexuality came from meat-eating; and his solution of the problem was to have all homosexuals put to death. But the subject, he went on to say, did not interest him; nor did he propose to give the meat-eaters (of whom he himself was one) any warning of their pathological danger, or of his proposed remedy for the pathological condition to which their meat-eating habits might bring them. Having escaped the infection himself, he was quite willing, apparently, to leave the rest to chance. It was, he had been told, very prevalent, but personally he had not come across it. And so he continued to interest himself in bacteriology, through which fame, wealth, and title had come to him.

As I left his consulting-room I felt as though I had just emerged from the Middle Ages, and from listening to the discourse of some learned theologian — a marvellous expert in the doctrine of the Incarnation and the Procession of the Holy Spirit, but still believing that the sun went round the earth, and that the earth was flat; and though — God aiding him — he would put to death anyone who thought otherwise, the subject did not interest him!

He remains to me a portentous example of how a really brilliant mind can totter into second infancy when called upon to dig for the roots of knowledge outside his own cabbage-patch in hitherto uncultivated ground.

What led me to this strange scientific experience was very much to the point. For it was just then, ten years ago, that I had been asked to join a society having for its object the formation of a more intelligent and less servile public opinion on this and various other difficult sex-problems which are part of human nature. I agreed to do so upon one condition — that membership should be open to men and women on equal terms, and that women should be upon the executive committee. Even in that comparatively enlightened group the proposal seemed revolutionary; and I was asked whether I realized that such things as homosexuality would have to be openly discussed. My answer was: 'That is why we must include women.' I contended that where a problem concerns both sexes alike, only by the full co-operation of both sexes can it be rightly solved.

My contention was admitted to be sound, and the society was formed on the equal basis I had advocated; and perhaps one of its best discoveries is that, in a body of social goodwill, there is no such thing as 'the unmentionable'. Since then, women have been called to juries, and it has become a duty of good citizenship for them to share with men the knowledge of things which the obscurantists, in order to keep them as a male perquisite, chose to describe as 'unmentionable'.

'E pur se muove': that wise old saying continues to have its application in every age. Always, at some contentious point in the affairs of men, belief in knowledge and belief in ignorance stand as antagonists. The nineteenth century had its superstitions, quite as much as the sixteenth and the seventeenth centuries, when loyalty to the Mosaic law made the persecution of witchcraft a religious duty. And a surviving superstition of our own time has been that false and foolish moral insistence on regarding certain maladjustments of nature as something too horrible to be mentioned, and therefore on putting the victims thereof in a class apart, rather lower than the ordinary criminal. The old theological idea that the world was flat reproduced itself in another form; and so, in spite of the advance of science, the moral world had to remain flat and simple, unencumbered by nature-problems, for fear of the terrible things it might have to contain and account for, if once admitted to be round.

Twentieth-century science is busy proving to us that the moral world is dangerously round; and it is no use trying to fall off it by walking about it with shut eyes. From a flat world that method of escape might be conceivably possible, but not from a round. A round world has us in its grip; and it is our duty, as intelligent human beings, to face the danger and get used to it.

What a strange irony of life, that the man who tried most to detach himself from the unlovely complications of modern civilization should have become the symbol, or the byword, of one of its least-solved problems; and that society's blind resentment towards the phenomenon it had not the patience or the charity to trace to its origin, should have supplied him so savagely with that 'complete life of the artist' which success could never have given him.

The Life of H.R.H. The Duke of Flamborough   (1928)

EDITOR'S FOOTNOTE

THIS is a valet's life of one who could have been no man's hero; but whose birth, nevertheless, brought him hazardously near to the throne of an ancient and wise people, and gave him, for the better part of two generations, the mismanagement of its army.

And had he come to the throne, the people would have accepted him, as they accept the conventions of institutional religion, with all the outward appearances of belief. And throughout his life a smoke-screen of fine phrases would have gone up concerning him, obscuring the fact of his more than average ordinariness, for the sake of the monarchical system which he stood to adorn.

. . . . . .

Without a glimmer of a notion that it meant double wastefulness, he gave to his own order the service that it required of him, believing heart and soul that the institution of Monarchy was the most useful of all devices to keep the world and religion and politics from going to the dogs.

And though to some its tendency may seem different and contrary, no one can deny that a use is still found for it; and many of its users will desperately cling to it, when the time comes for its removal, and perhaps even fight for it as the living symbol of all the atavisms of a system they still wish to preserve. And having so set their faith on it, and made it a part of their religion, they object to having it criticized. You may not even criticize it for the values it has lost under the commercial twist which vested interests have given it. Royalty, having been reduced to a safe average of ordinariness, is to stand representatively sacred, on a spot that has been well fenced-in; and the last thing it must ever do is to shock or startle the public conscience by a symbolic act of unexpected representativeness to which men's thoughts might unconventionally respond. We have a commercial, but we have no longer a courageous use for Royalty.

Yet the courage is sometimes there waiting to be used; and perhaps the best things done by Royalty in recent years have been things very unofficial and unrecorded.

And since I have thus ventured to criticize the impoverished use which the well-to-do mind of the Nation now makes of Royalty, I will give an instance the other way, of which perhaps very few will have heard.

To a hospital, on an official visit, goes a young Prince, charming, popular, with a gift for doing unconventional things which are sometimes a little embarrassing to the official mind. The hospital to be visited on this occasion was a hospital in which some hundreds of the most helpless and unpresentable victims of the War are to this day kept out of public sight, for fear lest we should realize in all its ghastliness what war means.

Into this receptacle of shelved humanity goes the young Prince. Officially received, officially conducted from ward to ward, he sees and speaks to some scores of the men by whose stripes in war the nation is supposed to have been healed. And having completed the official survey, he happens unconventionally to ask, 'Have I seen all?'

No; it is admitted by the officials that he has not been taken into a ward where the less presentable cases are congregated — cases too dreadful to look at and keep a good appetite afterwards. Contrary to official calculation no doubt, Royalty says: 'I must see them.' And does.

And that ordeal over, he asks again, 'Have I now seen all?'

Yes, really all this time, all except one: a case that nobody sees — a case unimaginably horrible to look at. And once more, contrary to official calculation, Royalty unexpectedly persists and does the courageous thing.

He goes in, and sees an object without eyes, without face; how much more of the body blown away — how little else left for life and the communications of life one does not know; whether able to be told, so as to understand, that the heir to the Throne had come to visit him, one does not know. Helpless before that spectacle of unhappy survival, helpless to do anything but to perform an act of human sympathy, the young Prince bent and kissed — what was left; and from that Presence went out white and shaken, but having done for the Nation the unexpectedly representative and the most truly royal thing which under the circumstances could be done.

.   .   .   .

There are times when great and immediate publicity is the essential accompaniment to an act royally conceived and performed; and times when the Nation greatly needs to have such an act done for it. Many years ago a King owned himself responsible for the murder of one of his subjects — a rather obstreperous and resisting one — did public penance for it, and was not less kingly in so doing. The act stands out in history.

In recent years a bloody and blundering crime was done by agents of this country, at a place called Amritsar. The Government denounced the act, and dismissed the perpetrator of it; the Country was ashamed of it; but nothing was done, sufficiently expressive of the Nation's sorrow and shame, to touch and convince the heart of the Indian people. Shortly after, we sent out the Prince of Wales as our representative to India. The ill done at Amritsar made the success of that official visit impossible; native feeling was expressed in a boycott which followed the Prince wherever he went.

It was then in our power to make Royalty the symbol of our conscience, for the reparation of a great wrong; but we had not the courage or the imagination to do it. But had the Prince, on his first coming, stood, as our representative, bare-headed on the site of the Amritsar massacre in a two minutes' silence, we should have found means once more to make a worthy and a courageous use of Royalty. It would have been an act of unendurable humiliation to certain people whom it would have been very good policy to humiliate; and — it would have won India.

A New Way with Crime by A Fenner Brockway   (1928)

PREFACE BY LAURENCE HOUSMAN

. . . Just as the self-righteousness of nations is a standing impediment to the abolition of war, so is the self-righteousness of society to penal reform. In each case there is a systematic refusal of nation or of society to take to itself any share in the responsibility for having brought war or crime into being; and from this refusal to admit a true share of responsibility, injustice is certain to result. It is impossible to have a just penal system which blinks the fact that society — augustly represented by its judges and magistrates — has very largely produced its own criminals; and every court of law which, by its high ritual and ceremony, conceals that fact and substitutes the fiction of a blameless and outraged society administering justice on men in whose guilt it has no share, is stamped with a lie.

This is not to say that there is never such a thing as a criminal, brutal, base, or mean, who is mainly if not entirely responsible for the crime of which he stands charged; but it is to say that the shared responsibility between society and the criminal varies through all degrees, and that we have stereotyped our formula of justice upon the false assumption that the criminal and not society is always to blame.

There have been occasions when a judge has honestly and bravely stated the case against society in his official capacity, and has given judgment accordingly. There is the famous instance of the judge who by his outspokenness, followed by a sentence of one day's imprisonment on a man found guilty of bigamy, caused an alteration of the law to make divorce a possibility for poor as well as rich; but such instances are rare, and belong too much to the past. The refusal of juries to convict for offences involving capital punishment brought society (and incidentally a very reluctant bench of judges) to throw over a penal code whose blind and stupid severities stood comparable to the atrocities perpetrated in war. . . .

A criminal is one who suffers from a defective sense of citizenship — a defect which we all share; it is merely a matter of degree. It has been produced, or has been encouraged, in a society whose sense of citizenship is also defective or incomplete; for until society stands for commonwealth and brotherhood, our individual citizenship is likely to be as defective as the social order in which it finds expression. The criminal, therefore, only expresses in a fuller degree, more representatively, and with a stronger focus of illicit action against its weak places, the defects of our social system; and we, taking hold of this deficient who is partly our own making, thrust him out of one defective social system into another still more deficient in the principles and incentives of good citizenship; and there, very effectively in fifty-five cases out of a hundred or thereabouts, we stereotype his defect into a habit, imposing on it such a rule of life that it becomes not merely an aberration from average decency of conduct, but a conformity to type; for prison can hardly by any chance develop a sense of citizenship — since from prison the sense of citizenship is not merely absent but systematically ruled out. Even kindness and friendship are forbidden, which is, in a damned nut-shell, about the best example of 'the sin against the Holy Ghost' which I know. And until we make our prisons a training-ground for citizenship — making the repair and mending of lives the be-all and end-all of the system — our prisons, like the society which has brought them into being, will themselves be mentally defective.

War-Letters of Fallen Englishmen   (1930)

INTRODUCTION

A BLOCK of stone, with hanging flags, stands in the centre of a London street — the very design suggestive of the silence which has fallen on the most monstrously devastating conflict that the history of man has ever known. On it only a few words; but because of what it stands for, even now, twelve years after the event, thousands salute as they pass daily.

That memorial, composed of a few hundred stones, represents over a million dead. And could each stone have a voice proportionate to the whole, it would cry out for a thousand lives laid down, with the hope held, or with the hope lost, that war might be no more.

But even among those stones there would be a divergent minority: a few, just a few, would cry that war in itself is a fine thing and worth while. They, and they only who have been through it, have the right to say so, and to be heard — not with agreement, but with respect.

Here, in these war-letters, the Cenotaph finds its two voices: the voice of a majority, the voice of a minority. A large majority, though firmly convinced that what they do is right — or right in the sense that it is inevitable — show their detestation of war in its operation. Yet some of these express the keen satisfaction it gives them as an individual experience — mainly as a test of themselves, of their power to conquer fear, to live at the full push of their energies, mental and physical. To them, individually, active warfare gives life a fuller expression; for it is a life lived daily in the power to face death.

Nobody can say that, for the individual, there is anything in that standpoint unworthy of noble minds. It led to great deeds of courage, tenderness, self-sacrifice. It produced some of the finest war-poems — the poems of Rupert Brooke and Julian Grenfell — the former a theoretical acceptance of war as a good thing; the latter a practical acceptance, after trial. At the back of both stands the conviction that, in this self-realization, they are serving the cause of their country, which they believe also to be the cause of humanity.

But alongside of this standpoint there are others equally worthy of respect — representative of other types of mind and character, of men who are not born fighters, men who have had a hard struggle to conquer their individual fears, temperaments, and disgusts, and have not come through with elation, or even with conviction. In some of these letters is the cry of a violated conscience, or at least of poignant doubt. In many — in some of the best — is the record of a diminishing hope: of men who went into the war with ideals, from which the reality (military and political combined) slowly crushed out the life.

Many of us, looking at the world to-day, will hold that those lost hopes came nearer the truth, as to the practical outcome of war, than the high elated expectation with which so many went into it.

But though the mind of the age is divided as to what war can or cannot do, few who read these letters will differ as to the high qualities of human nature, amazing in their beauty of staunchness, endurance, and tenderness, which the war tested and proved.

One of these letter-writers describes war as a thing of contradictions, full of beastliness, brutality, and many other things, a misery to mind and body, yet full of fineness as well. But that fineness is not of war, but of the human nature whose strong quality it tries out and reveals. To attribute any nobility to war itself is as much a confusion of thought as to attribute nobility to cancer or leprosy, because of the skill, devotion, and self-sacrifice of those who give up their lives to its cure, or because of the patient endurance of the sufferers. And this confusion of thought will be found in some of the writers of these letters. One — pre-eminently of the fighting class — writes that he 'adores war'; yet in the same letter he speaks of the hopeless misery inflicted by war on non-combatants: he writes that you never love your fellow-man so well as when you are out to kill him: yet tells later, when prisoners are taken, how 'one felt hatred for them as one thought of our dead.' But the story does not end there: human nature nobly contradicts itself, and reaches truth. He meets face to face a man as noble as himself, one of the enemy; tries to hate him and fails. The man salutes him. 'It made me feel terribly ashamed.'

What such men find 'adorable' in war is the tremendous test to which it puts all their powers, moral and physical; and so long as they can believe that the instrument by which they are tested can produce good results, commensurate to the accompanying horrors, war does not violate their conscience. That is a matter for the individual alone: it does not make war 'fine'.

These letters contain darker records of what war and obedience to authority require, not merely of a man's hand, but of his soul. Some of the most horrible things are told almost without comment; their reticence is eloquent. In one letter we read how a Winchester boy — almost a boy still — officer in a famous Highland regiment, goes out with a small bombing party to clear an enemy trench. The bombs are gas-bombs; and as the suffocating and helpless Germans emerge from the ground, they are all bayoneted — not on impulse, but on definite instructions from above, because men cannot be spared to take prisoners to the rear.

That was one of our 'military necessities' which were kept from our knowledge during the war; it was the sort of thing which was then supposed only to be done by Germans. It is well that we should be told of them now, for that truly is war. It is doubly well that the telling should be by men who died in war, accepting the dishonour it imposed on them as part of the sacrifice they must make while war remained the chosen instrument of their country's good.

But is that terrible acceptance still to be accepted by us who have not to do the horrible thing ourselves, but only ask that it shall be done for us? If such letters bring home to us the dishonour vicariously borne by men of noble character, who went into active service believing that war would call on them to do only honourable things, they will teach better wisdom to the race than those, of the more popular kind, which extol the 'fineness' of war because of the appeal which, in certain of its aspects, it makes to the adventurous courage of youth. To insist upon the truth that war is a beastliness and a blunder is not to detract from the high heroism with which the beastliness and the blunder were faced. It is right that human nature should be able to feel a fearful sort of joy when — put to the hardest task — it finds it has not failed. But all that nobility of courage — of the will to face death — which war brings out, does not make war a noble thing, does not make it more tolerable as an accepted means to high ends, any more than the perfect death of Christ upon the cross made crucifixion itself anything but a wickedly invented device for the punishing of criminals.

People deceive their consciences who think that the heroism of the men who faced out the horrors of war makes war itself less horrible, less brutal, less of a blunder. But with the baseness of war firmly fixed in our minds, what worth, what unexpected qualities in average human nature we see revealed against the darker background, made more prominent by the ugliness of their surroundings. The things here seen are not all of one kind; and often, in their abnormal setting, their values become changed. Kindness to a dog, for instance, is a small thing, and we think little of it; but in the account here given of the great charge at Thiepval, does it not catch one by the throat, that incident of the dog running out from the German lines, and of the man who, with comrades falling round him, stooped down and fondled it, and ran on, to be himself perhaps in another moment one of the dead? Or take that other incident of the two Irishmen, having a private quarrel of their own, who leapt out of their trench and fought in the open, with the German enemy cheering them on. Under such circumstances that fight goes up into the Heavens, a deed of unrepentant sinners fit to make angels rejoice. Here too we read, from one who took part in it, the account at once so humorous and pathetic of the Christmas Truce, which — winked at and condoned, in its first occurrence — was adjudged too dangerous for repetition, and so in the second year was not allowed.

These touches from life on its lighter side have here a moving beauty, coming with a difference across that face of storm.

War is an emergency; and in emergency human nature can be very wonderful — but also unexpected, not uniform. Amid the pressure of the emergency many phases arise, which all have their wonderfulness, yet may be almost contraries. For into this pit of destruction go all kinds, the clean and the unclean together, there to become more alike, or more different, as the case may be. None who has not been through it can know of the affinities between things honoured and despised which war reveals: and the charity towards human weakness of the fighting man, is often greater and of more understanding than the charity of the man who stays at home.

Courage itself is an enigma; it is not a simple virtue, for it does not come to all alike. Men achieve it differently. The man who is afraid of being afraid, the man who feels fear and shows it, but carries on; the man who feels fear and can hide it; the man who does not feel fear: all alike have the gift or grace of courage in them; but how differently it may act on their souls, coming to some easily as an instinct, to others as a hardly won escape from bitter temptation — sometimes only achieved at so great a strain that, in the end, they break. There is the further thought, unwelcome to some, that the man who falls to cowardice cannot always help himself: it may be a weakness lying beyond his nature to control.

Of the strengths and weaknesses of human nature, the war must have brought to many young minds a deeper experience and understanding than those outside can share or realize. Many must have had friends whose courage failed, and yet loved them, having a wiser pity for them than the contemptuous ignorant ones who sat in easy judgment at home.

A young man known to the present writer — utterly unfitted for war — of a temperament too highly strung, an artist, gifted with a wonderful voice — went into it, having no escape, war gave him no alternative. His muscles were sufficiently fit to pass the test; psychology did not count. He went out to the war in anguish of mind, just managed not to run away, got shot. A letter of his exists which cannot be printed here; it is too agonizing a confession of weakness; but he too is dead, and was not shot as a deserter. And he — or one like him — may be the 'Unknown Warrior' lying in Westminster Abbey. That representative of all the dead need not be a man who was specially brave, or brave at all in the accepted sense, but just one who managed to die at his post.

The agnosticism imposed on us by that memorial is good medicine.

The millions of our own countrymen who died in the war were not all brave, nor were they all willing to make that sacrifice which war required of them. They were not all lovers of war, or believers in war. In the four years while it lasted, many of them learned to hate war, from having known it, as they could not have hated it before. And they — those who so tasted war, and in their souls turned from it with loathing, not believing in it any more — have as much right to be remembered, and to claim that the Cenotaph is *their* memorial also, as those who died more happily, accepting war as a means, and believing that good might somehow come of it.

King John of Jingalo (1937)

PREFACE TO REPRINT

THIS study, written and published twenty-five years ago, of the subjection of a constitutional monarch to a craftily designed form of Cabinet government which called itself democratic, has not become less true with the passing of time; and the author may, perhaps, be allowed to congratulate himself that, without any gift for prophecy, but merely from an intelligent appreciation of the way in which the wheels within wheels of State-affairs are able to go round without the public knowing anything whatever about them, he was able, so long before the event, to tell a story of constitutional monarchy so closely paralleled by what has now actually happened.

For here is a King with a conscience, who, for the sake of that conscience, executes a deed of Abdication; and here is an heir to the throne whose left-wing tendencies in matters social and political give great uneasiness to Ministers whose tendencies are in a totally contrary direction; and here is an Archbishop who, though he would have turned a blind eye had the Prince kept a mistress in private, utters words of strong moral reprobation over a proposal of marriage which is deemed to be politically inexpedient, and does actually, to the best of his archiepiscopal ability, forbid the banns. And here, finally, is the meditation which the King, before committing his act of Abdication, addresses to the piebald ponies whose function it is to draw him, on the day of the opening of Parliament, to the delivery of a speech which is called 'the King's,' but not a word of it really his own:

'You and I, little brothers, are much of a muchness, and can sing our "Te Deum" or our "Nunc Dimittis" in almost the same words. We are both of a carefully selected breed and of a diminished usefulness. But because of our high position we are fed and housed not merely in comfort, but in luxury; and wherever we go crowds stand to gape at us, and applaud when we nod our heads at them. We live always in the purlieus of palaces, and never have we known what it is to throw up our heels in a green pasture, nor in our old age are we turned out comfortably to grass — only to Nebuchadnezzar by accident came that thing, and he did not appreciate it as he should have done. Never shall we go into battle to prove that we are worth our salt, and to say, "Ha, Ha" to the fighting and the captains; nor is it allowed to us to devour the ground with our speed: whenever we attempt such a thing it is cut from under us. Little brothers, it is before all things necessary that we should behave; for being once harnessed to the royal coach, if any one of us struck work or threw out our heels we should upset many apple-carts, and the machinery of the State would be dislocated. Let us thank God, therefore, that long habit and training have made us docile, and that our backs are strong enough to bear the load that is put upon them, and that if one of us goes another immediately fills his place so that he is not missed.'

And over that act of Abdication, when it has been presented to the astonished eyes of a flabbergasted Cabinet, here is the colloquy which takes place between the King and his Prime Minister:

'Your Majesty takes a course entirely without precedent.'

'What? Abdication?'

'Against the wish or consent of Parliament.'

'Ah, yes,' said the King, 'that is precisely the difference. Abdications have, like ministerial resignations, been forced upon us — I mean on kings in the past — at very unseasonable times and in most inconsiderate ways; and we kings have had to put up with it. Mr. Prime Minister, it is your turn now; and I only hope that you may find as clean a way out of your difficulty as I had to find out of mine when four months ago you threatened me with a resignation which you knew I could not accept.'

Yes; an author who wrote those two passages twenty-five years ago has a right to say, 'I was no fool when I wrote them'.

What Next?   (1938)

PREFACE

THE main aim of these tales is to show how easily faith can become a bad substitute for morals. One may write fairy-tales without believing in fairies, and similarly of other things which, while giving play to the imagination, can help to point a moral. That is the *raison d'être* of these miraculous tales. Miracles make good fairy-tales so long as one does not take them seriously, but they make bad theology; for either they are not miracles at all, but merely an imperfectly understood outcome of the law of man's being, or they are the capriciously bestowed favours of a licentious deity.

A certain soldier went out to war for his King and Country, with a heart full of faith and without fear, for he was a man of prayer. One day a bullet struck him. 'The God who can't stop a bullet is no God for me', he said; and died faithless.

The God who, in answer to prayer, *can* stop a bullet, and only does it by special favour, has become for a good many, to say the least of it, an uncertain character, producing in the minds of his would-be worshippers that attitude of 'I dunno' where He are' which is so prevalent to-day. Belief in material answer to prayer has, in its inevitable disappointments, provided the best possible grounds for honest doubt to become the generally accepted faith of the modern world.

A certain text of Scripture declares impartiality to be the essential characteristic of a weather-providing Deity — that without impartiality he would cease to be 'perfect'. Yet partiality towards favoured nations and persons is the underlying requirement of nearly all the prayers which go Heavenward — especially in wartime. And with partiality as their main aim and object, men are now providing themselves with new gods of whose partiality they can be sure. Polytheism, naked and unashamed, has taken hold of Western civilization, and race-worship is making nations more religious than ever they were before.

As a consequence Monotheism is dying — not of its virtues, but of the disease with which it has been persistently inoculated by its worshippers in increasing doses, ever since Christianity began paying spiritual tribute to Caesar; and that same disease has now become the life-force out of which the new Gods of the Nations are begotten — the law of their being, and the only reason for their existence.

In a world so situated, with partiality as the prevailing faith, with the Nations all following their god-led noses, and every nose out of joint, one may well ask 'What Next?' is going to happen to the human race.

The Preparation of Peace   (1940)

PREFACE

THE incredulous question of the first murderer, 'Am I my brother's keeper?' is a question which, from that time to this, others besides murderers have been reluctant to answer in the affirmative. Only very perfunctorily and gradually has our competitively organized society come to recognize that 'Devil take the hindmost' is not good political economy, and that as the needs and numbers of the 'Have nots' increase, so does the well-being and security of the 'Haves' diminish.

Not until we are ready to extend to other nations and races equal access to the means of prosperity which we ourselves enjoy, are they likely to credit us with the love for peace and liberty which we profess. To make peace and liberty secure, we must be willing to share also our prosperity. 'Collective Security' based upon the *status quo* of a world divided up by past conquests, with nearly one half of its surface held for the benefit of a few sovereign powers against the needs and growing pressure of population of other races — collective security on those terms is an impossibility.

Palestine Plays (1942)

PREFACE

THE history of the Israelites is the history of an extraordinarily God-conscious people; and the Old Testament is very largely a record of the long process of trial and error by which they arrived finally at a conception of God to which Christianity was able to attach itself. But that conception was only arrived at gradually and with difficulty, after many mistakes by the way. And because those mistakes became embedded in their Scriptures, and were vouched for as 'the Word of the Lord', Christianity, when it took over the Bible as the inspired Word of God, took over its defects as well as its excellencies — the misses as well as the hits; and as a result (even down to the present day) Bibliolatry has been one, of the greatest hindrances to Christianity: it has perpetuated many superstitions which would otherwise have died a natural death, and has imposed on the mind of each rising generation, as matter for unquestioning belief, things which the religious mind of to-day finds spiritually distasteful.

The reluctance of our theologians to throw over these vain beliefs has been largely responsible for the increasing neglect into which 'holy scriptures written for our learning' (and from which there is so much to learn) have fallen during the last two generations. Sound moral feeling quite as much as intellectual scepticism, has caused modern thinkers to regard as no longer worthy of respect a system of miraculous intervention which turns God into a showman performing tricks for the delectation of a small favoured tribe, providing it with short cuts to victory over its enemies, and special visitations of plague, pestilence, or famine whenever its rulers behave badly. Such a process of alternate coddling and bullying is no true education for man or nation: it only produces spoiled children; and until their later prophets taught them better, the Children of Israel were thoroughly spoiled children. Having decided that they were 'the Chosen People', they wrote their history in terms of tribal megalomania; and, as a consequence, ostentation and favouritism became divine attributes; and their extravagant taste for miraculous intervention, often on quite trivial occasions, has obscured the meaning and lessened the spiritual value of many a beautiful Old Testament story.

The best one can do for them to-day, to restore the respect they have lost, is to eliminate these useless excrescences. And so, in the Plays which here follow, the story is given without the miracle. The deep heart-searchings of Abraham to find in it the mind of God required the outside intervention of no Angel. The wrestling of Jacob with his shifty, time-serving conscience was an inward and solitary one. Micaiah's parable of the Lying Spirit — Jonah's of the Whale — belong to the prophetic technique of their day; and the puzzled inquiry which I put into Jonah's mouth, 'Is it not strange, Shemmel, that to make men believe the truth we prophets have to tell lies?' has its application even in the present day. Why is it that these old stories of miracle are still so insistently regarded, not as inventions quite natural in their day, but as religious truths which must not be questioned?

I cannot help feeling, therefore, that if these Plays cause offence to any, it is the surer proof that pious hindrance still stands in the way of a right understanding of what an old Preacher quaintly described as 'the better side of God's character'.